YOU'RE
ON THE AIR

To Sandy —
This goodsore " who sometimes
listened " — wife to his
wife Margaret
With much affection.

Callie Phillips

March 16, 2000

Canadian Cataloguing in Publication Data

Phillips, Sallie, 1910-
    You're on the air

    ISBN 1-55039-104-6

    I. Phillips, Sallie, 1910- 2. Interviews--British Columbia, 3.
British Columbia--Social conditions--1945-1991.* 4. British
Columbia--Biography. 5. Radio broadcasting--British Columbia--
Vancouver. I. Title
FC3827.1.A1P54 2000   971.1'04'0922   C00-910180-2
F1086.8.P54 2000

Sono Nis Press gratefully acknowledges the support of the
Canada Council for the Arts and the Province of British
Columbia, through the British Columbia Arts Council.

Cover design by Jim Brennan
Edited by Merrie-Ellen Wilcox
Copy edited by Dawn Loewen
Cover photo of Sallie Phillips by Lenare Photographers, Vancouver
Photo credits: All photos are from the collection of Dick and Sallie Phillips
    except: p. 73 (bottom), Dawn Loewen; p. 103 (top two), Selwyn Pullan;
    p. 143, Jack Lindsay Photographers, Vancouver

Published by
SONO NIS PRESS
PO Box 5550, Stn. B
Victoria, BC V8R 6S4
tel: (250) 598-7807
sono.nis@islandnet.com
http://www.islandnet.com/sononis/

PRINTED AND BOUND IN CANADA BY FRIESENS PRINTING

You're On The Air

Sallie Phillips

Sono
Nis
Press

VICTORIA, BRITISH COLUMBIA

Dedicated to those long-ago men and women
of the Canadian Broadcasting Corporation who
found my scripts worth broadcasting, and to my
godson, Sandy, who listened.

My warm appreciation goes to Jim Bisakowski for his interest and technical assistance in the early stages of this book; and to Merrie-Ellen Wilcox for her caring and inspired editing. In addition, I would like to express my deep appreciation to Diane Morriss for her continuing faith in this book and in my wish to preserve a small section of mid-twentieth-century life.

CONTENTS

Tuning in

We were very proud of that radio. I don't remember what it cost, but I know it was more than we could afford. It was a Majestic, and it stood about chest-high. Made of blond wood, it looked very modern in the late thirties. My husband Dick and I chose it because we thought it had a superior tone. It gave us a good reproduction of the Metropolitan Opera broadcast on Saturday and the New York Philharmonic Orchestra on Sunday, as well as "Fibber McGee and Molly," Bing Crosby, and all the others. In those first years of listening to our Majestic, it didn't occur to either Dick or me that one day it would be me who was "on the air."

The early 1940s—my early thirties—were a restless, unsettled time. I was a happily married, busy housewife with two small, active sons. I had spent eight years of my childhood in Australia, had a university degree in English and history, and a year's post-graduate study in Paris, but otherwise there were in my background the usual things for women of my kind: a correct but modest "coming out," the "right" marriage to the "right" man. We had watched our unmarried friends go off to war. Dick was a block warden; his duties included checking our neighbours' blackouts after the Japanese bombing scare at Estevan Point. I took the St. John Ambulance first aid and home nursing courses. Since there was a housing shortage for the families of war personnel, especially those with babies, we boarded a succession of them. Though a bit crowded, it was patriotic. We didn't have much money, but even that wasn't the problem. I needed more than marriage and motherhood. I needed to work outside my home, to do something that required thought and imagination. And as it turned out, those needs were fulfilled, through two different but sometimes connected careers—in radio and public relations—which were soon to fill my life with challenge and excitement.

In 1943, when I heard about a university extension course in parenting, I organized the mothers on our block in the Dunbar suburb of Vancouver to study with me. It was this course that indirectly launched me into both radio and public relations. A local radio personality, Hilda Browne, heard about our little group and asked me to discuss it with her on her program, "Around the Town with Hilda Browne." And about a year later, a friend of mine was coaching members of the very active Kerrisdale Parent-Teacher Association (PTA), including me. It was she who recognized the potential of my speaking voice. Together, we wrote a special program for PTA Week, and she persuaded a friend of hers at CBR—part of the Canadian Broadcasting Corporation's Trans-Canada Network—to broadcast it. That was when I lost my heart to radio.

The powers that be at CBR liked our little program. They also liked my voice. I overheard two producers saying, "She really can take it off the paper." I had finally found a place to act: I had tried acting on the stage, but my body would never do what I wanted it to; my voice, however, could do anything. So the CBR people suggested I think up a subject for a women's series. The subject I came up with was how the menfolk of my listeners earned their living, in logging, mining, fishing, and farming. Research for the programs required me to visit a logging camp, ride alone in a clanking ore bucket up the mountainside to the old Britannia mine, spend a day with the herring fleet, and tour a dairy farm on Lulu Island. Unfortunately, I didn't keep those four scripts, but they were to be the first of many—daily programs, weekly series, dramas, documentaries, and school broadcasts for the Department of Education—aired provincially, nationally, and even internationally. They were the beginning of six or seven years of intensive radio work.

In one way or another, I broadcast over most of Vancouver's radio stations. CKWX, where I made my first radio appearance, had aspirations for growth and grandeur, and had taken over the upstairs premises of the select women's club, the Georgian Club, on Seymour Street behind the Hudson's Bay. CKMO was in an old building on Robson Street. Both of these stations carried music, news, and local talk shows. CJOR was a CBC-affiliated station on the Dominion Network, carrying some network programs as well as local programs. It was in the basement of the Grosvenor Hotel on Howe Street. CBR, which was to become the most important to my broadcasting career, was housed at 701 Hornby Street, in an out-of-the-way corner of the then-new Hotel Vancouver, behind a red-painted door bearing the magic letters "CBC." That little red door was rather like Alice in Wonderland's door to the garden: if you didn't know it was there, you couldn't find it. But once you knew it was there, you knew that all the wonderland of radio lay behind it.

Meanwhile, in 1944, I fell into my first job. As a result of the parenting course, I had been asked to sit on a parent education committee. At the time, our older son Tony was at a boarding school in B.C.'s dry Interior, away from the damp coastal climate, in order to heal a perforated eardrum. The resulting strain on our already stretched family budget was almost insupportable. Through a casual conversation, another member of the parent education committee, the poet Dorothy Livesay McNair, learned of our financial woes. She said she had a part-time job doing public relations for the Welfare Council, and that she would be resigning at the end of the month. It didn't pay much, but it might help. Would I like the job?

I knew little about the Welfare Council, and nothing at all about public relations. But I did know the executive director, Edgar Brown, from my high school and university days. He gave me the job. A year later, when the Welfare Council merged with the Community Chest (now known as the United Way), I became the organization's first full-time public relations secretary, responsible for planning and implementing the annual fundraising campaign and other projects of the public relations committee. Amazingly, I proved to be a natural for the job. My professional business career had begun. Over the next twenty years, I did public relations work and publicity campaigns not only for the Community Chest, but also for the Vancouver Symphony, the Vancouver Opera Association, the Heart Fund campaign, the Children's Aid Society, the YWCA, the Vancouver Arts Council, the B.C. Department of Child Welfare, and others.

Public relations was a relatively new field in those days, and women in the field a rarity. I knew only two others: strong, independent women whose jobs were their livelihood. In those years, people were just beginning to think that women might have a place in the business world. Many men refused to accept the idea of a working wife. I was fortunate to have a husband who encouraged and praised me. However, I didn't take jobs that would interfere with our family life, particularly if they required that I work on weekends. Over the years I was offered many different jobs—like selling real estate, cars, and cosmetics; copywriting for an ad agency; and editing the *Vancouver Sun* social page—and I turned them all down for this reason.

Still, by the late 1940s, I had two jobs: my freelance radio work and public relations. Sometimes they overlapped. All of the Vancouver radio stations in those days were very generous in giving free air time to public service causes, whether through interviews or commercial announcements for non-profit fundraising campaigns and events. Sometimes they aired programs written for specific occasions. As public relations secretary for the Community Chest, I started "Treasure Chest," a daily five-minute program on CKWX that attempted to popularize the work of the Chest's member agencies. Later, part of my job with the Vancouver Symphony was doing advance publicity for the orchestra when it toured the province; for that I not only wrote commercial spots about the coming concerts, but was interviewed on stations in Victoria, Port Alberni, Prince George, Fort St. John, Pouce Coupé, Trail, Kimberley, and, since Grand Forks didn't have its own radio station, even across the border into Washington.

While I never entered the doors of New Westminster's station, CKNW, I did get interviewed by the station's popular announcer, Bill Hughes. Every morning he went down to the New Westminster bus station and talked to the travellers who were about to depart. Sometimes he would ask me to meet him on the bus, where he would briefly interview me about whatever cause I happened to be publicizing at the time. CKMO lent me its facilities for producing and airing documentaries like "So Many Children," and CJOR gave me public service airtime. It was also at CJOR that Jack Webster sometimes unbent to throw loaded questions at me. He was always very kind when interviewing me about a cause I was promoting, but I had to be very alert to field those questions.

By 1950, when I was forty, I was already adept at juggling home, marriage, and children; volunteer work on committees and non-profit boards; and a professional career in public relations and as a radio writer and broadcaster. It was hectic, but I was carried along by the excitement of new challenges. Every minute of every day was full of activity, and I loved it all.

*   *   *

The scripts in this book are only a small selection of the many I did over the years. Most of them are dated between 1946 and 1952. Some unfortunately aren't dated, but fall within the same period. (Actually, if it hadn't been for my orderly, patient, and most beloved husband, who gathered, sorted, and filed all the accumulated papers he could find in my chaotic little home office, there would not now be any record of all that activity.) I've chosen these scripts because I think they best reflect life in a particular time and place—mid-century British Columbia. They seem to fall into two groups: those which show us how much things have changed in fifty years, and those few in which we see that some things haven't changed at all!

What is especially interesting about these scripts is that they were made before tape-recording came into general use; in fact, they would probably never have been written or broadcast at all after the advent of taping, when the whole approach to broadcasting changed. Once taping came along, making a program was about making tapes and splicing them together. But before that, you had to have a very good reason for recording anything, or be a most important person: records were made on heavy black lacquer disks that were sixteen inches wide and could only be played on station equipment. It was the spoken word, read from a script, with occasional sound effects, that described people, places, and events, not recordings of them. So the scripts provide a special historical record of that short period when the speaker and the listener worked together to create the picture. Tape recording and television certainly changed all that.

I did eventually use a tape recorder. I got my first one in 1957, when I was commissioned by the CBC to make a documentary for a travel series. Each item of the series was called "Footloose in" some location—mine was Baja California. I couldn't afford the lovely Swiss tape recorder recommended by the station engineers, so I settled for their second choice, called a Tapak, a large, heavy, box-like object that had to be *wound up*. "It's used by reporters everywhere," they said, "because it's portable." Portable, but only just. One moonlit night on the heights above the beach at San Clemente, when we were on our way to Baja California with our little home-made trailer, we decided to practise recording—crickets, of all things. I was running ahead of Dick, holding the microphone like a flashlight in my outstretched hand. He followed, panting, crashing through the underbrush with the great awkward bulk of my new, portable machine, effectively silencing the crickets. But that's another story.

How I loved researching, writing, and broadcasting these scripts! A great many of them were for a program called "Morning Visit" on CBR. Every weekday morning, immediately after the CBC national time signal at ten o'clock Pacific standard time, the strains of Tchaikovsky's *Serenade for Strings* travelled the airwaves, and Morning Visit was on the air. I substituted for the regular host, Ellen

Harris, when she went away for the summer, took time off at Christmas, or was ill. The programs I wrote and broadcast for Morning Visit over a period of several years were a mix of reporting, personal anecdotes, and interviews, all very informal and conversational. Such fascinating people, interesting facts, exciting events!

Every weekday afternoon at two o'clock, the "British Columbia School Broadcast" was carried locally and by CBC booster stations and beamed to any schools that wanted it, particularly rural schools, even into the far northern reaches of the province. The programs included all kinds of material, much of it dramatized, and were an important addition to the curriculum in a one-room, one-teacher school, providing material that was a little different from the regular fare of "reading, writing, and 'rithmetic." In the files carefully compiled by my husband, there are a great many of these scripts—on everything from good bicycle manners to dramatized legends of the Pacific Basin to the history of the Hudson's Bay Fur Brigade Trail. The B.C. Department of Education didn't pay much for those programs, even allowing for the different money values of those years: twenty dollars for twenty minutes—and many hours of research and preparation. But they offered such an interesting challenge, conjuring up imaginative ways to present educational material.

I wrote three radio plays, which are too long to include in this book. Two of them were commissioned by the CBC and broadcast nationally. They were part of a series, "In Search of Citizens," conceived by the CBC after the war to help smooth the path of new Canadians in their chosen country. In 1949, I was asked to dramatize some of the difficulties faced by these new citizens in fulfilling the requirements set by the government of Canada, one of which stipu-lated that women must take jobs as household help for one year—perhaps to provide nursemaids, housemaids, lady's maids, and cook-generals for households that had been accustomed to having servants before the war. "The Dancing Shoes," about the way in which a Latvian woman and her daughter were affected by this requirement, was commended by the producers at UN Radio as being "touching and effective." They congratulated the writer and the CBC for "handling these social problems so deftly." I have a happy memory from that summer of rowing quietly on Lac Le Jeune, trolling a fishing line and in my head composing dialogue for "The Dancing Shoes." (I think that was the same year that I took a summer course in radio writing at the University of British Columbia. Lister Sinclair was the main instructor, along with Len Peterson, Mavor Moore and Lucio d'Agostino. How lucky we were!)

Over the years, I also wrote perhaps half a dozen documentaries. Some, like "So Many Children," which is included in this book, were written for non-profit organizations on whose boards I served as Public Relations Chairman. Everyone was very generous in their assistance with these programs: the CBC and CKMO for donating their facilities, and the many volunteers, including professional actors and actresses, board members, and technicians. What nerve I had, asking them all to give so freely of their time and talents, and presuming that I was able to produce and direct!

I laboriously typed all of my scripts in duplicate, using carbon paper, as often as not inserted wrong way up. I never took a business course, and so have typed all these years with one finger on each hand, and usually with half an eye watching the keys, but probably as fast as someone else using all fingers on both hands. My first typewriter was bequeathed to me by a departing friend of my mother's. It was a very early Remington, large and square and very noisy—a far cry from the Smith-Corona word processor I use now!

One of my "Morning Visit" scripts, dated July 6, 1949, was about the actual making of a broadcast. The script was addressed to my then six-and-a-half-year-old godson, Sandy, who often listened to the broadcasts and was very curious about them. It began by describing me rushing the family madly through breakfast, then racing for the 8:45 interurban tram and a bus—"one of those beautiful new creations that have recently made their appearance on Vancouver streets"—to get to the station in time for a run-through, even of ad-lib interviews, in order to check the content and timing of the program. Entering CBR through the little red door on Hornby Street, I hurried past the receptionist, through the ante-room where the actors for the dramas gathered between rehearsals, past the large studio where they worked, which was capable of holding a large dramatic cast or an orchestra, and upstairs to the other studios and offices.

The main control room was high above the large studio. This was where "the producer of all the dramatic plays and musical productions sits and tells the actors, actresses, and musicians what to do . . . and where the engineer—without whom there wouldn't be a drama or any other kind of broadcasts—twiddles his dials up and down, brings in the music, the voices, the whole production." There were at least two other studios. I did most of my broadcasting from a medium-sized one. It had big double doors, and a grand piano just inside, on which I left my hat, coat, and purse. It also had a booth for the engineer and producer, whom I could see through a large plate-glass window. I sat at a little table, over which hung a microphone. Microphones came in all shapes and sizes, and could be hung from the ceiling, stood up on adjustable stands, placed on tables, or handheld. In the script, I told the curious Sandy that the microphone I used was a "44 velocity— whatever *that* means!"

Sandy had asked me who or what a producer was. My producers in those days were people who were later to become big names in radio and television, like Ross McLean, Norm Campbell, and Doug Nixon. But my scripted answer to Sandy at the time was:

Well, Sandy, my producer is a man who sits behind that plate glass window I was telling you about. He has a stop-watch in his hand, and he tells me whether or not my story each day is too long or too short, or just right. Just after you hear the theme music for the program—you know, Tchaikovsky's waltz—and the introduction, when the announcer says "Sallie Phillips," the producer points his finger at me through the glass, and I start to talk . The red ON THE AIR sign goes on and no one can open the big double doors. All the time that I'm talking, the producer is timing me. If he thinks that my talk is going to be too long, he makes a round-and-round circle with his finger, and that means "Hurry up, Sallie!" If, though, he takes both hands and stretches them as though stretching a piece of elastic, that means "You're going too fast, Sallie! Go slower, and make it last!" And, if the script is just right for length and timing, he will put his finger on his nose, to say "On the nose." That's the sign that really makes me happy!

The script also described the engineer at the controls:

He has quite a job, too. He has to watch a little dial that wiggles as I talk. It goes up and down and shows him whether I'm talking too loudly or too softly. Part of his job in getting me over the air is to see that my voice is never either too loud or too soft. And there's another thing he does, something that for me is pretty important. Of course, you know that you're supposed to sound pretty perfect over the air. Well, there are times when maybe you need to clear your throat or cough. When that happens, all I have to do is look at the engineer, make a sign as though I were cutting my throat—I'm doing it now, drawing my finger across my throat—and he, believe it or not, can turn a switch and put me off the air for just the instant that it takes for me to go "ahem," and put me back on again!

When I was finished reading the script, the theme music came back on, and then the ON THE AIR light went out and I was finished for another day. One morning when the script had run shorter than it should have, I remember producer Ross McLean saying, "I think, Sallie, that you rather overworked Tchaikovsky this morning!"

* * *

In about 1952, CBR asked if I would be interested in doing a fifteen-minute program full-time. I said no. I didn't want to be tied to just one thing. And a full-time public relations job left no time for even summer substitutions.

It was also in those years that we got a television as a way to keep our sons home, since they always watched it at their friends' houses. They loved watching sports. Of course we still listened to the Opera and the Philharmonic on the radio, but television brought with it a whole new way of life.

While nothing can ever entirely dim the magic of radio, the use of taping, which became the norm within a few years, changed for me the whole approach to broadcasting. In 1957, when preparing "Footloose in Baja California," I did learn to work with tape. That was a saga in itself, some of it adventure, some of it sheer drudgery, as I tried to disentangle the hows and whys of tape editing by cutting and splicing the eleven fifteen-minute tapes I had produced with my "portable" Tapak, and connecting it all with commentary. But it wasn't the same: I no longer needed to create that special relationship between the written word and the listener.

Gradually my love affair with radio faded. Each script in this book is a piece of that love affair, and a record of life in this wonderful province fifty years ago.

1. PORTRAITS

WEST COAST WIVES

*IN 1948 OR 1949, I APPROACHED THE POWERS THAT BE AT CBR WITH THE
suggestion that some programs on the life of women up the rugged
B.C. coast might make an interesting weekly series. Powers that be
agreed, and I set out to get the material.*

*In the course of my work with the Community Chest, I had become
acquainted with the Reverend Alan Greene of the Columbia Coast
Mission. This agency ran the Anglican mission ship* Columbia *up the
coast from Alert Bay north to Belize Inlet, Sointula, and Cape Scott.
Graciously, Mr. Greene arranged for me to join the* Columbia *at Alert
Bay, travel on her for two weeks, and return to Vancouver on her.*

*It was March and quite cold, but the weather was fresh and
windy and sometimes even sunny. We steamed in and out of long
inlets, through narrow tidal passages, around islands large and
small, visiting floating communities and the families who lived
there; island communities like Minstrel Island and Simoon Sound,
and Port Neville on the mainland. Sadly, I wasn't taken ashore at
the Cape Scott lighthouse; the weather was too windy and the ocean
too rough. Neither did I go ashore at Sointula, because, I was told,
women were not welcome.*

*The programs described women's lives on the B.C. coast in the
1940s. All five of the scripts in the series are included here. Unfortunately, none are dated.*

*I didn't realize it then, but life was already changing on the
coast. In one script I mentioned Queen Charlotte Airlines and in
another place, radio telephone. In time, with changing transportation and communications, the work of the* Columbia *became
obsolete, although the Columbia Coast Mission did struggle on for
another thirty years or so, trying to adapt. But there was really no
longer a place for a hundred-foot boat built in 1910, nor even for
the two later, more modern ones that followed* Columbia.

I remember it well, though. Mug-ups in friendly floathouses. Our

little ship caught in the last of the raging tide in the Euclataws, swept
like a leaf completely around. Dear Heber Greene appearing one
morning in one brown sock and one black. Holy Communion held in
a firelit living room in Kingcome Inlet. Children in orange lifebelts
playing in floating play areas fenced with chicken wire. Two small girls
walking hand-in-hand down the street of a nearly deserted Indian
village, below towering snow-capped mountain peaks.

I. Ports of Call

HAVE YOU BEEN WONDERING WHY WEST COAST WIVES ARE DIFFERENT FROM
wives in other parts of Canada? Well, I don't think that they are so
very different, actually, but a good many of them have living conditions that make them seem different. If you're wondering why their
living conditions are different, get out a good big map of British
Columbia, and I think you'll see the reason. It's an amazing coastline,
isn't it? I don't suppose anybody ever actually measured the number
of miles of coast from Vancouver to Prince Rupert—a distance of
about five hundred miles as the crow flies—but it would be pretty
safe to say that if we followed every little bay, every sound and inlet,
it would be about seven times five hundred miles—about thirty-five
hundred miles. According to one authority I consulted, the entire B.C.
coastline, counting Vancouver Island in, too, measures some seven
thousand miles over all. In addition to its length, the coast is also, for
the most part, extremely rocky and precipitous. Beaches are few and
far between and beset with treacherous rocks, shoals, and tidal
currents.

    And yet, up these steep and rocky shores grows some of the
world's finest timber, and in these treacherous waters is found some
of the world's finest fishing. So men must go there to bring out the
timber, to catch the fish. And it's only natural that they have evolved
ways of building homes in order to have their wives and families near
them. Most of us, even here in Vancouver, know very little of the life
of the people up the coast. Some of us have perhaps stopped in at
Alert Bay on a pleasure cruise, or spent a summer holiday at Savary
Island, or cruised around the west coast of Vancouver Island, but you
don't get to know much about the way people live on trips like that.
You don't meet the families in the floating communities, in isolated

ranches at the head of fjord-like inlets, in Indian villages on lonely
barren points far from the nearest house. That's why, when Mr.
Greene of the Columbia Coast Mission asked me if I'd like to visit
these places on the hospital-mission ship *Columbia*, I jumped at the
chance. There just couldn't be any better way of finding out how families on the B.C. coast really live.

I joined the *Columbia* at Alert Bay, my head already buzzing with
information gleaned on the trip up. I had shared my cabin with a girl
from Sointula whose grandparents had come from Finland to help
establish on Malcolm Island one of the very first co-operative settlements, so I heard how pleasant life is in that thriving
community—which, by the way, is still co-operative. Later, when I
saw the place, I could well believe it: well-tended homes, neat
gardens, trim and spruce little fishboats moored in orderly rows in the
bay. I had heard, too, about the origin of the place names we passed.
The captain told me about the Spanish explorers and Captains Cook
and Vancouver, and about the Indian settlements. I had heard what a
growing and thriving centre Alert Bay had become, but I didn't have
a chance then to see the town. The *Columbia* had had an emergency
call from Port Neville, and was in a hurry to get away.

I was met at Alert Bay by Heber Greene, brother of the Mr.
Greene who had invited me to take the trip. Heber Greene is the
minister who travels with the *Columbia*. Fortunately, since we hadn't
arranged to wear carnations in our buttonholes or anything, I recognized him by his likeness to his brother, and perhaps, too, because
the pure white hair and humorously gentle face atop his short person
could not have belonged to anyone other than a clergyman. We
collected my suitcases and my typewriter and hurried around to
where the *Columbia* was moored. Within five minutes we had cast
off and were starting on our way. I asked what the emergency call
was—if it was serious—and was told that it was a sick child. That was
all they knew. Details, as I soon discovered, are often scanty and
practically non-existent for these calls, due to the fact that they often
have to be relayed through several points before they reach the ship
by radio-telephone. But it doesn't matter about details; the *Columbia*
always answers these calls, often travelling many miles, at night,
through dangerous waters.

I think perhaps a word of explanation about the job of the
hospital-mission ship herself would be a good idea at this point. Her
job is also a result of the geographical difficulties of the coastline. She

spends six weeks at a time, manned by her crew of minister, doctor, skipper, engineer, and cook, calling in at all the little isolated homes and communities that dot the rocky shores between, roughly speaking, Powell River and Seymour Inlet, including the coast of Vancouver Island that lies within the area, and the other islands. Her function, I should say, is threefold: she brings spiritual, physical, and social comfort to many people of all faiths and nationalities, although it is an Anglican mission. Church services are held in her roomy main cabin. Babies are weighed and checked, teeth are pulled, emergency treatment for injuries is given in the well-equipped surgery. A projector and reels of 16mm film are also part of the ship's equipment, and pictures are shown in the cabin. But, to me, the greatest job the *Columbia* does is the break her visits provide in the lives of those on whom she calls. She does an informal social work job, as well as a medical and spiritual one. And she is part of the life of that part of the B.C. coast. Do you wonder that I felt I couldn't have any better way of finding out about life up there?

During the two weeks that I spent on the *Columbia*, I met many people, all of whom were engaged in many different ways in the serious business of living. Since by far the greatest majority of the people we visited lived in floathouses, perhaps we should mention them first. Do you know that until just a very short time before I took off on my trip, I'd never heard of these floating communities, which is possibly a comment on the well-known statement that most of us know very little about the way other people live!

The finest stands of timber don't plan to grow where there's a convenient beach on which to build a house. And so, those who make their living by felling this timber put their houses on floats and, over a period of years, these floating communities have developed their way of living to such a point that many of them can rival land communities in comfort, convenience, and attractiveness.

Then there are the little centres dotted along the coast that serve as distribution points. These are usually on land, though we visited at least one, Dumaresque's in Seymour Inlet, that was all on floats. Mostly, these distribution points are on a rocky bit of laboriously cleared land in a sheltered bay on the mainland or on an island with a good convenient water supply. There's usually a good dock where the weekly boat can tie up and land supplies, a gasoline station, a general store and post office, a hotel and beer parlour, possibly a radio telephone, and a float to which the recently established Queen

Charlotte Airlines can moor their planes. To these centres on boat day come little work boats from an area that may include a hundred miles of coastline, and to these centres come entire families on the weekends when a dance is planned. Sometimes these dances are just held for the fun of it. Often, though, they are held to raise money for some charitable cause like the Red Cross or the Conquer Cancer campaign; they'll sometimes raise as much as six hundred dollars at a single dance. From early on Saturday morning, little boats may be seen chugging through the passages and channels towards their destination, each boat with its full complement of men, women, boys, girls, and little children. They will, of course, spend the night on their boat, and not attempt the homeward trip until the next morning. The general stores in these gathering spots are just like country stores everywhere: they sell everything from pins to home permanents, from baby food to oilskins. Around the central stove, local gossip is exchanged, weighty decisions are made; behind the racks of clothing a budding romance is shyly begun. . . .

The loveliest of these central gathering places, from the point of view of setting, was Fort Neville. The Hansens live at Fort Neville; they've lived there for many years. Only Mrs. Hansen and her daughter, Karen, occupy the house now. The others are scattered by marriage and death, although some of the sons and daughters have set up their homes on the wide, flat, cleared space where the old house stands. The house is built of hand-hewn logs, beautifully smoothed and fitted, and weathered by thirty years of wind and weather to a lovely silver-gray. There is a gravelly beach that winds around a little peninsula into a quiet lagoon. The clearing is planted with fruit trees and flowering shrubs, and when I was there it was gay with daffodils and crocuses shining in the early morning sun. The house served both as general store and dwelling, and the hospitable sound and pleasant smell of perking coffee greeted us in the roomy, old-fashioned kitchen with its high ceiling crossed by hand-made beams. On a cushion, a golden cat rose and stretched and jumped down to rub against our legs. I soon discovered that golden cats were a feature of the Hansens. Out on the back porch, where I presently went with Mrs. Hansen, there was, quite literally, a pile of golden cats and kittens who frolicked ahead of us as we made our rounds. Up on the hillside were drifts of white chickens, and every so often a loud clucking came to us as another egg was laid. Yes, Port Neville is a lovely place.

It was that same day that we met the Blairs. We had stopped in at another little centre, Jackson Bay, and the Blairs had landed in their little white open boat just before us. Of course, we started to talk, and right away discovered that we had mutual acquaintances. They were hungry for reading material, and since the *Columbia* carries lots of magazines and whodunits especially for people like them, we asked them on board to choose what they wanted. Then, finding that our course led us past their home, we offered to tow their boat behind and cast them off when the time came. On the way, we talked some more. I found that Mr. Blair had the job of looking after the FM booster for the coast radio station on a completely isolated point on Hardwicke Island, at least half an hour by water from their nearest neighbours. They were a lesson in how to live alone and like it! They had chosen the job with their eyes wide open to everything such a life would mean in isolation and possible loneliness. When I met them they had already spent a year on their rocky promontory and were calmly planning for at least another five. They live, just the two of them, in an attractive, up-to-the-minute pre-fabricated house, just above the high water mark with the ceaseless sound of the diesel motors in their ears. I asked them if the sound didn't bother them, but they said they'd miss it if it weren't there. Then I asked, "But what do you do all the time?" And it seems that there's never a dearth of things to do—painting, decorating, building additions to their house, reading, listening to the radio. Mrs. Blair said that she's never been so up-to-date in current affairs. She spoke of her enjoyment of the different people who come to use the telephone, their conversation, their personalities. I asked her if the winter hadn't been pretty grim, and she said that mostly they'd been warm and comfortable, but that once in a while when the wind blew from a certain direction, the waves were lashed right into the house, through windows that were tightly closed and under the front door.

During the two-week trip, we visited single floathouses like the Stasiuks', where the two little red-haired girls are getting their schooling by means of correspondence courses; little operations like the Soder-mans', where our welcome was heart-warming; and hospitable bigger ones like the Johnsons', who have the most wonderful establishment on floats that you can imagine. Like the Dumaresques', where Polly, the camp cook, regaled us with home-made bread and cake in her spotless mess house kitchen; like Hansens' and Wrights', where Mary Hansen manages to write beautiful poetry and run her home and bring up her little girl, and where ex-public health nurse Mrs. Wright has the most beautiful baby boy imaginable; like the Hallidays at the head of King-

come Inlet, who have farmed there for fifty-five years. All these we
visited and many more. Some of them you'll hear more about in the rest
of these broadcasts about the women who live on the wild and rocky
coast of British Columbia. For they have carved a way of life from what
would seem to be the most unpromising material, and have made it
more than just living—they've made living the vital, pleasant, enjoyable
business that it ought to be.

Until next Monday, then.

II. Life on the Ocean Wave

THE PHRASE "LIFE ON THE OCEAN WAVE" CONJURES UP A MENTAL PICTURE OF
ships and limitless horizons, and in our ears we hear the faint echo
of a sea shanty. The kind of life that I'm going to talk about today
isn't any of those things, and yet it's certainly life on the ocean wave!
The people up the coast of British Columbia who live in the so-called
"floating communities" have homes that are, for the most part, every
bit as comfortable as those in which we live in the city, and some of
them are far more luxurious. Their children go to school, they hang
their washing out to dry, they even have greenhouses and chicken
houses. And all on floats. Floats that rise and fall with the tide, that
rock with the waves when the wind blows strongly against the shore,
and that sometimes, when the tide is very low, find themselves
perched for a few hours on the land.

Perhaps you remember that in the first broadcast of this series, I
mentioned these floating communities. I pointed out that they had
developed as a result of the steep, rocky, sometimes almost inacces-
sible shores of this coast. Because great stands of valuable timber
grow in these places, men have built these floating communities so
that they can tow their homes to the selected site, moor them there
while they log the area, and, in time, move on to the next place.
When I first heard about them, it seemed to me in my ignorance that
there couldn't be any more uncomfortable way to live. I had
forgotten man's ingenuity when faced by necessity.

After the various dwellings and buildings, such as schools,
machine shop, mess hall, and bunkhouses, have been towed to the
logging site, some days are spent in arranging them in the best
possible order, with carefully laid planks connecting them; in clearing

the ocean bottom under them, so that at low tide an unfortunately placed rock won't upset the equilibrium of one of the buildings. Each building is connected to the electric plant. The water system is hooked up to the nearby stream—fresh water is the main essential next to the stand of timber—so that each house has running water in its kitchen and bathroom. Then, with everything shipshape, the serious business of getting out the logs is begun, and life settles down into an everyday routine that is not so very different to the life of us who live on land with a basement and a furnace.

Nearly every dwelling on floats has a good oil stove in the kitchen, and a good oil burner strategically placed somewhere else in the house, so that there's plenty of comfortable heat to cook and live by. Personally, the thing I'd miss most in such an existence would be an open fireplace for wet winter evenings, but that, of course, is impossible. Life in a floating community has other short-comings. Not the least of these is the difficulty of making it safe for children. Every child wears a life belt until he or she has arrived at years of discretion, and each home is built on a big enough float to provide play space for small boys and girls. The float is surrounded by a good, stout, high fence of chicken wire and a gate whose latch is out of reach of small fingers. Of course, the children still fall in, but it's remarkable how soon they learn to make their way around the floats with complete confidence, with the sure-footedness and balance of kittens. And there are very few tragedies. They do happen once in a while, but probably not as often as one of our city children falls under the wheels of a passing car.

I'll never forget the first child I saw in her life belt. It was the first morning after I had joined the mission ship *Columbia*. We had tied up at Bendicksons, a floating community engaged in logging in Port Neville. The sun was shining brightly, and in the flower boxes on the floats some early spring daffodils were blooming. Leaning over one of the yellow flowers was a little girl with long fair hair dressed in bright blue corduroy overalls, her small chest firmly encased in a bril-liant orange life belt. She might have stepped straight out of a painting by Van Gogh.

It was at Bendicksons, too, that I first saw the interior of one of these houses on floats. We arrived quite late the evening before, and darkness had already fallen. Inside the lighted windows as we came in to the dock, I could see here a woman washing the dinner dishes, there a couple of small faces pressed against the window watching

our arrival. The kitchen that we entered was a cheery place, spotlessly clean, gay with cherry-patterned oilcloth on the table, and
bright cups and saucers on the open shelves of a Welsh dresser in
the corner. The gleaming white enamel oil stove gave off a cozy heat,
and the smell of good cooking lingered in the air. We heard that there
had been a big birthday party in the afternoon. One of the small children in the household had celebrated her birthday with her little
cousin in a neighbouring floathouse. There had been thirty guests,
twenty of them children. Presently, we had very concrete evidence of
that party. The table was filled with wonderful home-made birthday
cake thickly spread with the icing children love, home-made cookies
of all kinds, fruit bread. We enjoyed the birthday party, too!

The next morning, Mr. Greene, who is the Anglican minister who
travels with the *Columbia*, and I went to visit the school. We found
a schoolroom flooded with sunshine, tulips cut from brightly
coloured paper pasted on the windows, a spring mural drawn on the
blackboard, and ten scrubbed and shining boys and girls. The teacher
asked Mr. Greene to speak to the children, and they watched him
eagerly as he explained to them, very simply, the beautiful meaning
of the Easter season.

When we left Bendicksons, I had done some very drastic revision
of my preconceived ideas about floating communities!

At Carter Bay, where we docked a day or so later, there is a large
land logging operation. The bunkhouses and other camp buildings
are built precariously on the edge of the shore, but the homes of the
five family units are on floats. It was here that I saw what ingenuity
can produce. Mr. Cook decided that he didn't want just any old house
on a float. He wanted something different. In the channel outside of
Carter Bay lie some small islands called the Broken Islands. On one
of these, appropriately named Mistake Island, he found what he was
looking for. Twenty-five years before, a man had established a mink
farm on Mistake Island and then built a log house, landscaped his
island until he had turned it into a veritable show place, married, and
brought his wife there. She, however, didn't like it—whether it was
the mink or the surroundings, I don't know, but whatever the reason,
they abandoned the project and went away, and the people round
about came to call the island "Mistake." Well, it was on Mistake Island
that Mr. Cook found the house he wanted. It was the log house built
twenty-five years before. Twenty-five years of deserted solitude hadn't
improved it: the roof was thick with moss, and young cedars were

flourishing in it. But the logs were still sound. Mr. Cook determined to get the house onto floats and tow it over to Carter Bay. Somehow he managed it, and he's turned it into something really unusual in the way of a floathouse. The outside logs he has painted white. The interior of the living room is panelled in knotty pine, the bedroom in natural cedar. The kitchen shines with white paint, and a window over the sink looks out over the water to the Broken Islands. A modern bathroom, complete with a shower, and the original "mistake" has turned into an attractive and comfortable home.

Mrs. Cook, who said she had been horrified when she first arrived to make her home up there, now enjoys her life so much that when she makes a trip to the city she can't wait to get back! That, as a matter of fact, was the attitude of every woman I met on my trip up the coast. It wasn't said just because they thought it was the thing to say, either. They really meant it. When, for instance, I asked Mrs. Cook how she and the four other women at Carter Bay got along together, she answered that they have their disagreements like the women on any city block, but that, on the whole, they managed very well. Those with electric refrigerators make room in them for the perishables of those who don't, and the two washing machines are worked on a regular schedule, so that every woman has the use of one or the other of them. And I heard how the men had got together and made a crib for an expected new arrival in one of the homes. I have yet to hear of neighbours on a city block enjoying such a community of spirit and material belongings!

Perhaps the most interesting thing of all about the Cook home was the fact that Mr. Cook had never before built anything, let alone completely remodel a house. "I enjoyed every minute of it," he said, "but I surely learned the hard way!" The Cooks urged me to visit the Taits, who lived next door. "That's the place you should see," they said, and told me that Mr. Tait had been a builder and had really gone to town on the interior of his place. And he had! Walking into the Tait home is like walking into the most ultra-modern ranch-type bungalow imaginable. There's a beautifully appointed cabinet kitchen, simply gleaming with paint and Arborite and enamel. At one end, where the windows overlook the water, is a breakfast table and chairs. The windows are complete with Venetian blinds and swag curtains made of silky plastic with a tiny pattern. The living room has a curved ceiling and big windows right across the front to take in the view. The floor is covered from wall to wall with soft green rug. The bedroom and the bathroom are the last word in comfort and modernity.

In the days that followed, I saw many other floating communities, some large and some small. Not all have a school, and where they don't, the parents teach their children from the excellent correspondence courses supplied by the Department of Education. Some of them are complete with a general store and gas station, as at Simoon Sound. At the Wrens', where they proudly call themselves the Gunnysack Logging Co., because they started from next to nothing the year before, they now have a schoolhouse, a machine shop, and several homes. And one of the lads who is getting married this year has laid the foundations of the home to which he will bring his bride, great fresh-cut logs floating on the water, on which he will place the stout planking and build the walls of his house.

But all the time, as the *Columbia* made her rounds, as we went into little bays and through tide-torn passages and up narrow inlets where the snow-covered flanks of the mountains rose steeply from the water, the skipper kept telling me about Belize Inlet. Wait till you see Belize Inlet and the Johnsons. Finally, almost at the very end of our trip, we went up Belize, one of the narrow stretches of the sea that opens off Seymour Inlet. And I met the Johnsons.

Oscar and Maude Johnson are grandparents. You'd never think it possible. They look younger and have more vitality and enthusiasm than most people in their twenties. And they have made their floating community as nearly perfect as anything can be. I believe their operation employs about twenty men, and they are twenty lucky men! The bunkhouses have rugs on the floor, and every man's bed has a different brightly coloured blanket on it. The mess house is bright and white and clean. The outside of the buildings is just as neat and fresh as the inside, with green paint and white trim.

But, it is the Johnsons' own house that is amazing. You walk to the back door through a trellised arch covered with a vine that in summer blooms with honeysuckle. Across the front of the house, boxes of earth are filled with bulbs and standard roses. At the other end, there is a clematis vine. Behind the house a small greenhouse is full of young plants, even healthy-looking young tomatoes. On a little float nearby, Maude keeps her chickens—plump New Hampshires—and her white pigeons. Three self-important Pekingese are also members of the household, and a number of white Persian pussies stretch lazily in the sun.

There's nothing formal about the Johnson home. It's as pleasant and as comfortable as time and thought can make it. Maude's cooking is famous, and justly so. Maude herself is slender and youthful and crisp-looking. She has a wonderful collection of Chinese figures and Dresden china, and on the kitchen windowsill, cactus. When we were setting out the cups and saucers and sand-wiches and cookies for the traditional mug-up—everywhere up the coast you are presented with mountains of delicious food—Maude showed me some delicate little silver coffee spoons that had come from Oscar's family in Sweden, and the pitcher from which his grand-mother had always poured the thick, rich cream into the good Swedish coffee. Now that the Johnsons' son is grown up and married and away from home, Oscar's sister, Mimi, has come out from Sweden to make her home with them. And, although she's only been in this country about six months, her English is extraordinarily good. Anyway, I like English with a little accent, don't you?

They showed me their new boat, too. She is called the *Tumte*, which, in Swedish, means Santa Claus. Built as a work boat, rather than for pleasure, she is sturdy and beautifully equipped with comfortable sleeping quarters and proper plumbing.

The morning after we arrived there, I awoke to find a heavy white mist lying over the water, but after a while the mist blew away in little wreaths up the mountainsides, and the sun came out and sparkled on the snow covering their sides and on the blue water. The whole Johnson camp shone, too, with its green and white paint and its neat orderliness. Everybody gathered on the float to wave goodbye to us as we steamed back down the inlet towards Alert Bay.

And I felt that nothing could be built on a float that would ever again surprise me!

III. Minstrel Island Goes to Town

TODAY I'M GOING TO TELL YOU HOW ONE SMALL COMMUNITY OF TWELVE families up the coast of British Columbia is really going to town. Have you got out that map of B.C. again? Then, look up the coast till you come to a very long inlet called Knight Inlet. At its mouth, you'll find a little round island that fits into two larger islands, rather like three pieces of a well-matched jigsaw puzzle. The two larger islands are Cracroft and Turnour; the small one is Minstrel Island. Tradition has it that Minstrel received its name because at the time the royal surveyors were giving names to islands and points and channels not already named, there was a minstrel ship at anchor in the island's bay. Other place names in the vicinity seem to bear out the story—Negro Rock, Sambo Point, Bones Bay. But, however it came by its name, the fact remains that, to me at any rate, the word has a lovely, musical sound.

Minstrel Island is one of those little centres I mentioned last week, where a weekly boat leaves supplies for distribution over a wide area, where dances are held, where there's a government dock, a mooring for planes, a radio telephone, a school, a general store, a hotel and beer parlour. But back in 1932, there wasn't much more than a makeshift dock for the weekly boat. Some of its growth just happened, the way "Topsy just grew." A lot of it is due to the highly developed community sense of the twelve families to whom Minstrel Island is home. And a lot of that community awareness is due to the driving energy and enthusiasm of a woman. Doris Murphy herself would be the first to deny that she had anything at all to do with it. I can imagine her indignant remarks! But certainly if what I saw and heard during the twelve or fifteen hours we spent there were any criterion, Doris Murphy has had a great deal to do with it.

Doris is one of those rare people who is able to infect those around her with her own enthusiasm. She's not an armchair planner; when she thinks something needs doing, she gets busy and does it, or if it's too big for her to tackle alone, it's not long before there's a whole group on the job. She's not an armchair critic, either. When she disapproves of something, from the state of a sidewalk to an article in the newspaper, she doesn't just sit back and say that something should be done. In the case of the sidewalk, there's a new boardwalk at Minstrel Island now. And in the case of the offending newspaper article, she actually had the editor eating humble pie in response to her spirited attack by letter.

It's interesting about that newspaper article. Everywhere I went up the coast, I found the wives and mothers and, in several cases, the men, too, highly incensed by a story in a local daily magazine supplement which purported to give an accurate picture of life up the coast. The writer was himself an up-coast dweller, and should have known whereof he spoke—anyway, the magazine section editor thought so. But the people up the way didn't. And the interesting thing is that, of all the people whom I heard indignantly deny his story, only one actually sat down and wrote to that magazine section editor and said why. That person was Doris Murphy of Minstrel Island. When I talked to Doris about it, she got indignant all over again, and the things she said painted such a vivid picture of life up the coast as it really is in the vast majority of cases, that I think I'll tell you a little about it.

Briefly, this article stated that life up the coast was a miserable affair. The people lived in shacks they lacked the money to insure. The children were a neglected, uneducated lot, brought up by inexperienced parents on inadequate diets. Most of the children, said the writer, had never seen an orange!

As Doris pointed out, the up-coast homes, for the most part, have modern plumbing and electric light. I know that's so, because I was in dozens of them. As for the children, said Doris heatedly, "I'm ashamed to say that the children up here waste more of even luxury food than most city children even see. I don't think there are any foods on the market that our children do not take as a matter of course. They have an abundance of fruit and vegetables, butter, and meat, and to date I haven't heard of any mothers up here who are waiting for the margarine ban to be lifted so as to have a spread for the children's bread." I can go along with Doris there, too, because I don't think there was a home I entered where there was not a big bowl of fresh fruit to be had for the taking. And never anywhere have I seen such wonderful food, beautifully prepared and served.

Getting madder as she went along, Doris said, "And what's more, our medicine cabinets are full of vitamin pills, and contrary to what that writer says, most mothers are skilled, not only in the care of their children, but also in home nursing. If the mothers up here are ignorant, then so are mothers everywhere, for they were drawn from the same stock. We didn't arise from barnacles, or come up out of the sea. Most of us came from cities or towns and had good educations. Many are nurses, teachers, and university graduates!"

Doris herself has lived in that part of the world for twenty-five years, and like almost everyone else I met on my two-week trip up the coast, she wouldn't live anywhere else on a bet. The Murphy home is on a float just across the narrow channel from the little town of Minstrel Island itself; her husband has a logging operation on the nearby shore. It is a roomy, comfortable house, with all the conveniences that we have in city homes. Her four children are a healthy, well-fed, well-behaved brood, the eldest about eight. Besides herself and her husband and children, there is room in her home for her mother, and room and board for the young teacher of the newly acquired Minstrel Island school. The atmosphere in her home is cheerful and informal; you feel comfortable and at ease the minute you

set foot inside the door. There's a pleasant confusion of people and
children and cats, all of them interested in and hospitable to the visitor.
A friendly cup of tea appears on the big kitchen table as if by magic.

As soon as Doris heard why I was travelling with the *Columbia*,
she told me there was a combined meeting of the Minstrel Island
Board of Trade and the Ladies' Club that night to discuss the building
of a community centre, and asked me if I'd like to go. Of course, I
jumped at the chance. So after supper, Mr. Murphy, the young school
teacher (whose name is Mr. Edge), Doris, and I climbed into the
Sardine, and putt-putted across the narrow channel to the Wilsons'.
The *Sardine*, by the way, is the family's equivalent of a car—an open
boat with an inboard motor and a definite personality of its own. It
doubles in the daytime as a school bus, ferrying the young Murphys
to school in the morning, and bringing them home at night.

Arrived at the Wilsons', we found the same cheerful clutter of
grown-ups and children, with Mrs. Wilson busy putting the younger
ones to bed. Then our ranks swelled with the addition of Mr. Wilson.
Mrs. Wilson would stay until the children were all in bed, and then
her husband would leave the meeting to do his stint of baby-sitting
while she went to the second half of the meeting. We walked over a
steep hill and down again into the little settlement of Minstrel Island.
In the darkness, buildings loomed up to the right and left of us: the
schoolhouse, the café, the new structure to house the radio-telephone, the big bulk of the hotel, and farther off to our right on the
shore, the machine shop, a dwelling, the dim length of the dock
stretching into the bay, the general store. Presently, a long building
loomed in front of us. It was a two-storied affair, the upper half used
as apartments, the lower as a meeting hall. It was because this place
is slowly falling to pieces from age and decrepitude that the meeting
was being held. I gathered from the conversation that the Ladies'
Club had asked the Board of Trade for this joint meeting to discuss
a new community centre, and that all the men were not in favour of
the project. It sounded as though it was going to be a good meeting!

In the hall a table with benches around it had been drawn over
by the stove, and a group of men and women were already sitting
around it. More people arrived until there were about fifteen present,
and the chairman, who in private life is the hotel owner, opened the
meeting. I sat quietly beside Doris and listened. The regular business
of the board was discussed first: the installation of the radio-telephone, freight rates on the boat bringing supplies from the city, some

difficulty with the dam behind the town that supplies the water. A new secretary-treasurer was elected, the young school teacher. Each item was well discussed, motions formally made, seconded, and passed. And then Doris Murphy was asked to take over the meeting for discussion of the community centre project. She demurred at first, and there was some heated informal discussion. When she realized that the cherished plan was receiving definite opposition, she leapt to battle. To the faint-hearted who wondered who was going to do the building and where the money was coming from, she pointed out that the whole community would do the building, and as to the money, they'd raise it, and anyway, the Ladies' Club had already received promises for donated logs. When someone asked if it wasn't a pretty big project for a community with only twelve permanent families, she wondered openly how these same twelve families had managed to get all the other improvements, such as the board sidewalks and the radio-telephone. When asked who would use the centre, she said that every man, woman, and child in the Minstrel Island area would use it for games like badminton, for meetings, for dances. And what was more, they'd all contribute to the cost of building it. She pointed out that with the unsafe condition of the hall they were in, there was nowhere to hold a dance, and added a pungent comment that a place to hold dances and moving picture shows would detract from the fascination of the beer parlour. It wasn't long before her enthusiasm had swept away all objections, and plans were discussed for beginning the project: the relative merits of various kinds of roofs, restrooms, land rights on the foreshore for a proposed building site. In no time at all, it was decided to call a big general meeting of everyone within a hundred-mile area to present the plans. A sub-committee was named to investigate the costs. Tentative suggestions were made as to how the centre would be run.

At the end of the meeting, everybody felt a little breathless and dazed except Doris, who was tired but triumphant. There was no doubt in anybody's mind. Minstrel Island would have a community centre. The Ladies' Club and Doris Murphy had done it again! The meeting around the table broke up, and the group dispersed in the darkness, calling friendly goodnights. We trudged back over the hill to the Wilsons', climbed into the *Sardine*, and putted back across the channel. The wind was cold and fresh in our faces and blew away the cobwebs from the meeting. Behind the little boat, phosphorescence sparkled and darted in the churning wake.

The next morning was one of bright sunshine and a fresh breeze. From the deck of the *Columbia*—we were moored to the Murphy float—I watched the young Murphys and the teacher sputter off in the *Sardine* across the water to school. Shortly after, we said goodbye to the adult Murphys, cast off our moorings, and went over to the big government dock. The little bay was full of activity. Boats chugged in and out, figures moved purposefully up and down the dock. The general store, where I presently made my way, was a hive of industry. I exchanged good mornings with faces familiar from the meeting the night before, and looked around. There was everything for sale in that store, Indian sweaters and ice cream included. I made my few purchases and wandered out into the morning sunshine. Up on the hillside, school was in session, with Mr. Edge leading his sixteen pupils up the thorny road of knowledge. Out on the bay, the Queen Charlotte Airlines plane roared down to its mooring. A boat went out to meet it. Along the board sidewalk, housewives were coming to the store for their daily shopping. The busy sound of a saw and hammer came from somewhere. Down on the shore, the waves lapped on the vacant place where sometime in the not-so-distant future the community centre would rise. Minstrel Island is going to town!

IV. Halliday House

THE MOUTH OF THE RIVER LOOKED FLAT AND MUDDY AND UNINTERESTING. Although it was a fine bright day, the damp and cold of many remembered days of rain and chill winds lay over the yellow salt marshes. The long-neglected totem on the riverbank looked somehow desolate and almost menacing. Obviously it was many years since the Indians who had conceived it had given it any meaning by painting it. On the flat landscape it stood grey and crude, the symbol of a long-vanished welcome.

The white boat with its outboard motor fussed importantly up the still water, sending clouds of wild seabirds from the surface into the bright cold air where they were soon lost against the dark mountains.

The mountains were very close. There was the flat expanse of salt marsh on either side of the river, and then the mountains rose, seemingly almost straight up, with patches of snow lying low on their sides, and a solid, smooth blanket of white on their summits.

Someone, I think it was the engineer, pointed out some geese to me. They had risen from the water and winged upwards to the mountains, frightened by the approach of our boat.

This, then, was the head of Kingcome Inlet. All morning we had steamed up the ever-narrowing reach of the sea between snow-capped peaks whose feet were washed by the breaking waves of the tides.

They told me on the *Columbia* that I was lucky that it wasn't raining. Perhaps because the mountains rise so steeply from the water, catching every rain cloud as it passes, Kingcome Inlet is often blanketed in rain, and cold winds from the snowy peaks blow down the valley that the river has carved for itself. But I was lucky. The day was cold, but it was bright and clear. In the little white boat from the *Columbia*, with its noisy outboard motor, there were: the doctor, complete with his bag of medicines and instruments; the minister, Heber Greene; the engineer; and myself. Leaving the *Columbia* safely moored in the deep water, we had launched the smaller boat and started on our way upriver to the Indian village.

The river wound and twisted its way between muddy banks where the reeds and sedges still lay flat and yellowed from the winter rain and snow. Ahead of us, beyond the flats, the banks were lined with alder. In the distance they lay like a rosy cloud. As we putted closer they took on form and colour, the trunks silvery-grey like birches, the branches hung with moss and with the pink catkins of spring. It was the catkins that in the distance had given them the rosy look.

We fussed on up the river, saw the Indian village of the Kwaki-utls, and in the late afternoon, put into shore again about two miles from the river's mouth. It was a somewhat precarious landing on a somewhat precarious dock. At some time the landing had been built with care, but the years had made the planks uneven and uncertain, and even I, who flatter myself that many seasons of shooting and fishing with my husband have accustomed me to all sorts of bridges, picked my way with unusual care along the dock and up and across the river bank.

Has all this so far sounded isolated and lonely and lost? I hope so, because that's the way it seemed to me. They had told me that the Hallidays lived here, and to me it seemed impossible that anyone would want to live in such a lost and forsaken place. The Indians, yes—this country was their country. They had lived here since time immemorial. But I couldn't imagine why anyone else would want to settle on the bank of that river at the head of Kingcome Inlet.

Nothing had prepared me for what I saw when we gained the top of the bank. Beyond the edge of pink-tipped alder and yellowed marsh grasses were lush fields that stretched across the flats to where the mountainside sprang upwards. I wish I could have seen those fields in summer. As it was, in the early spring, they lay slowly greening in the cold sunlight. They were wet and a little muddy and they smelled that lovely smell of land that is soon to provide crops for men and for animals. They were well-kept fields, with good fences. Across the way, in another field, cattle were grazing, and we looked across to where a big house and barn stood, tucked under the shoulder of the mountain.

It took us maybe ten minutes to walk over the intervening fields, through gates and over the little stream that wound its way through the pastures. And then we had arrived at the Hallidays': a tall grey barn, a big old house, and all the other buildings that go to make up a self-contained community of one family.

We went in the back way. As in any other country home, nobody ever uses the front door. Mrs. Halliday and Mr. Reg Halliday made us feel at home right away. And that's another thing: everywhere we went on that trip up the coast of B.C., we were made to feel at home right away, sometimes in the living room, but far more often in the kitchen. At the Hallidays', we were shown into the living room, but somehow it wasn't long before the Hallidays had found that we hadn't had lunch in the Indian village and that we were—and I mean it—starving! A huge lunch appeared in the kitchen as if by magic, and we proceeded to tuck it away with more gusto than manners. Meanwhile, I learned something about the Hallidays.

They had built their first house in 1893, just behind the site of the one we were in. Believe it or not, they had rowed from Comox all the way to the head of Kingcome Inlet. I asked Mr. Halliday—he's 83 now—how and why he had decided on that particular spot to settle, and he told me this story. "Back in 1893," he said, "we were living in Comox."—And at this point, I say, "Get out that map of B.C.!"—but to get back to Mr. Halliday, he said, "We got itchy feet, so I asked the land agent where was the very best land to start a farm. And he told me that at the head of Kingcome Inlet there was some of the best land he'd ever seen. So four of us rowed there!" If you've got that map in front of you, you can see that it was quite a row. Once they'd seen the situation, they decided to bring their families and make their home there. Their hope was that they would start a settlement, and I think that the fact that a settlement didn't start from their migration is probably one of Mr. Halliday's big disappointments in life. For a while, a big lumber company did make the Kingcome River a busy centre, with many families and a school and much coming and going, but they left in 1925. They decided that the area was logged out, and moved away. After that, the valley was left to the Indians and to the four original settlers. Of these settlers, today there remains only the Halliday family: Mr. and Mrs., a son, daughter-in-law, two grandsons, and the new wife of one of them.

Altogether, there are six living Halliday sons and daughters (there were eight born), fourteen grandchildren, three great-grandchildren. I wondered what arrangements they made when another Halliday child was expected, and Mrs. Halliday said that after the first two, who were born in Comox, she had her babies at home, there at the head of Kingcome Inlet. She told me about one of those trips to Comox. They started out in the rowboat, hoping to make the trip in a week at most, but they struck bad weather, wind and rain and storms. They were forced to camp uncomfortably on shore time after time, and finally arrived in Comox fourteen days later. Just by way of contrast, another time that Mr. Halliday made the journey on what I'm sure couldn't have been such an important mission, the wind and the tides were with them, and it took just three days of sturdy rowing.

Times like that I imagine they wondered why they had ever decided to live up Kingcome Inlet. Mostly, though life hasn't been easy, they've never regretted their decision. They've found a great deal of pleasure in the gradual development of their land, and there have been high spots, such as the time, some twenty-five years ago, when their dream of a big, comfortable, up-to-date house became a reality. Mrs. Halliday loves her garden, and took me out to see her early spring garden ablaze with purple and yellow crocuses, the gold of forsythia against the wall of the house, the slender whiteness of snowdrops. Mr. Halliday proudly showed me pictures of the incredible vegetable garden that he grows in a field below the house every year, incredible because everything—turnips, beets, and what-have-you—grow to such a tremendous size.

We stayed all night at the Hallidays'. The family hadn't had a church service for many months, and asked Heber Greene, the minister on the *Columbia*, to conduct one that evening. So we stayed. From the living room window I watched the daylight fade from the mountaintops across the valley, and heard how, if one watched carefully in the early morning, there were three sunrises, one behind each of three ascending peaks as the sun came up behind them. I heard, too, about the strange symmetrical square of light the moon threw sometimes on the mountain behind the house. Later in the evening, the fire was lighted in the big open fireplace. By its light, Heber Greene conducted the communion service. We sang hymns to the strains of the old harmonium played by Mrs. Reg., finishing with the familiar and lovely "Now the Day is Over." Afterwards we sat around the fire and talked of many things, about the early days, the original farmhouse of logs, and books, of which they have a large number, many of them about British Columbia and its history.

When Mrs. Reg. took me upstairs to my room, I spotted the strangest-looking object on the landing. It looked rather like one of those round Scotch loaves of bread, where two of the rounds have been placed one on top of the other and then baked. Overcome by curiosity, I asked what it was. "Why, it's a fungus!" replied Mrs. Reg. It was found growing on one of the trees back of the house many years ago, and brought into the house because it's such a strange shape, even for a fungus. For some reason, it hardened, until finally it became a plaything for the young Hallidays. Three generations of small children have played with that fungus. They've dropped it and rolled it, and even tried to hammer nails into it. They called it, still call it, for that matter, "Off-a-tree." And there "Off-a-tree" still sat in its corner, slightly scarred from its years of service, but waiting patiently for another generation of Hallidays to come along and play with it.

That overnight stay with the Hallidays of Kingcome Inlet was in some ways the high spot of my two-week trip up the coast. The story of a family has always fascinated me, and this family, against its background of rugged B.C. mountains, the solitary salt marshes, the old Indian village up the valley, the waters of the long narrow inlet below, winding to the open sea; this family with its story of fifty-five years of everyday living, of becoming a happy and self-sufficient unit in the wilderness, has more than usual interest. It is a story complete with a title: Halliday House.

V. In the Shadow of the Totem

*As you read this script, and some of the others in the book,
remember that it was written more than fifty years ago, when
understandings of and references to people and places were
very different.*

TOTEM POLES, STRANGE FLOWERING OF A NATIVE CIVILIZATION, CAST THEIR
shadows in many little Indian villages and settlements on the coast of
British Columbia. Too often these days they are ungainly shadows,
leaning a little to one side. The Indians are forgetting the meaning
they once held for them. The paint is weathering from them, too, the
bright colours dimming and wearing off. Just the carved outlines are
left, the crudely formalized raven heads, the bears, the whales, the
outstretched wings of the Thunderbird.

In the shadow of the totems live people who have taken on, in
very large measure, the way of life of the white race. The old tribal
distinctions, based as they were on family, are rapidly dying out. The
measure of success has become the ownership of the biggest car, the
fastest boat. The young people drift to the cities, and the villages are
largely left to the very young and the very old.

The day that I visited the Kwakiutl village at the head of Kingcome Inlet, the village was more than ever deserted. Everyone who
could possibly get away had gone digging clams. A few men were
sitting on a log on the riverbank, enjoying the pale warmth of the
early April sunshine. An old woman was preparing her garden for
vegetable planting. Two small girls, their button-black eyes bright
with shy curiosity, walked down the main street, clutching each other
firmly by the hand. Smoke was rising from a few of the chimneys; a
snowy line of washing fluttered in the wind.

We had come up the river in the longboat from the HMS
Columbia, winding between the high muddy banks, along a shallow
course that was so uncertain that at one point we ran aground on the
gravelly bottom and had to wait until the incoming tide raised the
level of the water enough to float us off again. On either side of the
valley the mountains rose, snow-covered. Here and there on the
banks, patches of snow still lay in sheltered places. We rounded a
bend in the river and came upon the village. A wide bar stretched

into the water, and drawn up on it were several dugout canoes. Beyond the bar and farther along the shore, the little white church stood out clearly in the sunshine against the dark mountainside. Beside it towered the great totem topped by the outstretched wings of the Thunderbird. The Indians of this village had raised the totem to commemorate King George the Fifth's silver jubilee. The colours on it are still bright and clear.

We landed, and while the doctor conducted a dental clinic on the front porch of one of the houses, Mr. Greene (the minister of the *Columbia*) and I walked over to the church. Built by the Indians themselves, it is a lovely little building with, on the altar, some beautiful examples of Indian carving at its best. I was enormously interested in the way they had managed to impart the essential quality of their own art to the furnishings of this Christian house of worship. Presently, Mr. Greene disappeared with Mr. Christmas, the missionary who, with his wife, looks after the state of spiritual grace of these Kwakiutls. So I wandered back to the village and presently discovered the old community house.

The community house was once the main unit of Indian village life. Built ingeniously of hand-hewn planks with tremendous heavy adzed beams, it housed many families, each family having a certain space allotted for its use. There were no room divisions, no privacy. On special occasions, it became the centre of community festivities, dancing and feasting going on around the fires lighted on the hard-packed earth floor.

The door of this particular community house stood open, so I went in. I blinked in the sudden gloom after the sunlight outside. But as my eyes became accustomed to the semi-darkness, I looked around. The only light came from the space between the planks that ran the length of the ridge-pole above my head, and from the open door behind me. Snow was still heaped on the floor under the central opening in the roof. Drawn well to one side lay a great war canoe, hollowed from a huge single tree trunk. The upright poles that supported the great ceiling beams were carved in the same strange forms as adorn the outside totems. Stored on either side of the doorway were things that looked for all the world like very big bath-tubs. They were carved in the likeness of a hollowed-out, semi-crouching human form, high at one end, quite low at the other. For a few minutes, I was really puzzled. I couldn't imagine what they were for. Then I remembered. Of course. They were food containers for the potlatch feasts that had at one time played such an important part in Indian community living.

Potlatches have been outlawed now, although lenient authorities occasionally close their eyes when one is held. The potlatch is based on a primitive concept of insurance, a concept which worked in theory, but which in practice often defeated its purpose, especially as the Indians became more civilized and potlatches became mostly an excuse for one enormous party. The idea, roughly, is this. A man decides to give a potlatch, perhaps to celebrate the coming of age of his son. For weeks and months he has been collecting food and drink and suitable presents for his guests. If he is a chief, these presents must be fine enough to maintain his prestige in his own and neighbouring tribes; they used to be furs and weapons and food, but of recent years they have become extraordinary things such as bundles and bundles of drawer handles, or hundreds of pounds of flour. He then issues his invitations. And when his guests arrive, there is dancing and feasting for many days, or until the host runs completely out of supplies. Then the guests leave, taking their presents with them, and leaving their host so impoverished that it takes months for him to get back on his feet again. Since each of his guests is also expected to give a potlatch sooner or later, the original idea was that the host would in turn receive many presents and, in this way, provide for himself and his family a fairly steady supply of food, furs, and so forth. In practice, though, and in recent years, a man would entertain at a potlatch, but very often his guests did not entertain in their turn, and the host would be really poor. Also, the feasts became pretty riotous affairs, and the government finally banned them altogether. It was for these feasts that the great hollowed-out containers had been made.

Presently, I went outside again and stood looking up at the dilapidated totem that guarded the door. Down the street came the two small girls I'd seen earlier. This time they stopped and essayed a smile. I tried a little conversation, admiring the delicate little earrings one small girl was wearing in her pierced ears. I didn't get very far, though. So we walked down the street in companionable silence.

The houses were, for the most part, pretty rundown and uncared for. Some of them were obviously deserted. All of them were raised a good two feet from the ground, probably a relic from the days when good Kwakiutl residences were sometimes as much as thirty feet above the ground. Possibly, too, the position of this village on the bank of the Kingcome River made it subject to occasional flooding when the river was very high. Here and there, however, were new homes. These were built in the modern manner with neat clapboards and composition roofs.

Judging by the fish bones that I saw in piles on the riverbank, salmon still forms a large part of an Indian's diet, although he is fondest of those little silver fish called oolichans. Oolichans are rich in oil, and the oil has, or used to have, many uses, from fuelling lamps to preserving berries and shellfish. It was an inherited privilege attached to the chieftainship among the Kwakiutls to dip the net in which the first oolichan of the season was caught. Today, of course, many Indians of the coast own excellent fish boats, and many of them in recent years have become really wealthy from the development of the fishing industry. They still, however, take advantage of the privilege that belongs to them alone, that of spearing salmon as they go up the rivers to spawn. The salmon are then smoked and laid out on big racks on the bank to dry. I remember what an indelible impression of wild beauty and strangeness I got one night driving down the Fraser River canyon, when, as we rounded a curve in the road, we came upon a party of Indians engaged in this age-old pursuit, everything glowing redly in the light of a huge bonfire.

I must admit that I found that village of the Kwakiutls up King-come Inlet depressing. It looked like a place that life was passing by. Everywhere were signs of neglect and desertion. Except for the totem by the church, all the others standing so forlornly outside the houses hadn't been painted or tended. The community house was obviously disused. The great feast dishes had lain forgotten in the dim corners where I found them for many a day. And I wonder how long it's been since the great war canoe slipped through the water, propelled by strong young men?

The B.C. coast Indian of today, though, is learning to take the best as well as the worst of the white men's civilization. He has worked for, and at last obtained, the vote. He will vote in these elections for the first time. He is learning to make his living, to want education, to stand as a Canadian citizen, the original Canadian citizen, beside his brother Canadians of every race and creed.

It is sad that the old picturesque customs are dying, but there seems to be no midway point of compromise, except during the painful and unhappy period of transition from one life to another. You couldn't wish that state on your worst enemy, let alone these essentially fine people who lived on these shores long before the white man came.

It's interesting to note in this connection a widespread revival of interest in preserving the relics of this vanished way of life. At the University of British Columbia at the present time, many of the best totems have been collected and are being carefully and painstakingly restored. There is a real attempt being made to collect the old legends before they have vanished from men's memories forever. I would like to see a picture made for posterity of some outpost where the old way still persists. And we have, of course, the immortal canvases of Emily Carr, who captured in her paintings the real spirit of the Indian as he was.

Nevertheless, it was with a feeling of sadness that I left the village of the Kwakiutls and started down the river once more. As we rounded the bend, I turned and looked back. Mellowed by distance, the grey houses and leaning totems looked peaceful in the afternoon sun. On the log on the riverbank, the men still sat sunning themselves. In her little patch of garden, the old woman still worked, and up the street were walking the same two small girls, intent on some childish errand.

We rounded the bend, and all that I could see were some wisps of lazy smoke rising from unseen chimneys.

The river received us and bore us swiftly back down to the sea.

UP-COUNTRY PIONEERS

*The "West Coast Wives" series was a success, and so I suggested
another weekly series, this time about up-country pioneers. This
became a reality in the autumn of 1950. I spent a happy September,
first taking a bus trip to gather material and then writing the four
scripts.*

*September can be a beautiful month in the upper country, and
September 1950 must have been one of the loveliest: crisp, frosty
mornings; clear, warm sunny days; star-filled nights. The leaves on
the cottonwood trees had been turned into golden dollars by the
frost, and the huckleberry bushes growing in the gullies that cut
through the barren brown hills were now scarlet flames licking up
the hillsides.*

*I had never travelled the Fraser Canyon on a bus before. Seated
up high, I could look down in places to three old roads below, each
one an improvement on the one just below it. Running right along
the hewn-out banks of the river, the railroads, of course, twisted and
turned, the CPR on one bank, the later-built CNR on the other. Just
above the rails were small snatches of the oldest road of all, the
canyon trail travelled by the motley crowd of gold seekers in the
Gold Rush of 1858. Above that, the first motor road. How well I
remember driving on that narrow, largely unpaved road—as early
as 1928. Creeping around hairpin curves, passing a bus on one of
the wooden scaffoldings built precariously out over the river where
there simply wasn't room for a road on the precipitous cliff face,
and where, as we inched past the great bulk of the bus on one side
and hundreds of feet of nothingness on the other side, we used to
say there wasn't room for a piece of paper between us.*

*I have very clear memories of my information-gathering bus trip.
I remember riding across a high plateau one moonlit night when the
huge stars hung low above me, and the headlights of the bus swung
around a curve and lighted up the ghostly white trunks of a grove of
those cottonwood trees. Winding through the lodgepole pine forest on*

*the reddish dirt road above Lytton. Driving past the deserted,
tumbledown log cabin that Edith Wallace Wilson told me was the
prototype of Hetty Dorval's cabin (Hetty, of course, was the heroine
of that famous Canadian's first novel of the same name). I
remember my visit to Dr. Margaret Ormsby at her home partway up
Okanagan Lake, and how graciously she gave of her time and
knowledge to answer my questions about the Hudson's Bay Fur
Brigade Trail, facts that I badly needed for a B.C. School Broadcast I
had been commissioned to write for the Department of Education.*

*Then there was the night that a bus dropped me at eleven o'clock
in a darkened village. I went into the dim-lit, shabby lobby of the
only hotel that graced the place. No one stood behind the desk. No
one answered the tinny bell standing on the counter. More than a
little panic-stricken, I picked up my suitcase and my typewriter and
stood uncertainly under the pale street light on the corner. What was
I to do? The headlights of a car drove slowly down the street. Should
I hail it? The car stopped. The front window rolled down. A face
looked out. "Sallie! What on earth are you doing here?" It was an
old friend who had recently moved to the valley in which the little
village stood. I was rescued!*

Lovely memories . . .

I. Mamit Valley

October 6, 1950

THE FIRST THING WE SAW IN THE FARMHOUSE KITCHEN WAS THE STATELY,
gleaming-white bulk of the new refrigerator. Its sleek smoothness,
built for modern efficiency, looked almost self-conscious in its functional simplicity, self-conscious because, although its surroundings
were freshly painted white and spotlessly clean, the kitchen was large
and airy and comfortably non-functional. The mistress of the kitchen,
Miss Sophia Steffens, was understandably proud of her new possession, and we inspected the freezing compartment and the shining
shelves, and peered into the interior workings of the refrigerator,
interested by the fact that even such mammoth modern objects have
been adapted to farmhouse use. You see, there's no electricity in the
house where Miss Sophia Steffens lives with her brother, Rupert, and

so the beautiful new refrigerator works on a little coal-oil flame.

Miss Steffens has lived in the valley since 1904 when she and her sister, Pauline, rode bumpily up the Nicola Valley in the stagecoach to the little town of Lower Nicola. Today, the road through the Mamit Lake valley leaves the highway that runs between Spences Bridge and Merritt at Lower Nicola and winds up across rolling, bare brown hills to the high, upland valley of Mamit Lake. Up there, three thousand feet or so above sea level, the hills are thickly timbered with jack and ponderosa pine, and along the creek beds cluster the white trunks of the cottonwoods, their round green leaves whispering and rustling to every passing breeze. The musical singing of the cottonwood leaves always makes me think of Chinese windbells. Perhaps they are a sort of rustic, natural windbell of B.C.'s up-country.

Are you wondering what B.C.'s up-country is? Well, it's the interior of the westernmost of Canada's provinces. We coast-dwellers always talk about going up-country when we speak of leaving the seacoast and crossing the mountains of the Coast Range to the dry plateau that forms so much of the British Columbia hinterland. It's rather like travelling to a different country. Down here on the coast, the air is mild and humid and it's never very hot or very cold. The vegetation is thick and lush, with much tangled undergrowth of bramble and bracken. Up-country, the air is clear and dry, very hot in summer and cold in winter. The rolling land is open, with few trees, except where there is water, and on the slopes grow bunchgrass and sage and cactus. At higher altitudes the trees begin, mostly pine and fir. But there's no undergrowth here, just long, shining mountain grass that in the early summer is starred with the crimson of Indian paintbrush, the vivid blue of wild lupine and the orange of tiger lilies.

The Steffens' land in the Mamit Valley is like that, except that they have cleared much of it into wide, rolling meadows for hay and grain. I came there one summer afternoon and for a minute before entering the comfortable, white farmhouse I stood quite still and let my eyes rest on the scene. The rolling fields first, with the young green of the half-grown wheat, the cluster of deeper green that marked the course of the creek through the valley bottom, the dark green of the pines that climbed the steep rise on the other side of the valley. The sunlight lay clear and golden over it all, and everything—house and outbuildings, fields and wooded hills—seemed held in a deep summer silence.

Round the corner of the house trotted a friendly dog, wagging his tail inquiringly. Then a cat stalked across the driveway, looking majestic and unconcerned. I made my way to the back door, met Miss Steffens, and was invited into the kitchen where the refrigerator stood. Over cups of tea and thick slices of buttered toast, we talked about the past.

It was on May 23, 1887, on the first through train to the Pacific coast, that Sophia Steffens's mother arrived in Ashcroft from England to join her husband in making a home in this wild new country. For a year they lived uneasily in the barren little town, and then moved down to Lytton, where the bright, peacock-blue waters of the Thompson River tumble into and lose themselves in the muddy Fraser. Here the Steffenses opened a store and began to raise a family, and quite a family it was, too: thirteen altogether, nine boys and four girls. It began to be apparent that the store could never support them all, and finally Mr. Steffens decided to take up land. An Indian had told him one day of some fine land in the Mamit Lake valley, so with the Indian as guide, and taking along his eldest son, Mr. Steffens rode over the mountain to the place. But it was not for another three years that the move was finally made. It was in 1904 that Sophia and her sister, Pauline, after leaving the stagecoach at Lower Nicola, rode in and camped under a tree, and the next morning their father waved his hand over the valley and said, "Well, girls, this is where it will be." The next morning they rode down through the trees, for the land was then still uncleared, and chose the site for their new home. The old log cabin still stands, unused now, for the present farmhouse was built twenty-nine years ago of trees cut by the Steffens boys and made into boards with the saw and planer that they bought for the purpose. They hired a neighbour to design and build the house, and when it was finished, the family moved in. Today, all but Sophia and her brother, Rupert, have married and moved away.

Life in the new country wasn't easy for Sophia's mother. She was afraid of many things, of snakes, of the wild-looking cattle that soon roamed the range on the land they had pre-empted. She was afraid of the deep pools in the creek where the boys sometimes fished. But there were many things she loved about the new life, too. She loved to look across the valley as we had done that afternoon. She loved the changing seasons and the deep quiet, so different from the noise of towns and cities. She even liked the small, seemingly endless household tasks, tasks that were performed without any of the labour-saving devices that city-dwellers take for granted, without running water, without electricity. And before they moved into the new house, these tasks were performed in a log cabin roofed with mud, with a floor of bare scrubbed boards, and, of course, without a bathroom of any description. Most of all, though, I think Mrs. Steffens loved her husband. If you're wondering how I could possibly know this, let me tell you something. Mrs. Steffens wrote a book. It was never published, although I think perhaps it might be someday. It's the simply told story of her life, for, although her heroine is a woman called Aggie, it's impossible to miss the fact that it's largely autobiographical. It's to that book that I am indebted for knowing about things like her fear of snakes, and it's because of the book that I think she loved her husband above everything else.

Claud Paul Henry Steffens was a story in himself. Born in Denmark, he entered the German navy. Because he worked hard and studied, he was promoted and set to teaching some Polish conscripts. He had some trouble with one of them and, as a result, found himself thrown in the brig. Upon his release, he and a friend jumped ship in South America. By devious ways he found his way to England, met and married Sophia's mother, and came, eventually, to western Canada. There's an interesting story of how, many years later, a certain German baron came a-hunting in the mountains around Lytton. At that time, one of the Steffens sisters was helping in a halfway house on the old Fraser Canyon trail. The baron met her there, and asked her if by any chance her father was Harry Steffens. When she said that was his name, the baron asked to meet him, saying that he was an old shipmate of her father's. He had been, apparently, an officer of the ship Harry Steffens had left so unceremoniously so many years before! Wasn't it strange that they should meet again in such an out-of-the-way spot? Who will deny the saying that it's a small world?

Well. If Sophia's mother loved her father, Harry Steffens also deeply loved his wife. He shared all his problems and his hopes with her. Together they discussed the irrigation of the land, the clearing of more fields. Together they talked about their children, and although Mrs. Steffens thought her husband very strict with the children, she realized that unless each had his allotted tasks, the business of building a life in the isolated valley would be quite impossible. And they were building a home. They earned the right to own the land they had pre-empted.

Then, in 1910, Harry Steffens died and was buried on his own land. After that, changes came to the home in Mamit Lake Valley. Sophia went to work at the new coal mines that, along with the lumber mills and the coming of railroad, were bringing the town of Merritt into existence. She worked there for two long, unhappy years. Then for another period of several years, she waited table in the old Coldwater Hotel in Merritt. There she met many of the colourful figures of the time, men and women who helped to open the Nicola Valley. Two years after the hospital was opened in 1912—it was the only hospital closer than Kamloops—Sophia went into training as a nurse. Sophia Steffens didn't tell me much about the years that followed. The ranch prospered, of course, and the new house was built. Mrs. Steffens died, leaving behind her some beautiful needle-work and the unpublished book, and leaving only Sophia and her unmarried brother, Rupert, on the original land. They are a contented pair. Sophia acts as hostess for all the money-raising teas in the district. She has many friends. She writes a little and paints a little, paintings that catch, in some indefinable way, the very essence of her surroundings. For Miss Sophia Steffens loves the country she lives in, particularly what she calls "our valley," and longs for the outside world to know its story and its beauty.

But she's a very practical dreamer. She's proud of the fact that this year there are sixteen children attending the little school in our valley, even though some of them, maybe most of them, are strangers, strangers being newcomers of less than, oh, ten years. She's proud of her beautiful new refrigerator, and that her large and comfortable kitchen will soon be transformed into a modern miracle of streamlined cupboards and chromium-banded working areas. She's neat and quick and capable, and I imagine that her brother Rupert gets his meals on time and that they're good meals, too! And the ranch continues to prosper. There's a lot more land now than the original pre-emption. For one thing, another of the Steffens sons has built his home farther back up the hill behind the original homestead, and his acres are part of the whole.

I think—don't you?—that Miss Steffens must like to look back over the years of her life. They've been full years and busy years, with plenty of hard work and some hardship. But she sees those years as a procession of progress. They're coloured with her love of the place and the people, for Sophia Steffens knows that the story of her family is a happy one and a successful one, too. In its own small way, the Steffens family is helping to build not only "our valley," but a nation.

The present is a good time, too. Filled with small important happenings, brightened by a good radio program or a congenial book or the finding of the right word for a poem she is making up as she goes about her work, beautified by her never-dimmed appreciation of the loveliness of her surroundings—lovely things like blue moon-shadows on the snow in winter, or ground covered with the bright gold coins of the fallen cottonwood leaves in the fall, or the sweetness of a meadowlark's song in the early-morning stillness of a summer day, or the scent of sagebrush after spring rain . . .

There's no need to look into the future. That's the solace of unhappy people.

II. Penticton's First Good Citizen

October 13, 1950

JUST OFF PENTICTON'S MAIN STREET THERE'S A LARGE, COMFORTABLE-LOOKING house. It's not in any way remarkable, this house, but for many years it was the home of Dr. Reginald Brant White and his wife, Hester. Almost every country town these days has its doctor, and the lives of most of them are unwritten stories of service to others. Most of them never receive any particular recognition for the work, recognition such as came Dr. White's way just two years before his death when, in 1948, he was named Penticton's first Good Citizen.

If there hadn't been a Second World War with its resulting boom for the little towns of the Okanagan Valley, and if it hadn't been for Penticton's growing consciousness of itself as a community, the townspeople might never have thought of naming a Good Citizen, and the man whose favourite saying was "The kindlier the deed, the better the day" would not have achieved even the distinction of having his name head the roll of distinguished citizens of the city of Penticton.

Where is Penticton? It lies at the head of Okanagan Lake in the valley that has become world-famous for its wonderful orchards. Many years before the miracle of irrigation made the valley bloom, though, it was part of the southern end of the famous Hudson's Bay

Fur Brigade Trail, the route established by the old fur traders back in 1811 from Astoria, at the mouth of the Columbia River, to Fort St. James and Jasper House, far in the northern interior of British Columbia. Penticton comes from the Indian "Pen-a-tic-tin," meaning a permanent abode, where water always runs, where people always live.

The town is built on a strip of flat, rich land that lies between the head of Okanagan Lake and another, smaller lake that is now known as Skaha, but which used to be called Lac du Chien, or just plain Dog Lake. It is green with fruit trees, apple, peach, and apricot. Orchards cover the benchlands above the town, too, and behind them rise the bare brown hills so characteristic of up-country. The incredibly blue up-country sky is reflected in the waters of the lakes by day, and by night the brilliant stars hang close to the earth, so that if you are standing above the town, they shine as brightly above as the twinkling lights of the town below.

When I met Hester White, Dr. White's wife, this summer, it was not in the large house near the centre of town, but in a trim small cottage on the shores of Skaha Lake. We sat and talked in a sun-filled window that looked down on the blue water. Our talk was a revelation to me. I've always been fascinated by the wealth of human and historical material that lies untouched in the memories of the up-country old-timers, and have thought what a pity it was that someone didn't get busy and write those memories down before their owners slipped away forever. But here was a woman who, herself an old-timer—she was the fourth white child to be born in Osoyoos, among the first to be born in the valley—felt the same way. Mrs. White doesn't care particularly about dates and facts, although her dates and facts are always strictly accurate (she spends hours on research, verifying and checking). What she does care about is recapturing the feeling of the past, that special flavour that manifests itself in small everyday happenings and through personalities. For that reason, her writings have been criticized as too full of irrelevant details and description to be historically sound. That may be true enough, but when she speaks of the grey snake-rail fences winding in friendly fashion down the hillside, or when she talks about the "caribou" wind, the bitter north wind of winter, she conveys something of the spirit of the country as well as its history. And when she told me of the difficulties Dr. White encountered making his rounds in his buggy drawn by one horse, and explained that the reason for his difficulty was because his was the first vehicle in the district to be drawn by one animal, she created in my mind the picture of the poor doctor in his buggy bumping along in the deep ruts made by wagons drawn by a yoke of oxen, while the even more unfortunate horse struggled to make its way along the high ridge between the ruts. And if that's not part of the history of progress, what is?

Hester Haynes, born, as I said before, in Osoyoos, was the daughter of an Irishman who later became known far and wide as Judge Haynes. Mr. Haynes arrived in Victoria on the same sailing ship as the first governor of B.C., and was promptly set to establishing law and order along the unruly Fraser Canyon Trail. Later, when gold was found at Fairview, near the southern end of the Okanagan Valley, he went there, and was so taken by the land at Osoyoos—which means in English, where two lakes come together—that he established his home there, and a very comfortable home it must have been, too.

A vivid description of Christmas at the Haynes' was written by his daughter: "It is Christmas, 1885, evening time, the lamps are lighted. Mr. Haynes is sitting on the far side of the large stove with the mica front, through which the fire casts a rosy glow. The table is laid. The glasses gleam, the silver sparkles, and the two old port and sherry decanters lend cheer to the room." Then Mrs. White describes the wonderful three-layer Christmas cake. "Matilda had cut the sides and bottoms out of coal-oil tins, made holes in them with a nail, and then laced them together with fine wire. Raisins had to be stoned, currants washed and dried, spices pounded in the pestle and mortar—the almonds, too, for the icing. The butter from Grand Forks, the eggs put away in salt after being smeared with beef fat, for the barnyard biddies only laid when they felt like it in those days. . . . Santa Claus stands on the top, his red face all smiles and his red coat and cap sprinkled with sugar snow. French creams, glacé fruits and chocolate creams decorate the cake, so that with each slice one gets a precious piece of candy." The Haynes had music that Christmas because Mr. Haynes had bought, through one Hiram Smith, a small organ from Walla Walla. "When it arrived," said Mrs. White, "Mother spent hours singing and playing. Someone gave her 'The Treasury of Song' by Morrison, full of lovely songs." One day while Mrs. Haynes was playing, she heard a sound and looked up to see a pack horse, complete with pack, leaning soulfully against the dining room table, absorbed in the music. They had to remove the pack to get the horse out. Mrs. White remembers that that Christmas she and her sisters and brother found dolls with wax faces on the Christmas tree, and cap pistols, sleighs, and a woolly lamb, which, when its head was bent down, gave a mournful baa. Many years later, this lamb came to light in the loft of the harness room. Moths had eaten all the wool, but, said Mrs. White, "It could still baa!"

When you talk to someone about his or her own life, you always fill in some of the gaps in the story with your own imagination. And I imagine Mrs. White, alone in the big comfortable old house, or later in the cottage on the shore of Skaha, waiting for the doctor to come home from a long journey over the rough country roads, writing down her memories, colouring them with descriptive words, perhaps smiling to herself as she remembered some long-ago incident that lived only in her memory. But she would write with decision. Mrs. White is a decisive woman. Tall and spare and upright even now, she is a force to be reckoned with in the community, on the school board, and at the meetings of the many organizations of which she is a member.

She must have been alone a good deal of the time, for Dr. White is remembered as the doctor who never refused a call. He went on horseback, by buggy. Even, when he was CPR doctor at the turn of the century, by hand speeder on the railway track. And he attended prospectors, Indians, isolated farmhouses, travelling up and down the valleys to Camp McKinley, Osoyoos, Keremeos, Olalla, up the precipitous trails of Anarchist Mountain, or the narrow track to the Nickel Plate Mine. For some years before his death, he was the oldest practising physician in the province of British Columbia, and many and varied were the stories he could tell about his experiences. One of the most amusing concerned an Indian. It appears that the Indian met with an accident. The doctor was called and in the emergency had to amputate the Indian's leg with a jack-knife and tie up the arteries with string. Then, characteristically, he set to work to raise the money for a wooden leg for the man. Years later, the Indian's wife came into the doctor's office bearing a large paper-wrapped parcel. She told him that her husband was dead, and, undoing the parcel, showed him the wooden leg, and tried to sell it back to him for twenty dollars!

In 1918, the year of the Spanish influenza, Doctor White was the only doctor in the valley left on his feet. He toiled day and night until the worst of the epidemic was over. It is due to his unflagging efforts during that period that many of the valley people are alive today.

Dr. White died this spring, still serving the people of the district he had come to in 1897. For fifty-three years, he brought medical aid and comfort to the men, women, and children of the Okanagan. He left a son in Penticton, another Dr. White, to carry on his father's tradition of never refusing a call. From the little cottage on the lakeshore, alone now, Mrs. White carries on her community activities, and in the sun-filled window she continues to write her stories and articles about the colourful past.

III. Inland Empire

October 20, 1950

MUCH OF THE DRIVE FROM MERRITT OUT TO THE GUICHON RANCH LAY ALONG the shore of Nicola Lake. It was a clear, bright day in late September, and looking back over the way we had come, I could see how the dust raised by our passing had drifted out over the water and lay like a mist over the sparkling water of the lake. It was dry—too dry, the ranchers said to each other as they discussed the crops and the progress of the threshing. And when it's too dry in the upper country, the hot, bare hillsides lie scorched and shimmering under the relentless sun. The dirt roads crumble into deep fine dust that the passing wind whirls into eddying dust devils. The dust gets into everything, and lays a fine grey powder over furniture and people and food.

The hills of this ideal cattle country are covered with bunch grass for grazing herds. Their shoulders are smooth and rounded, covered in a cloak of gentle green in the spring, brown-clad at high summer and in the autumn, mantled in white during the winter months. Marshy land around the lakes and along the creek beds provides fertile hayfields for winter fodder. Here the beef cattle grow sleek and fat.

The Guichon homestead, set back from the road in a little oasis of cool green, was restful to my eyes, though even here the sun lay harshly on the white brightness of the new building we approached. Farther away, under the trees, I could see other, older buildings, but they looked shadowed and cool. The new one, which we entered, seemed somehow to focus all the sun's intensity. And inside, although it was cool, the rooms seemed to have that peculiar impersonality that is a quality of the very new. We waited for Mr. Guichon in one of these well-furnished, impersonal rooms, a room that somehow had no feeling of being lived in. The big, quiet man who presently came in and sat down and began to talk to us in a quiet voice, was impersonal, too. Perhaps, I thought, because he was accustomed to business dealings with many people in his position as virtual ruler of this inland empire. This man was kind, yes, and humorous, but somehow I had the feeling that although he was quite willing to answer my numerous questions, his heart wasn't in it. It wasn't until later on, when Mr. Guichon had left the room for a few minutes, and my companion leaned over to whisper to me that Mrs. Guichon had died ten years ago that week, that I was able to put my finger on it. This was a womanless household. I don't mean by that that there aren't any women there, but this new house had no mistress. There was no feminine clutter. There were no homey touches, such as only the mistress of a house can add.

After the interview was over, we went over to the old homestead for tea, and what a contrast it was! On the pathway to the door, two small children were playing. On our way through the dining room to the living room, I saw a cache of toy trucks and airplanes and dolls under the dining table. The living room was comfortable and used-looking, there were pictures and photographs, and the chairs and couch seemed to say, "Come and sit down and relax, lots of other people have." In this home lived Mr. Guichon's son and daughter-in-law and their children. In this home Mr. Guichon had lived, too, until the completion of his shining new house. He had lived there until he had realized the age-old truth that a family should have a place of its own, that no matter how deep the bonds of affection between older and younger generations, they are better under separate roofs. Grandfather was a welcome guest in this household; the children followed him in and told him all about their small doings. His daughter-in-law, Ruth, plied him with tea and sandwiches. Everybody's conversation was warm and haphazard and pleasant. This wasn't an interview. This was family discussion, friendly and informal.

The Guichon Ranch is one of B.C.'s great cattle ranches. Its land adjoins the enormous Douglas Lake holdings, one of the largest on the continent. It is not the largest in B.C., but it is one of very few of the big holdings still operated by the original owners. Most of them are run now by companies or are owned by wealthy city dwellers, but the Guichons' is still run by Guichons, all forty thousand acres of it. Yes, there are forty thousand acres of Guichon land, not counting the land leased yearly, and there are four thousand head of cattle on the land.

It all began back in 1886, when Joseph Guichon bought a hundred acres from the government at a dollar an acre and put a hundred head of cattle on it. It wasn't just happenstance, either, that Joseph Guichon picked this cool green oasis called by the Indians "Katalma"—open space with rose bushes. It wasn't by accident that he built the great square post-house at "Quilshenah"—the place to catch fish—either. Because Joseph Guichon had by that time been more than twenty years in British Columbia, and he had travelled the country. He had walked, with his belongings on his back, the length of the Cariboo Trail; he had driven mule trains, two trips a year, from Yale to Omineca. He had stayed at Savona on Kamloops Lake; he had taken up land on Mamit Lake in '77; he had been at Douglas Lake when it began in '83. So when he finally settled at Quilshenah and began to build his inland empire, he chose carefully and well. In country where water is always a problem, here are streams that run all year and little lakes where the water is always sweet and fresh, and the big expanse of Nicola Lake might almost be said to form one boundary of his property. All this, of course, was acquired gradually, and not all, by any means, during the lifetime of Joseph Guichon. But he began it all when, way back in 1864, he crossed the ocean from France, travelled from New York to the Isthmus of Panama, crossed it, and made his way up the Pacific coast to British Columbia in search of gold. He found it, too, and made as much as $1,000 in a single week. But it was spent almost as quickly as it was made, for in those days a sack of flour or a shovel cost an ounce of gold. Two of those early years Joseph Guichon spent driving mule trains for that colourful figure, Cataline, whose booming voice and burly figure encircled always with a scarlet sash was a highlight of the motley throng that travelled the Cariboo Gold Trail. There are those living who actually saw Cataline pour liquor on his abundant head of hair and rub it in, a sort of unusual hair tonic to which he attributed its luxuriant growth! It was an almost legendary time, a time of adventure and murder and robbery, a far cry from the quiet retreat where Joseph Guichon settled down at last. He had married in 1878, and he had seven children, of which Laurence Guichon, my host that afternoon, was the eldest.

The children went to school at Spences Bridge and later down the Fraser River to boarding school at New Westminster. It was in New

Westminster that Laurence Guichon met his future wife. He said of her, "She had such beautiful hair, in two long braids." And that was all he did say about his wife. It was from someone else that I learned how the big, quiet man had shyly paid court to the girl with the lovely hair and had taken his bride back with him to Quilshenah. And it was from someone else that I learned of his devotion to her, and how, since her death, he has become even quieter and more reserved. I mentioned in an earlier broadcast how one is apt to fill in gaps in a story with one's imagination; well, one's imagination can lead one very far astray sometimes! Looking at Laurence Guichon, at his big frame, I imagined him gladly undertaking the long rides after cattle, the horse-breaking, the branding, all the duties that would fall on him as the eldest of Joseph Guichon's sons. Well, I made a remark to the effect that I supposed he had done a great deal of riding, and to my surprise he told me that, on the contrary, he had done very little. He didn't like riding much; an injury when he was young had quite taken away his taste for it. "I left the riding to the rest of the family," he said, smiling in his gentle way.

Well, there are enough Guichons for each one to do the job he most prefers on the great ranch. One of Laurence's brothers runs the ranch store. We stopped in there to meet him that day. There's nothing quite like a country store, is there? With everything from saddles to soap, from lettuce to lingerie on its shelves. And this one was no exception, except that it was tidier than most. The store had been built many years ago, at the same time as the Quilshenah post-house. Its interior is dim and cool, with a high ceiling and a broad, shallow staircase rising from the far end and leading up to the offices. My companions chatted with this Guichon brother in a desultory way about the crops and the weather. They spoke of a Guichon sister who was even then in Rome, a Holy Year visitor to the Vatican City, and I thought of the little white church with its wooden cross that stands on a corner of the Katalma property, and of the black-robed priests who, through the years, had periodically brought the comfort of Mother Church to Guichons old and young. Laurence Guichon had told me of the visits of Father LeJeune, one of the first priests to enter the country, who, during his many years of service had learned every Indian dialect of the district, and who was revered and loved by white man and Indian alike, whatever their creed. When Father LeJeune died some years ago, there died with him the story of an era, the opening chapters of the story of British Columbia.

At last it was time to go. I said goodbye with regret to the Guichons—to Ruth, from whose big white modernized kitchen savory dinner smells were beginning to waft, to the small brother and sister, playing happily outside at stone hauling on an old rock sledge, to Laurence Guichon, warm in his invitation to return, to the whole quiet homestead, whose peace and quiet conceals the smooth-running wheels of the organization of one of B.C.'s great inland empires, the Guichon Ranch.

IV. Ashcroft Manor

October 27, 1950

I CAME TO ASHCROFT MANOR IN THE DUSK OF EARLY EVENING, PUSHED OPEN the garden gate with a sense of adventure, walked up the path in the friendly light from the open door and into the life of the Cornwalls. I came with a sense of adventure because, although I'd passed the Manor many times—it lies right on the main highway to the Cariboo, and traffic swishes past it day and night—and I'd even stopped in there briefly years ago, this arrival was different. This time I was, as I said before, walking into the life of the Cornwalls. Walking into anyone's life is an adventure, but when the people you are going to meet are part of the warp and woof of history in the making, it is adventure, indeed!

Not that these people were in any way different from other people, perhaps just a little more charming than many, that's all. Neither is there anything of the historic ruin about Ashcroft Manor itself. It, too, has developed a graciousness and charm with the years. But don't for a minute think that it's the sort of charm that goes with lavender and old lace and quiet folded hands. On the contrary, life in the Manor is brisk and busy and bustling. That's because today the old post-house is operated as a combination auto court and summer resort, and in a set-up like that, everyone is always busy.

From post-house to auto court. That conjures up a picture for the eyes and ears of the imagination, doesn't it? From the raucous braying of irate mules, the snap and crackle of the bull-whip, the shouts of men in English, French, Chinese, Chinook; from dust clouds rising from the hot, baked earth, from the glow of campfires at night. To the swish, swish of speeding traffic along the crowded highway as it passes the old building set so close to the road, the distant thunder of a huge truck gradually growing to a roar in the quiet night, and then fading away in the distance, its powerful headlights momentarily lighting up the sagebrush that grows along the roadside, turning it into strange, unreal shapes, like coral growing on the ocean floor.

In the daytime, the sun shines on the parched earth, and makes little heat mirages shimmer above the black, unwinding ribbon of the black-top highway. The people who travel the highway, though, aren't the same. Gone is the motley crew who went through the incredible hardships of travelling the Cariboo Trail in search of gold. The travellers of today are mostly seekers for another kind of treasure. They are looking for fish and game, and they come armed with fishing rods and shotguns and rifles. There is one similarity, though. Those early travellers came from all over the world, and so do today's tourists. Cars with licence plates from every state in the Union and every province in Canada pass this way in search of some of the world's finest fishing and shooting. Up the precipitous Fraser Canyon they come, following the once-narrow and winding old trail that the stagecoaches and mule trains and foot-travellers used. At Ashcroft Manor enough passersby have always turned aside for a day or a night to keep the hostelry in a continual hum of activity.

I was glad that I had arrived in the evening. The rush of the evening meal was over, and there was time to talk. We sat in the big comfortable living room, with its white-painted walls, pleasant fireplace, and gracious bow window. This room, I was told, used to be the barroom. Along here had run the long bar. See this trapdoor cut in the floor? Below that door, the liquor was kept in the roaring gold rush days. And see these delicate scales on the mantel? Those used to stand on the bar, and were used to weigh the gold-dust from the prospectors' pokes—so many ounces, so many drinks. Of course, there'd been no fireplace then. A large, barrel stove stood at one end of the room and the floor had been well adorned with spittoons.

When the two Cornwall brothers, Clement and Henry, heard about the Thompson River valley back in 1862, it wasn't the promise of gold that interested them, but tales of the rich bunch grass that grew there. And perhaps, too, the thought of adventure in a new land, far from the restrictions and conventions of their life in England. They sailed from Southampton on April 1, 1862, and, travelling via the Panama, landed at Esquimalt in June. There they bought horses and provisions and started for the Cariboo. In the days that followed, they looked over land here and there, and finally, on June 30 they noticed, and I'm quoting now, "a desirable-looking flat watered by two streams with a fine surrounding range for cattle." The next day, they rode back to explore it and decided to pre-empt three hundred and twenty acres. Clement rode to Cook's Ferry, as Spences Bridge was then called, crossed the river in a canoe, and walked twenty-three hot and dusty miles into Lytton to record their claim. It was there that he learned that the new Cariboo road would pass through their property. When he returned, the brothers began at once to build a house of logs on the larger of the two creeks, to put in a garden, and to erect sheds and corrals. They bought horses, mostly breeding stock, and oxen for farm work.

Many people passed through their land on their way to and from the Cariboo: miners, packers, road-builders, and government officials. It was an excellent position for a stopping place, so they decided to build a road-house. It was built in 1863, and became known as the 104 Mile House. This is the Ashcroft Manor of today. Later they bought another eighteen hundred acres of land, and later still bought more and leased some on Hat Creek for summer range. They called their ranch "Ashcroft" after their old home in England. It wasn't until much later that "Manor" was added, to prevent confusion concerning the postal address of the ranch and of people in the town of Ashcroft, which had grown up on the new transcontinental railroad. The town continued to be called Ashcroft, and the ranch homestead was from then on known as Ashcroft Manor.

For a long time after the post-house was built, it was operated by a man who was not a relative of Clement and Henry Cornwall. It was quite a separate and distinct entity from the big comfortable home that nestled under the shadow of Cornwall Mountain. The two places came in time to be known as the House of Lords and the House of Commons, and as the years passed and Clement's and Henry's children grew up, they were forbidden, on pain of severe punishment, to go near the House of Commons. You can imagine what a delicious excitement it was to sneak away from home and to mingle among the men who camped around the post-house, and sometimes, greatly daring, to peek through the windows into the barroom and watch the noisy crowd within. After a while, though, the homestead became too small for the growing families of the two brothers, and Henry, the younger, moved down to the House of Commons to live. From then until his death, when his widow moved her family to Cherry Creek, the post-house was a dwelling. When it again opened its doors to travellers, they were travellers of a different era.

During my all-too-short stay at Ashcroft Manor, I was able to talk with Jack Cornwall, son of the Henry who came from England so long ago, and to Dede Parker, a Cornwall granddaughter. Jack Cornwall told me many stories of the old days. He remembered seeing the famous mule-packer, Cataline. He had tasted the forbidden delight of peeking through the windows of the House of Commons. He had watched his father and uncle ride with horses and hounds after coyotes in the manner of English fox hunts, until the coming of fences and the railroad spoiled the sport in the 1880s. And he told me of a hair-raising experience that his mother had when she first arrived from England, "green as grass," as Jack Cornwall put it. They were sitting around the fire one evening soon after her arrival, just chatting, when suddenly the door opened and several Indians filed silently into the room. She was terrified, and it took considerable explaining to make her understand that the Indians had only come to welcome her, and that the dusky visitors just didn't know that doors were meant to be knocked upon before they were opened.

I talked to Dede Parker, too, but only in snatches. There are very few quiet moments in her day, for hers is the responsibility of seeing that the Manor runs smoothly, that meals are cooked and served on time, that bedrooms are kept fresh and aired, that the linen is changed and washed, that accounts are made up. But, you know, I think there must be something about really hard work that enhances good looks. Mrs. Parker may be harried and hurried, but you'd never know it, and I'll swear she looks younger and more attractive than she did when I first saw her ten years ago. Dede Parker told me about the fire. Yes, there was a tragic fire on the ranch some years ago, when the old House of Lords burned down. All the men were away haying, and only Dede and another woman were about the place. The old house was tinder-dry and went up in a sheet of flame that destroyed the gardens and tennis courts and all the fine old trees planted so long ago by Clement and Henry. Today there is a raw new farmhouse on the old site, but the land has passed from the hands of the Cornwall family. All that now remains to them is the old post-house, with its wide green lawns and big shade trees, its rambling outbuildings and the prim little row of neat tourist cabins.

Just before I caught the bus to Vancouver, Jack Cornwall drove me up Radio Hill, a steep little rise topped with the tall towers of the radio beam mechanism for passing airplanes flying blind. Up there, we picked our way over the heat-cracked ground, avoiding the sharp spines of cactus and smelling the pungent odour of the sun-warmed sagebrush, to a spot where the ground fell away sharply to the Thompson River far below. Spread around us was the whole panorama of the upper country. The rose and purple stone walls of the river canyon. The bare, brown hills rising barren and treeless with, here and there, the sudden green of a homestead on one of the flat benchlands. The waters of the river, rushing and tumbling away down there, were peacock blue, white-tipped. Overhead the sky was blue, a deep endless depth of blueness. And over it all lay the clear light of the autumn sunshine. This is B.C.'s up-country, the land that lays its magic spell on all who visit there; the land of which it is said that if you have once lived there, you'll always go back. And I believe it's a true saying.

THE PHILLIPS FAMILY

August 7, 1950

GOOD MORNING. SINCE I'M GOING TO BE TALKING WITH YOU FOR THE NEXT four weeks, I thought that perhaps you'd like to know something about the Phillips family generally, a sort of introduction. Some of you, of course, have met us before, because this is the third year now that I've helped fill in the summer months while Ellen is away with her family, enjoying a well-earned holiday.

Where to begin? Well, there are four of us: me, my husband Dick, and our two sons, Tony, aged fifteen, very big for his age, with simply enormous feet, and a voice that has just about settled in the lower registers; and Ted, aged thirteen, who is smallish for his age, and who evidences, at the moment, a tendency toward plumpness. The plumpness is a source of amazement to us, since no member of the family has ever been plump. However, it'll probably pass off.

But the family doesn't end there. In addition, there are three dogs. Yes, three! It's fortunate that we have a largish house, otherwise there simply wouldn't be room for all of us. Rocky is the senior member of this trio. He's a six-year-old Labrador, and he weighs eighty-five pounds. We've had Rocky since he was five weeks old. The other two are very new arrivals on the family scene. Mike, a seven-month-old golden cocker spaniel, has attached himself, body and soul, to our elder son, Tony. He is still enough of a pup to chew shoes, socks, blankets, and ankles with delightful impartiality. The third member of our canine family is Mrs. Sara Binks. Binks is a mongrel, a bright-eyed, alert dog who's a cross between a Boston bull and a fox terrier. At least that's what we think she is. We acquired her, or she acquired us, about a month ago when we were on holidays. It happened that we were staying at an auto camp in Nicola. Someone had just left Binks there. Can you understand how anyone can go off and leave a little dog behind? We couldn't. Especially Binks. So she became a member of the family, too, the special care and responsibility of Ted, who promptly bought her a very beautiful tartan collar and a leash with a red plastic handle. Last Friday, Binks was in an accident, we don't know just how seriously she was hurt, but we think it's a broken leg, and hope that it won't be long before she's as good as new again.

Then, of course, there are the birds, two of them. Polly is a somewhat cantankerous green South American parrot. Polly has belonged to one branch or another of the family for nearly forty years, but since we understand that parrots quite often live to be a hundred, she's really just in her heyday now. Her vocabulary isn't very large, but it's fairly varied, and she can always be depended upon to start talking at the top of her voice when I begin an important telephone conversation. For some reason, she has steadfastly resisted all attempts to teach her the odd swear word or two; we feel that she must be an innately respectable old bird, in spite of her raucous voice and raffish appearance.

The other bird is a budgie. Tippy is almost a year old now, and has quite a vocabulary of his own. He is a source of endless pleasure and amusement to us. It seems extraordinary that anything so small can be the possessor of so much personality. Unfortunately, Polly is violently jealous of Tippy, and would love to remove him from the scene, so life is one long and continuous effort to keep them separated.

No description of the Phillips family would be complete without mentioning Rudy, the ruby-eyed rat, and Marmaduke, the circus mouse. Rudy is a large white rat, and Marmaduke is a small beige-coloured mouse. They both belong to Ted, and he can be seen at any time with one or the other sitting on his shoulder while he sits quietly reading the funnies or wanders around the house. With the exception of a number of transient residents, such as large numbers of tadpoles or small frogs or fish in assorted jars, that completes the family picture. And you'll be quite correct if you assume that there's rarely a dull moment in the Phillips household.

Well, now about the things we like to do. Mostly, I guess, we like to camp—certainly that's what we like to do in the summertime. After we've solved the ever-present problem of where to park the assorted livestock, we like to take off, even if it's only for a weekend, hitching our equipment trailer onto our faithful old car. The car, by the way, really deserves mention as a member of the family. She rejoices in the name of Dodo, and has transported us loyally into all sorts of nooks and crannies of this province of ours for the last ten years. On this last trip, she turned 73,000 miles, and she's still going strong. And when you consider that we usually weigh in at the Pattullo Bridge at the start of our holidays in the neighbourhood of 5,500 pounds, that's saying something!

Anyway, as I was saying, we like to hitch the equipment trailer onto the car, complete with tents, sleeping bags, camp stoves, etc., tie the boat on top of the car, pile the boys and the dogs inside, and go somewhere to camp. Once a year, of course, we go off for our holidays—holidays that seem to be over before they've begun. And then, the whole family likes to fish. And Dick and I for many years now have tramped the fields in the autumn and early winter for ducks and pheasants. This fall, though, it looks very much as though I'll be minus my gun. Dick feels that Tony is arriving at the years of discretion, and he will be allowed to carry a gun next season. For this year anyway, it will be my gun. I'm going to miss the long tramps over the stubble fields, watching the dawn come over salty marshes, crouching behind cover on the bank of a slough while the birds circle over the decoys and set their wings to come in, and hearing the wings of the ducks as the evening flight comes whizzing past us in the early dark. Just talking about it makes me think that maybe Tony'll have to get a gun of his own, after all.

There are things we like to do at home, too. Dick's vegetable garden is his pride and joy every year. And because he always plants more than any one family can possibly eat, even if we became vegetarians, there are always lots of fruit and vegetables to can. When the salmon are running, we spend a day fishing, and when our luck is good, there are rows of jars of salmon on our shelves. How good it tastes during the winter, too!

We like to listen to our records during the long winter evenings. The Phillips family really just discovered music a little over two years ago, when we bought our record player, and now the record cabinet that we bought at the same time has overflowed. Back then we wondered how we'd ever fill the wide expanse of empty shelves; now we wonder how we could ever have thought they'd be big enough. We don't know a great deal about music—technically, that is—but we're getting so that we have a pretty wide acquaintance with it. All kinds, from Spike Jones to Beethoven, from Shostakovich to Sibelius, to Bloch, to Mozart. We can't imagine how we ever managed to get along without our record player. Probably the most gratifying result of all is the way that the boys have come to enjoy it, too. Sometimes we have guessing games. One member of the family plays a recording, and the rest of us have to guess what it is. You can rarely trip the boys on Beethoven or Tchaikovsky.

But that is only sometimes. The boys always have so much to do, there's not often much time for musical guessing games. They each have a paper route and, as a result, a growing bank account. Each month, they keep out so much for repairs to their bicycles and for their personal expenses, and the rest is building up towards that university course they each hope to take some day. By the way, paper routes, we think, are a grand way to help growing youngsters develop a sense of responsibility and an idea of the value of money, but they have a secondary, and very definite effect on the senior members of the family: route lists get tangled up and have to be straightened out by the accountant in the family—that's not me—and on very wet or snowy winter evenings, when deliveries are some-times unavoidably late, Ma and Pa have to be able to do a deft public relations job soothing irate customers who phone and want to know why their paper hasn't arrived yet. One dreadful night when it was pouring rain and blowing a gale, we coped with upwards of thirty such calls. I bet the daily papers haven't the least idea what a large part parents play in maintaining satisfied customers! These paper routes also cause complications on our weekend camping trips and during summer holidays: inevitably the substitutes get things muddled up, in spite of having the best intentions in the world, and the united efforts of the whole family are needed for placating in all directions. I speak with considerable feeling at this point, because we've been back from our holidays several days, and only now is a tangle getting straightened out.

We had a wonderful holiday this year, three whole weeks of it. We travelled over the Hope–Princeton Highway for the first time, and were fortunate enough to see the wild rhododendrons in full flower, lovely pale pink blossoms, something I've never seen before. It's a lovely route altogether, just as different as can be from the canyon route to the Interior. The country's entirely different and very beau-tiful. Then we drove on through the Similkameen Valley to Penticton, and on up through the Okanagan Valley to Sorrento on Shuswap Lake. It was hot. That wonderful dry heat that seems to make you feel energetic instead of sapping you of all desire to do anything. And the valley looked beautiful. We were saddened, though, to see how many of the fruit trees had been killed by the bitter cold last winter.

It was curious, too, to see how the cold had struck: perhaps one tree in a row, or one whole row in a whole orchard. There didn't seem to be any rhyme or reason to it. Some of the trees had managed to keep a little flicker of life, and we'd see a pathetic little bunch of wan green leaves at the end of a branch on a tree that was otherwise stark and bare.

After Sorrento, we drove on to Kamloops and laid in supplies for a week, and drove to Lac Le Jeune. We've fished that lake for many years, and always look forward to pitching our tents among the whispering cottonwoods and casting a fly into well-known waters for the silvery trout—not to mention eating them later, sizzling hot from the pan. We had eight days there, and then moved on down into the Nicola Valley, where we explored country that we'd never seen before. If you ever go up that way, it's very worthwhile to make a side trip into the Douglas Lake country. Nowhere else have I seen such wonderful rangeland! No wonder Douglas Lake is the centre for the biggest cattle ranch in B.C.—in fact, one of the biggest on the continent, about 175,000 acres. We came home through the Fraser Canyon, where the tremendous job of widening the highway is still going on. When it's finished, it's going to be something pretty special in the way of a road. A far cry from twenty years ago when we first drove up there, and had to back and fill to get our cumbersome old car around one of the hairpin turns on the old road between Ashcroft and Savona, with the Thompson River at least a hundred feet straight below!

Well, we're home again now for another year, our suntans already growing a little faded, as we try desperately to catch up with a vegetable garden that decided, in our absence, to turn into a jungle. I'll let you know later on if any of our mammoth tomato plants come to anything. Meanwhile, we're canning like mad and feasting on huge helpings of peas and beans and lettuce and carrots and beets.

And now you've met the Phillips family. I hope you like us, because, here and there during the next four weeks, you'll probably hear more about us. Tomorrow, though, I have a guest who is going to tell us about life down under. He's Mr. Barnett, from the city of Auckland, in New Zealand. He is visiting Vancouver, and wants to tell us why he thinks we should visit Auckland.

Till tomorrow, then.

Rocky

August 10, 1950

YOU MAY REMEMBER THAT ON MONDAY I TOLD YOU THAT ONE OF THE CANINE members of our family, Binks, who belongs to my younger son, had been in an accident. Well, it turned out that Binks was too badly injured to recover, and poor little Binks was put to sleep. Ted was bereft. So we put our heads together to try to decide what we could do to cheer him up. And decided to get him a puppy. An ad in the paper was offering Labrador pups for sale. We went to see them, and came home with a small black roly-poly of a pup that is the funniest miniature edition of Rocky that you can possibly imagine. Perhaps that's what made me remember Rocky's puppyhood again. Anyway, Rocky became a member of the family six years ago last winter. We had finally, and painfully, decided that Peg, our portly lady spaniel, had seen her last days in the field, at least as far as shooting was concerned. There just wasn't any question that age, fat, and, I suspect, too many families, had taken their toll. Peg simply was no longer a hunting dog. We had to find one.

One night in the newspaper we saw an ad. It said, "Black Labrador pups for sale." Now, Dick had long cherished the ambition to train a dog himself. He knew it would have to be from puppyhood, and that is why, when he saw the ad, he insisted on driving out to the place, even though it was far enough out of town to be annoying. We drove and drove. And when we did arrive and were shown the pups, I think there were seven of them, we had no more idea than the man in the moon how to pick which one we would take. Seven identical, scrambling, rambling pups! Well, we finally did what no one is ever supposed to do: we chose for our own the largest pup of the whole lot. We've always heard that the smallest of a litter is probably the best, but we just forgot all we'd been told, and took the biggest. We've never been sorry.

On the drive home, the pup finally settled down and went to sleep. He fitted very comfortably into the round made by my two hands. Once home, we put him into a carton with a piece of old

1 • Portraits 69

cloth and a hot water bottle, and didn't hear anything from him until about six the next morning, by which time the hot water bottle was cold—poor little pup. He was feeling lost and miserable, and his cries of woe rent the air. I don't know what the neighbours thought—although I can imagine—but it took about a week for Rocky to become a reasonably silent member of the Phillips household. At that point, he had discovered that he could climb the stairs, and we had them barricaded with planks of wood and everything we could find that made an effective barrier. Of course, the fact that somehow Mama had to get up and down was quite beside the point; she leapt over everything!

When Rocky was about two months old, he began to learn. After all, he was supposed to be a retriever, and so he learned to retrieve. It didn't take him long to catch on to picking up things that were thrown to him, but it did take a while to teach him all the other things, things like to sit, to hold, and to hand. And it took a very long time to teach him not to shake after a water retrieve—that is, after he had fetched something from the water and brought it back to us, to hand it to us without first shaking the water off his coat. Dick spent hours and hours, nights and nights on that training process. He took Rocky up to the pool in the neighbouring park. He rigged up a pretend bird of sticks and feathers. He threw it far out into the pool, and Rocky responded nobly: he always brought it back.

Then came the day when we really asked him to retrieve a bird. We were driving into Clinton early on the morning of the opening day for shooting ducks. There is a chain of small lakes just this side of Clinton. We hadn't done any shooting. We were concentrating on getting into the Dog Creek country, where we hoped to get our shooting. But other people had been shooting those small lakes. Among them were three or four men without a dog. They had brought down a duck, and it had fallen into the exact centre of the largest of these little lakes. There it was, floating gently, well out of reach of anyone. These people flagged us down. We stopped. "Have you got a dog?" they said. "Can it get that bird for us?" Dick said, in a very superior manner, "Yes, we have a dog, and of course he will get your bird for you."

Well, for twenty minutes we sent Rocky after that bird. I might as well say right now that he never did get it, and after a while the men left, disgusted. The reason? Well, Rocky went into the water, all right, but I guess he was looking for Dick's pretend bird. He followed all the stones and so on that Dick threw in to guide him, but he simply didn't recognize the duck as the thing he was supposed to bring back. He swam all around that duck—he even nosed it—and left it again to try and retrieve the stone that was thrown to guide him to the bird. The men weren't the only disgusted people. So was Dick. For the next ten days, he pretended he didn't even have a dog. It devolved upon me to make Rocky heel, sit, and all the many things that a hunting dog must learn in the field, not only in theory, but in practice.

Perhaps that's why now he works for me almost as well as he works for my husband. Whatever it is, I know that Rocky is the first dog we've ever had who works just as well for me as he does for Dick. Not only does he retrieve the very infrequent birds that I bring down, he retrieves birds that neither Dick nor I ever shot! Out in the field, Rocky will suddenly disappear, to return later with a duck that somebody else shot and didn't pick up.

This isn't as perfect as it sounds. There was the time that Dick took an ill-advised potshot at a merganser and brought it down. It happened in the middle of winter, and on the slough we were shooting over, the ice was pretty solid for about fifty yards offshore. Well, Rocky was out to retrieve that bird before we could say Fetch. He slithered across the ice until it was too thin to take his weight. Then into the water he went, and broke his way through the thin ice to the bird with his forepaws, collected it, and came back, still breaking his way with his paws. He brought it in beautifully—didn't stop to shake the icy water from his coat or anything—sat and handed it to Dick in the most proper manner you can imagine. Of course, Dick appreciated his efforts, thanked him, wrung the merganser's neck, and tossed it aside. But mergansers don't die as easily as that. This one shortly arose and flew back to approximately the same place from which Rocky had retrieved it before. And, once again, before we could do anything about it, out went Rocky, bent on bringing back the bird! Across the ice, breaking the way with his forepaws. But when he had picked up the bird, he demonstrated the fact that dogs do learn. Instead of breaking a fresh path back, he carefully found his outward path, and came in the same way.

One of Rocky's most endearing habits is the way he always comes to meet you with a little gift in his mouth. With welcome in every wriggle of his body, he comes tearing towards you, only stopping long enough for his little gift. And he never forgets the gift. Usually it's a stone, but it may be anything—a stick, a piece of paper, an old tin can. And you are definitely expected to accept his present, too. He marches proudly around you, and finally sits and hands it to you. It is the welcome ceremony. If you are carrying anything, bundles large or small, or the evening paper, he would prefer to carry it for you. He makes a rush and grabs it from your hand. This is the habit that has been misunderstood by numerous people, especially the postman, who, probably from bitter experience, was convinced that the dog was attacking him. It was quite a long time before we were able to persuade him that all Rocky wanted was to carry the mail in for him. Now the postie gives Rocky a letter to carry, and relations are extremely amiable all around.

We only feed Rocky once a day, in the evening, after our own dinner. Comes dinner time, and Rocky lies patiently on the floor, paws crossed, his brown eyes following every move. When we say "Fetch dish!" he galvanizes into action, tears down the basement stairs, and shortly reappears carrying his large enamel bowl in his mouth, then sits watching while his dinner is prepared. Upon occasion, he finishes his meal and brings the dish back again. Sits with it in his mouth, looking hopefully for a second helping.

Rocky is a wonder in the field, but he has only one parlour trick. This one trick never fails to rouse the admiration of all beholders. We put an open carton of beer on the floor in the kitchen and retire to the living room for a little conversation. After an interval, we say, "Rocky, go fetch beer!" And Rocky does just that. We hear scrabblings going on in the kitchen—it's Rocky opening the carton—and in a minute he appears back in the living room, proudly carrying a bottle of beer. It's not everyone who has their beer brought to them in such style!

This habit of bringing us things has its drawbacks, too. There was the time when we were camping at a certain lake. There were other campers nearby. Early one sunny morning, Rocky came into camp carrying a large paper-wrapped parcel. He handed it to us with a proud look of accomplishment. We accepted it with some bewilderment, and unwrapped the parcel to find one of the largest and most delectable steaks that I have ever seen. Rocky had quietly gone to the other camp, helped himself to the steak, and brought it to us. There was no question of his eating the steak himself. His teeth hadn't even marked the paper wrapping. He was just bringing his family a present. Hurriedly, we returned the parcel to its owner. Unfortunately, however, the owners didn't see the humour in the situation. Nor were they impressed by Rocky's retrieving ability. They were merely annoyed.

And there was the other time when he flushed a grouse, out of season, and pursued it through heavy underbrush and, somehow, managed to scare it into the lake, where he dived in after it, and came back carrying it. Happily for us, there were no game wardens in our immediate vicinity.

While Rocky would rather fetch birds than everything else in the world, he's interested in other creatures, too: rats. One year, we were camping at a lake where there happened to be a large pile of old fence posts nearby. Rocky smelled rats. And it was the most amazing thing you ever saw to watch him tear that pile of fence posts to pieces. Quite literally. He didn't just dislodge them. He disintegrated them, splinter by splinter. Of course, they were pretty old and rotten, but he went right at them and tore them to bits. He got his rats. Great big packrats with huge bushy tails, a whole family of them.

Rocky loves to go camping. For days before we leave, he watches our preparations eagerly, and we can't open the car door without Rocky leaping in it and sitting there looking expectant. He is terrified that somehow or other we might leave him behind. And he's as stubborn as a mule about getting out again. On the actual trip, even on the occasional 300-mile, non-stop drive we've taken, he's as good as gold. He lies quietly at our feet and never budges. He seems to make himself as small as possible. And there's nothing small about eighty-five pounds of black Labrador!

Yes, Rocky weighs eighty-five pounds. When he wags that great black tail of his, all ornaments and bric-a-brac on low tables fly in every direction. We have long ago given up all attempts to have decorative objects at low levels in our house. Because of his size, it's rather disconcerting to have him decide that he's a Pekingese lapdog, and try to climb into your lap while you're peacefully reading the evening paper. He frequently does this. And his feelings are very hurt when you point out that he is not, after all, a lapdog, and refuse to allow him to settle in your lap.

Rocky has one or two special tastes: raspberries, for instance. It's quite a sight to see him moving slowly down the row of bushes, delicately picking a berry here and a berry there. And eating them! Most of all, however, he likes pancakes. On pancake mornings, he sits through breakfast with his eyes glued to the dish of pancakes. And we wouldn't dream of eating them all. If necessary, we even make more, just so Rocky can have his. And they disappear in one large gulp. I've often wondered why he loves them so much, because I'm quite sure he never gets a taste of them. They go down too fast.

And that's Rocky, our black Labrador. Very big, very black, and altogether lovable!

2. ALL AROUND US

WILDFLOWERS

In the years since this script was broadcast, we have indeed learned many of the proper names of the wildflowers we've seen. We've also gone as far afield as Greece to see them. The importance of learning these names is that, with there being so many "common" names for the same flower, the correct and, yes, usually Latin, name is its only sure means of identification.

But what's in a name? Each flower remains its own lovely self.

I SUPPOSE IF ONE TALKS ABOUT WILDFLOWERS, ONE SHOULD REALLY KNOW something about them. I mean, technical things like the long and correct Latin names, and to what family they belong. I certainly don't, but I do love wildflowers, and in the course of considerable wandering around this province of ours, I've seen a good many different kinds, and have never failed to wonder at their beauty and variety.

As a matter of fact, we came back just a while ago from a long-weekend trip to a lake near Kamloops and, although our primary interest was fishing, we took time out to see the wildflowers that are still blooming under the trees around the edge of the lake. I guess that's what started me thinking about all the flowers we've seen on other expeditions.

The lake we went to last weekend is high—over four thousand feet—so the flowers that are over now in lower altitudes are still blooming up there. At that high altitude, too, there is practically no underbrush, and so the flowers look as though they were growing through the long green grass of tree-dotted parkland. There is blue lupine, and the speckled orange of tiger lilies, and the fragile red and yellow of the delicate wild columbine. Paintbrush, that strange scarlet flower that seems to rise straight from its leaves, looking for all the world just like a brush freshly dipped in a pot of red paint, grows in clumps, and proves how well it has been named. And then, if you bend down close to the ground, you will find tiny, pale pink twin-flowers, and the small white stars of the flower of the wild straw-berry. It won't be long now before the tiny, deliciously sweet fruit of the strawberry will be found hiding modestly under the green of its leaves. Is there anything in the world like the fragrance of crushed wild strawberries on your fingers?

On the hot brown barrenness of the hills just above the town of Kamloops itself, the mariposa lilies are beginning to appear. I've often wondered how this seemingly tender bulb ever manages to survive on those inhospitable slopes. But survive it does, and the pale, almost whited mauve petals are little patches of unexpected beauty.

Last year, at just about this time, I had one of the most unforget-table experiences of my life. I'm sure you remember what a cold, wet summer we had. Well, up on the mountaintops the summer came very late, and that is how it happened that even though it was in the middle of July, up on the more than four-thousand-foot summit of Apex Mountain it was still early spring. And that is why, for the first time, I saw the carpets of alpine flowers one is always hearing about. Apex Mountain is not far from Penticton, where I was staying with my sister. The way up lies along a winding track with edges blurred by the scrab-bling of the sheep that graze there. The track leaves the valley with its chuckling stream, and rises quickly and steeply across open slopes from which the view downward is like looking through the wrong end of a telescope. It passes through thick stands of scrubby fir and pine. It follows the course of a tumbling mountain stream, and crosses it without benefit of bridge. Then, once again, there is a view, this time of far-off valleys where the treetops stand in pointed rows and the light catches the gleam of water where a mountain lake lies cupped among the hills. Clouds were lying low on the surrounding peaks, and a light rain was falling. A sudden turn, a last steep climb, and the track disap-peared. It was the summit. We got out and thankfully stretched our stiff legs, inwardly (as far as I was concerned, at any rate) heaving a large sigh of relief. It had been quite a ride!

Then, for the first time, I really looked around me. Spring had come to Apex Mountain. Flowers were blooming everywhere. Hundreds and hundreds of tiny blossoms with names only known to botanists spread a gentle cloak of colour across the weather-beaten shoulders of the mountain. And all the more familiar flowers were in miniature, tiny replicas of their usual selves. And, possibly by reason of one of Mother Nature's laws of compensation, their colouring was more brilliant than anything I had ever seen. There was vivid lupine.

There was Indian paintbrush, its scarlet a licking tongue of flame across the hillside. There were everlastings of every shape and colour. Tiny blue violets grew in tight little clumps. Strange white lilies lifted their heads in the marshy places near the mountain spring. And in great drifts, some of purest white, and some shading from pale pink to deep rose, the heather covered the unfriendly rocks and grew to the very edge of the snow patches that were still lying on the topmost summit. Moving slowly—I had to move slowly because the altitude makes it hard to breathe, and the rare mountain air was so clear and cold it almost hurt my throat—I was enchanted by this wealth of flowers. I even counted twenty-five different varieties in an area no more than three or four feet square, and most of them I'd never seen before.

I remember another day when the wildflowers took my breath away. It was when we were living on Vancouver Island, and had driven up to the Cowichan River for a day's fishing. Vancouver Island people have a right to boast about the beauty of their spring. Driving up the highway, the dogwood was in bloom, and great masses of pale, starry blooms hung over the road, not just in a few places, but all the way along. No wonder the dogwood is the flower of British Columbia.

Later, scrambling over the rocks along the edge of the river, we saw all sorts of other flowers, from the humble yellow of bacon and eggs, to the svelte pointed blossoms of the shooting star. In woodsy places, we found white trilliums, and once in a while, a patch of dogtooth violets, creamy and delicate with their strange brown-spotted leaves. We even found blue and white and yellow violets that day. I'm afraid we didn't do much fishing, but we did store up a memory for what Wordsworth calls "that inward eye" to feast upon for a long, long time.

I suppose since I'm talking about wildflowers I shouldn't mention another strange flowering in the wilds that we came upon one time— but to me they were as beautiful in their own way as flowers.

Each summer the Phillips family goes camping, sometimes for a weekend, sometimes for two weeks. On this particular occasion we were far from home on a two-week vacation camping trip. Our campsite was on the lakeshore in a little grove of cottonwoods. We like to camp in cottonwoods because of the way their leaves sound in the wind. They sing a different tune to every passing breeze. Anyway, behind this little grove was another, larger one, of thickly growing evergreens. Through their branches even the brilliant sun of the Cariboo couldn't penetrate. It had been a season of much rain, and it was damp and soggy under the trees. And everywhere there were toadstools. That was one time that I wished I had a book on fungi. I'm sure there were real mushrooms among them, but we didn't dare take any chances. If I hadn't seen them, I wouldn't have believed that so many kinds of toadstools could grow in one place. They were all sizes and colours and shapes. There were little pointed ones, like half-open umbrellas, and other little ones that looked like the straw hats worn by the Chinese in the rice fields. There were clusters of pale-red ones, so small that unless you looked closely at the mossy trunks of the fallen trees on which they grew, you wouldn't see them at all. Every so often we came upon a magic circle of just ordinary toadstools, and then upon a huge monstrosity of vivid orange, or a group of white puffballs looking like a handful of golf balls dropped negligently upon the ground. Maybe you don't like toadstools. I don't either, much; but none of us will ever forget that strange flowering in a wood that must surely have been haunted by witches and pixies.

This is one family that is eagerly looking forward to the day when the Hope-Princeton Highway will be completed, chiefly because of an unexpected experience we once had up that way. We hadn't intended driving as far as that, but we kept deciding to go just a little further, and eventually we found ourselves driving up the Coquihalla Valley on a beautiful stretch of the new highway. On and on we went, until the highway ended and we were on the old road. Even then, we kept on over twenty miles of some of the worst road it's ever been my misfortune to drive on, until we finally arrived at a forest ranger's cabin close to the banks of the Skagit River. It was built in a forest of the highest, straightest cedars I've ever seen. Up and up they went without a branch for hundreds of feet. And then their branches formed what seemed like the vaulted roof of a cathedral. Through the branches, long shafts of late afternoon sun slanted down to light up banks and banks of maidenhair fern. They lighted up great clumps of devil's club, too. But the wonder to us was the incredible quantity of maidenhair. Looking back on it, we wonder if there could really have been as much as we remember. When the highway is opened this fall, we're going back to see.

You know, it seems to me that the wildflowers are part of the treasure of this province of ours, treasure that is just as worthy of conservation and protection as our fish and game. And in the same way that preserving our fish and game is the individual responsibility of each one of us who goes into the woods, so is it the individual responsibility of each one of us to help preserve the wildflowers. I guess the law against picking dogwood has helped to save it from extinction, but nowadays it's pretty hard to find wildflowers—except buttercups and maybe daisies—within a radius of many miles around the cities. Doesn't it seem too bad that thoughtless people who pull them up by the roots and otherwise destroy them couldn't leave them where they grow for the pleasure of everyone?

Because I thought you might be interested in finding out some of the more technical facts about the wildflowers of B.C., I phoned the reference department of the library and found out the names of some books that might be helpful. The first one and, I think, the most interesting is one that was published just this year. It is called *Wildflowers in the Rockies*, and it's by two B.C. people, Mr. and Mrs. Hardy. It is full of beautiful illustrations painted by William Beele, paintings so outstanding that they were exhibited in the Vancouver Art Gallery a short while ago. Next in this little bibliography, and included because many people are interested in herbs these days, and also just might share my interest in edible mushrooms, is a book by Anderson called *Trees and Shrubs, Food, Medicinal, and Poisonous Plants of B.C.* Then there is *Wildflowers of the Pacific Coast*, by Haskins, and although this deals mainly with the flowers of Oregon and Washington, still much of it applies to B.C. Next on my list are two books, one by a husband, and the other by his wife. The first is called *Flora of Southern B.C. and Vancouver Island*, and the other is *Collecting Plants Beyond the Frontier in Northern B.C.* Last on the list is a highly technical work called *Alpine Flora of the Canadian Rockies*, which, though it was published in 1907, still remains the authority on the subject. All these books are available in the science department of the Vancouver library. If any of you are interested in getting those titles again, I'll be glad to let you have them. Just write or phone me, and I'll see that you get them.

And now, goodbye until tomorrow.

O CHRISTMAS TREE!

December 15, 1949

I did this piece for a series on CBR called "Behind the Scenes."

> O fir tree green, O fir tree green,
> I still shall love you dearly.
> How oft to me on Christmas night
> Your laden boughs have brought delight.

I FIRST HEARD THAT LOVELY OLD GERMAN CAROL ON MY VERY FIRST REALLY white Christmas. It was the year that I went to college in the middle-western states, and when the snow came just before December twenty-fifth, it was the crispy, crunchy kind that sparkles in the sun. Long icicles hung from the eaves of the houses. The air was so cold to breathe that it almost hurt, and everybody's nose was red-tipped. Everybody felt simply wonderful. And the college glee club sang "O fir tree green."

It's strange, isn't it, the way we've made the Christmas tree into one of the symbols of Christmastime? Its original association with a pagan religious festival had something, I believe, to do with a feast for Freya, the Norse goddess of plenty. And in those long-ago times, the fir tree was hung with cornucopias of fruit and good things to eat. As a matter of fact, we still hang cornucopias on our trees, but we have adapted the old custom to our Christian festival by placing on the tip of the tree the shining star of the East that guided the Wise Men to Bethlehem, and piled underneath its branches the gifts that are the symbol of our goodwill to men.

Here in Vancouver during the last two weeks we have been reminded of our goodwill to men by a huge Christmas tree that glitters with thousands of lights in the middle of the great open space in the heart of the city, where the old Hotel Vancouver used to stand. At first I must confess that our giant Christmas tree seemed pretty much like just another publicity stunt. We would have the highest

Christmas tree in the world—or anyway on the Pacific coast—higher than the hundred-foot-high one in Los Angeles. Ours was one hundred and ten feet and two inches high. But then it turned out to be a publicity stunt with a purpose. Our giant tree would be the gathering place for everyone's gifts for our war veterans in hospital. And so it didn't matter that a few days later, Bellingham announced that they would have the tallest tree of all. Theirs was one hundred and fifty feet high! No, it didn't matter, because the height of our Christmas tree isn't really measured in feet and inches; it's measured by the goodwill of the citizens of Vancouver towards those men and women who once upon a time fought a war so that goodwill might continue on earth, and who are still fighting a war that will never be over. Under that Christmas tree we may place our gifts for those hospitalized veterans. We may do our part to see that they have a truly merry Christmas. There are fourteen hundred of these men and women. The project of the giant Christmas tree was organized by a Vancouver man, Roy Sim, who, seven years ago, founded the St. John's canteen to provide entertainment for the men and women of the Armed Forces hospitalized in Shaughnessy Military Hospital and Hycroft. The canteen was and is a project of the St. John's Men's Service Club.

And that is why Vancouver has a giant Christmas tree, one hundred and ten feet and two inches tall, in the middle of the spot where the old Hotel Vancouver used to stand. That's the story "behind the scenes."

Last week I watched the official lighting of the Christmas tree. I stood in the early evening darkness with the rumble of home-going traffic all around me and listened to the voices of a choir rise clear and true over the roar of motors, the blare of horns, the screech of brakes, the shrill blast of the policeman's whistle at Georgia and Hornby. The choir sang "Hark the Herald Angels Sing" and I could hear every word in the cold air. When the time came to light the tree for the first time, I watched the strings of coloured lights come on, one by one, and the great glowing star at its tip, until all the towering graceful height of the tree was revealed.

There's another "behind the scenes" story about the Christmas tree, too. It's the story of community co-operation and generosity in the finding of the tree; felling it; bringing it to its present site; raising it; and decorating it. It's been estimated that about ten thousand dollars' worth of labour and materials went into that. And it was all done for free.

It seems fitting, too, that the tree itself was a gift of the Capilano Indians. It was cut on their reservation at the mouth of the Capilano River, and presented by Chief Matthias Joe. Under the giant Christmas tree the pile of gifts is growing. It should be a merry Christmas for hospital veterans.

This year, Christmas trees large and small have more than just a one-occasion importance to the people of B.C. The first time that this was forcibly brought home to me was some years ago when my husband and I had gone into the Copper Creek country back of Savona for some duck shooting. There was a heavy storm just before we started home along the narrow winding road, which was not much more than a dirt track and was our one link with civilization. Thunder and lightning and a high wind. Part of the way was through a stretch of sturdy up-country fir and pine, and it wasn't long before we came across evidence that more than one tree had fallen across the road and had been expertly sawed through and removed. Pretty soon we caught up with the car that was apparently making the path so much easier for us. Its driver was out in the road, busily sawing away at yet another fallen tree. We stopped—we had to, even if we hadn't wanted to—and fell into conversation with him. It turned out that our good Samaritan had been travelling through the country marking Christmas trees. That was the first time I realized that B.C. made more than a local thing out of selling Christmas trees. Last year, as I discovered from the Forestry Service, B.C. shipped 2,129,169 Christmas trees out of the province, trees whose sale realized $470,000. When I asked where they all went to, I learned that they were sent to the States. Mostly to California, but some go as far as New York. I wonder how many families gathered around their trees in that faraway city know that the tree standing in their living room was cut out here in British Columbia?

One reason I asked where they went was that I wondered if perhaps some of them went to Australia. Of course they don't. They wouldn't last the three-week journey across the sea and the Christmas season as well. But I asked because I remembered the difficulty our family had years ago when we were living in Melbourne, and, being true products of the North American continent, wanted an evergreen Christmas tree. (You know, of course, that Christmas down under falls in the middle of the summer, and at that time, nobody bothers very much about evergreen Christmas trees. They're too busy just trying to keep cool!) But my father was determined to celebrate

Christmas the way he always had. We even had a roaring fire in the
fireplace, although Mother threatened to bring chunks of ice for us
to sit on while gathered around the rosy flames. Finally, after a great
deal of arranging, Father had a tree shipped to us, roots and all! Yes,
he did. And we planted it in the back garden and dug it up and put
it in a box and brought it into the house at Christmas. And afterwards
planted it back in the garden again. We kept that tree for the eight
years we lived there, and when we left we gave it to another tree-
hungry family from this side of the ocean. By then it had grown
considerably. I wonder what finally became of it? We never heard.

But to get back to our own B.C. Christmas trees. I learned that
most of the trees that are cut commercially come from around
Kamloops and Nelson. Cutting young firs is not permitted on the
Crown lands on the coast. Of course, there's nothing to stop individual landowners here and on the Island from letting the two main
firms who handle the trees cut trees on their own lands, but as they
said in the Forest Service, "Down here on the coast we prefer to let
our trees grow to more than Christmas tree size, and reforestation is
quite enough of a problem as it is." I was told about a telegram that
had arrived that morning telling of a forest warden who had inter-
cepted some enterprising person on the Island who had driven onto
one of the reforestation plantations and cut a truckload of young firs.
"They will do it," he said ruefully, "in spite of all we try to do to point
out why we don't allow it."

Apparently the trees up-country, those cut and exported, are
about one hundred per cent firs and have no other commercial value.
They are scrub timber. But even these trees are cut with an eye to
the future. It seems that they are always cut about three feet above
the ground, being sure to leave at least one branch on the stump. The
branches so left are then bent upwards, and in three or four years,
there are sometimes as many as four new Christmas trees where one
grew before. That's something to remember, isn't it? Because if your
family, like ours and many thousands of others in B.C., makes an
expedition to get your own tree each year, it's satisfactory to know
that you're not depleting the stock of future Christmas trees if you just
cut them the right way. I've always felt just a little guilty about cutting
down our tree. Now that I know that by leaving at least one branch
behind on the stump we're not really destroying anything, I feel
much better about the whole thing.

The Phillips family went out en masse last Sunday to get its

Christmas tree, and really, it was one of the most satisfactory tree expeditions we've ever had. Not only did we get a lovely pine—and we are particularly fond of pine—but the setting was just right. On the way to our very secret source of supply, we heard the United Nations broadcast on the car radio. We heard Bernstein's inspiring music and the wonderful voice of Sir Laurence Olivier reciting the Preamble to the Declaration of Human Rights. In the marshy place where we get our tree, the pools were covered with a thin film of ice. Frost had painted the salal leaves silver white. The air was cold and full of the pungent fragrance of crushed Labrador tea leaves and the scent of cut cedar as we gathered our greens. On our way back to the car, the boys bearing the tree, our arms full of cedar and salal, a gentle powdery snow began to sift down and fall silently on everything. If I could sing I would have paraphrased the old German carol: "O pine tree green, O pine tree green, I still shall love you dearly. How oft to me on Christmas night, your laden boughs have brought delight."

BIZ: *Fade into music of "O Tannenbaum."*

CASCARA AND OTHER MEDICINAL PLANTS IN B.C.

August 15, 1950

How things do change! The demand for ginseng has done anything but wane, among both Chinese and non-Chinese, and ginseng now occupies an esteemed place on every health food store's shelves. Perhaps the Chinese man questioned by Professor Davidson was just trying to keep a secret.

GOOD MORNING. I DO HOPE THAT THE TITLE OF MY TALK WITH YOU THIS morning hasn't scared you away from your radio, but it seemed to me that it would be interesting to explore the possibilities of medicinal plants in B.C., not only those native to our province, but others that might be raised here. It wasn't an original idea; it was brought on by seeing a letter in the "Letters to the Editor" column of one of our daily newspapers a week or two ago requesting information about a certain plant for which a large order had been placed, and which there was difficulty in finding. The letter was signed by John Davidson, with a Vancouver address, and I thought to myself, "there's someone I must look up." And I did. Imagine my surprise at finding plain John Davidson to be none other than the distinguished botanist, Professor Davidson, of the University of British Columbia, with a string of letters after his name that would have completely overawed me had I known in advance that they were there. I never would have dared just to pick up the phone and call him and ask him if I might have a talk with him about medicinal plants for a talk on "Morning Visit." I would at least have acquired a highly formal introduction!

But I needn't have worried. Professor Davidson is a most approachable person, and apparently didn't in the least mind having his brains picked by a mere layman. We spent a most delightful afternoon; my only complaint was that the time went too quickly. Professor Davidson told me of some of his early experiences in tracking down B.C. flora, of the interesting relationship he was able to establish with the Indians through the medium of an interpreter named Teit. (The story of Teit, by the way, tells like a movie about the pioneers. It's a story that should be told someday.) And the professor told me how his work with plants tied in through the similarity of native plant names with work being done by other men busy tracing ethnic origins and relationships.

When we finally brought ourselves back to a strictly medicinal plants basis—almost with reluctance, we were having such a pleasant time talking about other things—the first one mentioned, because it is by far B.C.'s most important native medicinal plant, was the cascara tree. Most of us have, I think, heard something about the value of the bark of this tree, which grows naturally and easily in—in fact is native to—B.C. But I wonder how many of us know all the facts. And especially I wonder how many of us know about some of the more recent discoveries about this tree made by Professor Davidson and some of his colleagues at the university.

My knowledge of the subject was pretty vague, to say the least, so I asked the only question that occurred to me as a pertinent one. I asked, "When the bark is stripped from a cascara tree, doesn't the tree die, and doesn't this do dreadful things eventually to the supply of cascara?" And then I had a short and very elementary lesson on the way a tree lives and grows. I had always thought that the roots of the tree were the vital parts for its life, but I learned that the leaves have a far more important part to play. And that, while certainly the tree dies when the bark is stripped from it, it's not because the sap can't get up through the bark to the leaves, but mostly because the food that is produced by the leaves can't get back to the roots! Professor Davidson said that years ago a tremendous number of trees in the neighbourhood of Haney were stripped as they stood and left standing stark and bare and dead. Now, in that neighbourhood, while it is true that there are a few cascara trees left, they are only a few. And so, since 1914, about ninety per cent of our original supply has been wastefully depleted in this way, because, as a result of meeting the world's requirements of between one and two thousand tons of bark each year, about three hundred thousand trees have died each year.

But research at the university showed that if the trees are cut down before the bark is stripped, the stumps sprout new shoots and these, in a few years, produce flowers and berries for future propagation. The new sprouts will probably never have any bark worth stripping, but the production of flowers and berries does mean that the seeds for future trees will be sown by birds and wind. That phrase, "research at the university," covers an interesting little story. Apparently Professor Davidson saw some men clearing a vacant lot one day some years ago. It was a lot that contained a number of cascara trees. The men were felling the trees and burning them in connection with a city-wide cleanup of vacant lots to prevent the spread of a bad plague of tent caterpillars. The professor went up to the men and told them that they were destroying perfectly good money. They looked at him unbelievingly. When they were finally convinced and figured out just what they had destroyed in good hard cash, they were completely abashed. Some time later, the professor had occasion to pass by the same lot again and noticed that new sprouts were springing up from the stumps of the felled cascara trees, and he realized that there was the answer to the depletion of the source of supply of the bark. Now it is provincial law that a tree must be felled before it is stripped.

More research has since proved that the wood of the cascara tree contains the medicine also—in fact, that there is as much cascara in two pounds of wood, and of the same quality, as is contained in one pound of the bark. If it were possible to sell cascara trees by the cord to a manufacturing druggist right here in the province, it would be entirely possible to ship out the completed extract. Unfortunately, we do not have such manufacturing druggists in the province. It is unfortunate for another reason, too. If we did have such a drug factory, it would then be profitable for drug farmers and collectors to go ahead with their work. Until this sort of a factory is established, we shall go on using one-sixth of our cascara resources and wasting five-sixths, and there won't be real profit, at least not a livelihood in drug farming or collecting.

It is very important to us here in B.C. to remember that our province is almost the sole supplier of cascara at present. Supplies in Washington and Oregon have been practically used up. It is particularly important to those people who collect and dry the bark and sell it to wholesalers, simply because of the need for watching market prices. It is also a fact that if B.C. had a manufacturing drug concern, the province could prepare enough extract in two months to supply the world demand. I asked the professor how much a person could reasonably be expected to make in a day collecting cascara bark, and he told me that in a good district he could make five or ten dollars a day. But that wouldn't be so if everyone suddenly started collecting it, for the market would be very quickly glutted.

Because of the importance of cascara and B.C.'s virtual corner on the supply, B.C.'s future in drug farming hinges on the establishment of a drug manufacturing factory. B.C. has everything else necessary to make this kind of farming profitable, starting with a longer growing season and milder winters than any other part of Canada. Goldenseal, a plant native to eastern Canada, much used for gastrointestinal remedies, and also for nasal catarrh, grows very easily here. So does digitalis, or foxglove, used for heart ailments. Another is henbane, and yet another is Datura, or jimson weed, which is used for asthma. At some time during our conversation, I asked Professor Davidson if he had had many answers to his letter in the paper. He told me sixty-four by the latest count, and that they had come from as far north as Quesnel, as far east as the Arrow Lakes, and from many parts of the Okanagan, the Fraser Valley, and points on the Island. He told me, too, that he had written these enquirers and told them that drug farming is "no get-rich-quick" scheme, but assured them that after some experience in growing and drying, they might be assured of a profitable return. I suppose he meant that would be so if and when a manufacturing drug factory is established here. In any case, I'm sure he'd be glad to answer much more fully than I can any questions you might have about the possibilities of drug farming.

You know, when I first got the idea of a talk on medicinal plants, I was haunted with memories of those books by Gene Stratton Porter. Do you remember? *Girl of the Limberlost* and *The Harvester*. And how the characters in the book made a fortune from ginseng? Well, imagine my surprise when Professor Davidson told me that ginseng has no medicinal qualities whatever! Then he went on to tell me a very amusing story about how one day, a certain Chinese gentleman came to get some information from him. Professor Davidson, who, after all, is a canny Scot, said, "I'll give you the information you want if you'll tell me something I want to know." The Chinese smiled and nodded, and the professor said, "Will you tell me what it is that the Chinese use ginseng for?" The Chinese hesitated and looked a bit doubtful. "Come on," urged the professor, "fair exchange is no robbery. Do you use it for medicine?" The Chinese shook his head. "Do you use it for food?" Again the Chinese shook his head. "Well, what then?" Finally the Chinese said, "We use it for charm. When Chinese girl get married, her friends give her ginseng for luck and happiness and many children." So much for the medicinal properties of ginseng! The professor also told me that the more like a human figure the root, the higher price it commands among the Chinese. He said he knew of one root that brought fifty dollars in Vancouver's Chinatown. However, with the development of western ways of living, the Chinese demand for ginseng is waning.

It is strange, though, that many people still chew ginseng root in the belief that it will make them feel better. The same is true of devil's club root, which was thought for a time to cure diabetes. Although it has been conclusively proved that this root doesn't contain a single sugar-reducing property, many people are still under the impression that medicine containing it will help their diabetes. Lots of people, too, chew slippery elm for general health, and while it's quite pleasant to chew, it definitely is not an aid to better health. The addition of Labrador tea to your own pleasant pot of morning tea won't have any noticeable effect on your well-being either, although it's supposed to.

However, there are in B.C. some fifty species of plants mentioned in the pharmacopoeia growing wild, some in great abundance, others too sparsely distributed to be collected in quantity. Some are worth only a few cents a pound and are not worth the costs of shipping to eastern firms. Once again, the establishment of a local manufacturing concern would make the collecting worthwhile. So don't do anything rash about establishing a drug farm or rushing out enthusiastically to collect medicinal plants until you've inquired more closely into all the possibilities. And if you want to do that, let me know and I'll pass along your questions to Professor Davidson. Sometime I'd like to tell you his story of Botanie Valley, and his interpreter's tale of how Kaiser Wilhelm's son came a-hunting big game specimens for German museums in B.C. back in the early years of the century. But those stories will have to wait until another time.

Till tomorrow then.

THE CHALLENGER RELIEF MAP

August 28, 1950

The Challenger relief map remained in the B.C. Pavillion at the PNE (Pacific National Exhibition) until early 1998, when the building was torn down. The map was dismantled and put into storage while the Challenger family and the City of Vancouver look for a new permanent home for it. Let's hope it happens.

GOOD MORNING. TODAY I FEEL AS THOUGH I HAD ACQUIRED A DEEPER knowledge and understanding of this province that we live in, than I ever had before. Ever since we came to this country to live I've been aware of a certain quality, that for want of a better term, might be called the "romance" of British Columbia. It's a quality, I think, born of its scenery partly, and partly due to the fact that here we still seem to be very close to the early days when history was in the making. But I had never quite realized that, geographically speaking, B.C. is the very essence of romance. We can travel through the province and be continually amazed at the contrasts the country presents to us. We can look at maps and be impressed by the ruggedness of the coastline, the magnitude of the area that is B.C. We can be roused to excitement by stories of the early days. But it wasn't until I saw the Challenger relief map that I understood that all these romantic qualities spring quite naturally from one source: its geography.

When we look at flat maps, it's impossible to relate them to the bits and pieces of the country that we see; whereas this wonderful map makes that relationship immediately evident. This was the first time that I'd seen the Challenger map, although it has been on display—or those parts of it that were completed at the time have been on display—at the Pacific National Exhibition for the past two years. Two years ago, sixteen panels had been completed, last year forty-two were finished, this year there are seventy-five, and next year the completed map will contain one hundred thirty-one panels, covering the entire province. This year, these separate panels have been joined together to form four huge sections—for example, one

section covers from Victoria to Campbell River and east to Fernie—
representing 345,600 square miles. It occupies one whole wing of the
Industrial Building.

It's not easy to convey to you just how the relief map gives one
such a greater understanding of what our province is like. But when
you see it, it's impossible not to be aware of the height of our mountains, of the way in which the rivers wind through the deep valleys,
of the immensity of the Chilcotin rangelands, of the fjord-like ruggedness of our long coastline. You immediately understand just why the
old Indian and fur-trappers' trails followed certain routes. You appreciate the tremendous difficulties that faced the engineers constructing
the railroads, and the hazards faced by our coastal boats as they navi-
gate the narrow waterways from Vancouver to the Alaska border. You
get this understanding, I think, because not only can you see the
country in relief, but each level of altitude is most subtly coloured to
create a clear visual impression of varying heights, from sea-level to
the towering peaks of the Rocky Mountains. Such a variation in colour
would be quite impossible to obtain in an ordinary clay relief map. It
is only possible in the Challenger map because each level is formed
of separate and individually cut pieces of plywood, ingeniously glued
and nailed together, until the required altitude of each and every little
rise, every hill and mountain and plateau and plain, has been reached.

It doesn't seem possible, does it, that such a colossal task could
ever be accomplished? And yet, already the map contains over six
hundred thousand individually cut pieces of plywood. Individually
cut, moreover, only by Mr. Challenger and his son, because they felt
that only by doing it themselves could they be sure of the accuracy
that to them was absolutely essential. And not one of those six
hundred thousand pieces exactly resembles any other piece—"at
least," said Mr. Challenger, "not that I know of." And he should know,
if anyone does, because he and his son spent endless hours guiding
the little electrically powered jigsaw around the contours of each
layer of plywood that forms each altitude level of each and every rise
in the ground in the 345,600 square miles. In the map, as it is
displayed this year, there has been over a hundred miles of actual
cutting of the individual pieces! Although, as Mr. Challenger told me,
the building of the map has been a truly family affair, with each
member of the family—four sons and a daughter—helping at one
time or another. There have at times been as many as twenty-two
people engaged in putting it together. To date, there have been

34,500 man-hours of labour put into the task, and when the map is finally finished, it will have been six years in the making.

I like one little glimpse that Mr. Challenger gave me of just how the map is a family affair. He said that, night after night, the only view that the rest of the family had of his daughter was a rear elevation as she perched on a ladder, ten feet in the air, laboriously plastering on pieces of wood.

I asked Mr. Challenger how he came to undertake the project, and he told me that for forty years he had been making relief maps for mining and logging and other engineering projects in the province, maps that entailed travelling the length and breadth of the province by canoe and boat and on horseback, and many, many miles by foot. So that his knowledge of the topography of B.C. is probably more intimate and detailed than that of any other single person. And, more than most people, he has in this way acquired a stronger feeling for the romance of our province. Then, during World War II, he was, as he himself put it, "dug out" of retirement to make relief maps for civilian defence. One night during this period, Mr. MacCorkindale, superintendent of the Vancouver School Board, idly remarked how wonderful it would be if a relief map of the whole province could be made to help students in their social studies, saying that he felt it would prove very valuable, not only to the students, but to the teachers as well. And so the idea was planted in Mr. Challenger's mind. He began drawing master maps. If the result was to be worth the labour, everything must be as accurate as was possible from the data available. And Mr. Challenger said to me that, except for a variation of maybe one degree here and there in slope, the detail of the map is absolutely correct. (Perhaps right here I should mention that the scale of the map is one mile to one inch horizontally and one thousand feet to one inch vertically. The differential in the scale is intended to give a more realistic visual conception.)

Well, those master maps took seven long years to complete, and Mr. Challenger celebrated his seventieth birthday with their completion. July of next year should be a still bigger celebration, for it is then that the map will be entirely finished, including some big panels without relief that will mark the prairies and the Pacific Ocean. And all of this for the benefit of the students in our schools and as a public service to the people of British Columbia and visitors to the province. The map itself is, of course, the property of Mr. Challenger's company, Challenger Cartographers Ltd. It has been shown to the public for the last three years through the co-operation of the H. R. MacMillan Export

Company, the British Columbia Packers Ltd., and the Pacific National
Exhibition. But Mr. Challenger's dream of making it available for the
instruction of school students is going to be realized. All next winter
the map will be kept available in the Industrial Building, where it is
now, for the use of the schools and the general public, and eventually it will be placed in a building especially designed for it.

The arrangements for this coming winter were made possible
through the kindness and interest of five prominent B.C. industrialists
and businessmen, and the building which is to be built to house it
permanently will be a Pacific National Exhibition building, the British
Columbia Building, erected on the fairgrounds. There's a wonderful
little model of this proposed building on view with the map at the PNE.
It shows an eighty-foot glass tower—glass, that is—on three sides; the
fourth is the map, rising above the main body of the building. Inside
the tower a ramp winds upward so that visitors looking at the map
may examine each section in detail. Of course, we must remember that
this building is only proposed as yet, but it would be a terrible thing if
such a valuable contribution to education and general knowledge were
not to have adequate housing to make it available to everybody. Let's
hope that the British Columbia Building doesn't remain in the dream
world of proposed things too long; let's hope that it becomes a reality,
and as soon as possible, too. Think, for instance, how wonderful it
would be to have the map, completed and properly set up in the
proper surroundings when thousands of visitors troop to Vancouver in
1954 for the next British Empire Games. Among the many compliments
that Mr. Challenger has received about his map, about its usefulness
now and in the future, and its contribution to education and general
knowledge, the one that he himself values most was spoken by Mr.
H. R. MacMillan. He said, "If that map had been made forty-one years
ago when I was made Chief Forester of British Columbia, there
would be today a different and better forest industry and a different
and better forest branch." When you see the map, you will, I'm sure,
understand what prompted those words of Mr. MacMillan's.

Seeing the province through the Challenger relief map is to get an
entirely new perspective of it, a sort of four-dimensional view that even
at the first glance revises all one's previous conceptions. For instance,
we have a friend who made a most unusual trip about a year ago. He
made a boat, a very superior boat, big enough for all the equipment
necessary for a two-week trip far from civilization of any kind, and yet
light enough for a short portage, and manoeuvrable enough even to

shoot rapids if need be. Then he and his companion put the boat on a small trailer and drove up to Ootsa Lake, where they launched it and set out on their journey—up Ootsa to Whitesail Lake, up Whitesail, and after a portage, up Eutsuk Lake to Tetachuk, through the Tetachuk rapids into Natalkuz Lake, and finally up Natalkuz and back to Ootsa again. Well, I heard in detail the story of the trip, of the hardships they encountered, of the wonderful country through which they travelled. I even saw many very beautiful coloured pictures that they took on their way, but I never really understood or realized just what they had done in making that trip until I saw the Challenger relief map.

This summer, too, we went into the Douglas Lake country for the first time. We were lost in wonder at the beautiful rangeland in there. But before I saw the map I had no real idea of why the country is the way it is; one look at the map, though, and you can clearly see the plateau formation that runs through, between Nicola Lake and behind Okanagan Lake and upwards towards Armstrong and Salmon Arm.

And it's quite amazing, too, to see how Lillooet is set deep within the mountain walls in the bottom of the gorge cut by the Fraser River. Of course, the only thing to do is to see it for yourself, so that you, too, may pick out the spots that interest you and see what an entirely new vision it gives you. The grand thing about that is you don't have to live in Vancouver to see it, and you don't even have to visit Vancouver during the time of the Pacific National Exhibition; you can see it any time that you happen to be in the city. Because don't forget that the map will be on display in the Industrial Building all next winter and spring, and that if all goes well, it will soon have a permanent building where the completed map will be placed for the benefit of students and the people of B.C. and visitors to the province alike. So that all of us may learn better to appreciate the wonder of this province that we live in—with, I think, a great deal of gratitude to Mr. Challenger.

If, however, you are going to the PNE during this next week, and would like to make the map your first port of call, here's the best way to find it. Instead of entering the grounds by the main entrance, go on up Renfrew Street to the entrance, just about opposite Callister Park, the one marked with a big sign that says Rollerland. Turn hard left immediately inside the gate, and follow the sawdust track that runs between the fence and the backs of various and sundry tents. Walk into the doorway that faces you at the end of the path, turn right inside the building, and there's the map!

Until tomorrow then.

IMPERIAL CANNERY, STEVESTON

August 30, 1950

GOOD MORNING. EVERYTHING TO ME THIS MORNING STILL HAS A FAINT FISHY smell. No, I didn't go fishing yesterday, but I did visit the Imperial Fish Cannery out at Steveston, and for the first time got a real idea of the story back of a can of salmon. When we see the bright rows of canned salmon on the grocery shelves, we seldom stop to think how they arrived there, and really, it's a fascinating story.

The tale begins, of course, long before the fish arrive at the cannery stage; it goes back, for these particular fish in this particular cannery on the Fraser River, to the early years of the last century—back to 1829—when the Indians first began commercial salmon fishing on the river. By 1863, Fraser River salmon was being salted down in large casks for trade with, of all places, the Hawaiian Islands. In 1867, the first salmon to be hermetically sealed in metal containers were displayed at the Agricultural Exhibition held in New Westminster and, since that time, the fishing industry has grown and developed, until today all kinds of processed fish from British Columbia waters are marketed in all parts of the world.

The next chapter of the story is one of near disaster. Between 1900 and 1913, the Fraser River emerged as the main producer of B.C.'s fishery wealth—in fact, as the mightiest salmon-producing river in the world. And then, in 1913, a rock slide at Hell's Gate in the canyon of the Fraser partially blocked the passage of the fish to their spawning grounds. It so happened that in that year there occurred the largest run of sockeye salmon ever recorded in the river. The slide made it impossible for most of the fish to pass the obstruction, and the salmon died by the millions without ever reaching their spawning grounds. For the next 25 years, the Fraser declined steadily as an important producer of salmon. Then, in 1937, a treaty was concluded between Canada and the United States providing for an International Commission to study the situation and, if possible, to take steps to restore the river to its former glory. The Hell's Gate Fish-ways—or as we know them better, the Hell's Gate Fish Ladders—were the main result of this investigation. The Fishways first went into operation in 1945, and since then have completely justified their installation. As most of us know, the salmon spawns in four-year cycles, and an actual count of certain runs before and after the Fishways were constructed proved this most dramatically. For instance, in 1941, the Stuart Lake run of fish that actually reached their spawning grounds in the Stuart Lake area totalled something like 6,300 fish. In the next cycle year, 1945, with the aid of the Fishways, the number had increased to 28,000, and in 1949, which was the next cycle year for that particular run, at least 400,000 fish returned to Stuart Lake!

This year, the Adams River run, which is actually the biggest run of all, has been expected to top all records and put to the greatest test of all the adequacy of the Hell's Gate Fishways. But so far, the expected run has not materialized. When I reached the cannery yesterday afternoon, instead of a seething hive of activity, the plant was running at about one-tenth of its capacity, and everybody was looking a little worried. Where is the run? You wouldn't think that a delay of a day or two would prove worrying, would you, and yet it is a curious fact that salmon runs can be predicted almost to the hour—that is, they usually can. Now, in 1946, the last cycle year of the Adams River run, the fish arrived on August 27, and people are beginning to speculate as to whether something has happened. One theory that's being advanced is that the fingerlings—the baby fish, born of that last spawning cycle four years ago—were due to come down the river again on their way to the sea in 1948, the year of the great Fraser River flood. Could the flood have affected the fingerlings? Perhaps they died from too much oxygen, or perhaps they smothered in the river silt that poured down the flooded river. No one knows. But the fish still haven't arrived.

However, there was still plenty to be seen at the cannery. Under the wing of Mr. Payne, my genial guide, I saw so much and learned so much in a short time that my mind is still whirling with facts and statistics, and filled with pictures of everything from fish to machinery to tins to nets. Some of the pictures are lovely ones. It was a beautiful day, clear and sunny with a fresh breeze, and after we had passed between the cannery buildings, bright with their white paint and green trim and brilliant notes of colour in window boxes, and passed the totem poles before the door of the company store, we came out to the dock. The wind was really blowing there, whipping the muddy yellow Fraser into choppy waves. Boats were purposefully passing up and down, seiners and little fish boats and packers.

Tied to the dock was a fish carrier, a boat whose master takes it to the fishing grounds, buys the fish from the fisherman, and then sells them to the cannery. In the uncovered hold were big bins of salmon, mostly white springs. They were being weighed and unloaded. Everything was shining in the sun, the flags flipping at the mastheads, the white paint of the cannery buildings, the outspread wings of the wheeling, screaming gulls.

Then we started through the cannery. I saw salmon being deftly filleted and packed in boxes, then wrapped in cellophane by an automatic wrapping machine, looking when they emerged, as my guide put it, for all the world like boxes of chocolate rather than salmon. These fillets were due to be quickly frozen in a deep freeze. A little farther on, where fish are smoked with oak sawdust, I appreciatively sniffed the wonderful aroma. I raced through the cold storage rooms capable of storing two million pounds of fish. I raced, not because I wasn't interested, but because it was so cold—brrr—so cold that we hadn't been inside but a minute before the inside of my nose went all stiff and crackly, and the tips of my ears began to tingle, and by the time we came out again, I was cold clear through. So cold that the wind that had felt just the least bit chilly before going in now felt like a soft tropical breeze.

In the cold storage rooms, though, it was like walking through a frozen wonderland. We passed down aisles between shelves of huge salmon, staked high and frozen solid, and covered with a whiskery coating of white frost. We saw the huge frozen carcass of a two-hundred-twenty-eight-pound sturgeon, and the great flat expanse of a halibut that weighed one hundred seventy-eight pounds. Near the sturgeon there was the stiff and frozen body of a strange deep-sea creature called a sawfish, with great flat round eyes and a long thin body edged with fins that looked exactly like the teeth of a big crosscut saw; it looked even stranger, covered as it was, like everything else, with its coating of white.

Outside again, we blew our noses lustily as we thawed out, and moved on to where Indian women were packing quarter-pound tins of salmon by hand; there was no automatic packing going on yesterday at all. But I saw the big machines, the "Iron Chubs," that automatically cut off the heads and tails and fins, clean out the insides, and separate the fish and the cleanings, sending the fish on its way for packing, with the offal swishing down troughs of water sluiced with high-pressure hoses on its way to the reduction plant.

Nothing of the salmon, except possibly a little steam, is wasted in this cannery. I was interested in the reduction process, so Mr. Payne, after warning me, "This is going to be smelly," took me into the building where the offal is collected and steam-cooked, the water removed in a great furnace, and then dried in long tubes, in which are long shafts like enormous augers, and finally pulverized and run off into hundred-pound sacks of fishmeal. I mentally held my nose and inspected it all. Then I was shown where the water is churned and the oil removed from it, the remaining water mixed with sulphuric acid, churned again, and more oil—more grease than oil this time—taken off, and finally the last residue of water, called "stick water," is pumped into the evaporation plant for a process just like evaporating milk, from which a product called "fish soluble" is obtained. This fish soluble is shipped out in tank cars and used to spray on cattle feed to give cattle a balanced diet. Of course, though, before the fish cleanings go through this reduction process, the livers are removed and sent to another plant where they are used for medicinal purposes.

One thing that impressed me very much about the cannery was its cleanliness. With so much fish around, one would expect lots of flies; but everything is kept so clean and fresh that there are actually no flies at all!

After the rattle and clatter of the canning machinery and the pervasive smells of the reduction plant, it was infinitely pleasant to climb the stairs up to the net loft. Up in this high, airy place the nets are unpacked and prepared for use. Those that I saw were all gill nets, twelve hundred feet long and twenty-eight feet wide, valued at six hundred dollars each. They all come from Scotland and Ireland, tightly packed in large bales. They are beautifully made of linen thread, so strong that they last for about three years, unless, that is, they are torn by the strugglings of a huge salmon. Usually such damage can be repaired, but it takes many hours of patient work. When I said that the nets are prepared for use in the net loft, I meant that up here they are selvaged with a heavy cotton string, and the oval cedar floats strung through one end and the silver lead weights through the other. I wish you could have seen the net loft: high-roofed, as I said, with sunlight streaming down through windows set far up the walls, and the gossamer lengths of the nets draped like lacy cobwebs from beams placed across from wall to wall way up in the roof, and sitting on stools in a row on the floor, the women, skilled pieceworkers every one, their fingers flying in and out as they deftly weave the selvage on the nets.

Through a window at one end of the loft we could see across to another dock where the fishermen, careful to protect their investment, were spreading their pale green nets to dry in the sun. When the nets arrive, they are a natural linen colour, but here they are dyed brown to match the colour of stream water, or a soft green that may deceive the fish down in the green ocean depths. Last evening, when I was recounting the day's experiences to the family, my younger son said, "Mummy, I read a joke about nets in a joke book. It said, how do you make nets?" And the answer was, "You make nets by taking a handful of holes and sewing them together."

Well, when we left the net loft, we crossed the dock to another building. In here, the windows were long and low and looked out over the river with its moving boats and wheeling gulls. On the other wall were great bricked-in cauldrons of molten lead. In this place a man was pouring the little oval silver weights that are strung through the nets. First of all, he fixed the cord so that it passed a certain number of times through the mould, then he closed the mould and poured in a ladle of the liquid lead. After he had given it a minute to set, he opened the mould again, first prying off the excess metal and returning it to the cauldron, and there, beautifully wrapped around the cord, were half a dozen of the little weights. He hammered them gently to make sure that they were securely held in place, trimmed them so that they were smooth, and then proceeded to repeat the process with the next length of cord. It was a fascinating business. I could have watched him for hours.

Finally, I reluctantly tore myself away, and we went down to the other end of the long dock, stopping in on the way to watch pound tins of salmon being ingeniously labelled by machinery that seemed almost human—slap the glue, slap the label, a rub around a metal cylinder to complete the job. Then the tins, ready for packaging, ran along a conveyor, stacked in the right number of layers for a carton, boxed and sent on their way along another conveyor to another machine that closed the cartons. And the fish was ready for shipment.

Down at the other end of the dock, we climbed some more stairs to another bright, airy place, the laboratory of the research chemist. Glass test tubes and retorts lined the wall. There was a bottle containing a baby whale that had been taken from the body of its mother, and a bottle full of sample slices of salmon, and still another bottle with what looked like a trout in it. In a little kitchen at the far end of the lab was a dish of jellied tuna. I sampled it, and it was delicious. Jellied tuna is the latest delicacy to be evolved by the chemist at the cannery: the oil is removed, and a delicately spiced jelly surrounds the tuna in the tin. You'll be able to buy it in the stores this fall.

And that was my visit to the cannery. There are six thousand people engaged in work in the canneries of B.C. Twelve thousand fishermen supply them. Directly and indirectly, the fishing industry, fourth in importance in our province, employs seventy-five thousand people. So when you see a can of salmon on the grocery shelf now, you'll know that it represents a whole lot more than just a tin of fish!

Wild HORSES

August 16, 1957

This is a piece I did for a CBR series called "Western Magazine."

ABOVE THE VALLEY OF HAT CREEK AND THE BRILLIANT BLUE WATER OF PAVILION Lake towers the limestone-marble barrier of Pavilion Mountain. Some twenty-two hundred feet up is a steep, narrow pass which may once upon a time have been the route of an Indian trail across the mountain into the valley. On its rocky walls, in red that has weathered goodness knows how many hundreds of seasons of sun and rain and snow, are several groups of vividly drawn pictographs. Until about ten years ago, very few people knew they existed, for even the Indians had forgotten that they were there.

Today, the messages they carried are unknown, for nobody has been able to decipher their exact meaning or that of other such groups that have been found near Naramata, Skaha Lake, Vaseux Lake, and other places in southern B.C. It seems to me, however, that to an imaginative eye, the Pavilion Mountain pictographs had a very clear message: the figure of a crudely drawn man, the arrow in his stretched bow pointing to the valley below, said, "We have passed this way." A painted circle divided into segments could have been a sort of sundial that said, "Ten hours to the west the hunting is good"—the hunting shown as the outlines of several animals.

Some people have thought the drawings were part of the old Indian rituals of initiating boys into manhood; in other words, that one of the first tests of courage was to send the boy, armed with a little pot of paint, out into the night to a designated spot, and, to prove that he had been there, he drew something on a rock. Others have thought that they were merely the outpourings of Indians with artistic leanings, and others that the symbols bear a marked resemblance to the highly developed pictographs of the early Mexicans. This last idea seems to me to be the most likely when linked to the fact that horses, many horses, were found by the first white men who came to B.C. They were not like those of the prairie Indians, but showed signs of an Arab strain, descendants, perhaps, of the horses Cortez brought to Mexico in 1519 and which were ridden up the Pacific coast by wandering Mexican peons. Or did an expedition of white men and Mexicans precede the arrival of the fur traders? It is true, too, that the pictographs are always found along old trails, and it doesn't seem too unlikely to assume that they were the road signs of an earlier day.

Well, we may never know the exact answers to either the pictographs or the horses, although both are still part of the British Columbia scene. The first, however, are gradually being destroyed by vandals and curio hunters armed with picks, and the horses, the wild horses, are present in enough numbers to constitute, at times, such a real nuisance to ranchers that permits are issued to shoot them, expeditions are organized to destroy them, and there has even been a bounty of five dollars paid for a pair of horse's ears.

The wild horses of today are mostly a pretty sorry lot, the result of turning loose the culls from the ranchers' herds. Sometimes, though, especially in the Kootenays, there are some with evidence of good breeding. I guess, however, that it would take a lot of study to determine whether evidence like that was the result of accidental breeding with good modern stock, or the recurrence of an Arab strain brought up from Mexico. Nevertheless, herds of wild horses still wander in British Columbia, in the Kootenays and the Chilcotins, in the Clinton area, and around the valleys of the Nicola and the Similkameen.

Some years ago in the Nicola Valley we were told of one expedition organized by ranchers tired of having their water holes fouled and of providing free grazing land badly needed by their cattle. Hundreds of wild horses were rounded up and the ranchers were well pleased. The Indians of the valley, however, were not pleased at all. They claimed that the horses belonged to them by hereditary right and that the ranchers had no right to deprive them of this source of revenue and of free locomotion and transport. I never heard the result of this dispute, if indeed it had a result.

That the wild horses did sometimes provide a means of revenue for Indians and white men alike is quite true, for, as I mentioned earlier, there has sometimes been a bounty of five dollars for a pair of ears. The system of bounties is looked upon with great disfavour by all who know good game management, because it can be so misused. The Game Commission tells a story about wild horses that is a case in point. In 1945–46, the range was closed to horses, and shortly afterwards a newcomer to the Clinton area applied for a permit to shoot them. A few days later, he appeared before Ranger Robertson with a sackful of ears and demanded the bounty. The ranger was suspicious. First, the man was very new in the district; second, his permit had only been issued a few days earlier; and third, the ears in the sack were mouldy. Ranger Robertson made inquiries and it was found that the man had a partner at the coast in whose possession they found twelve hundred scalps and ears—scavenged from a local slaughterhouse. A neat scheme for cashing in on the bounty on wild horses!

I had one very dramatic encounter with wild horses, one which I will never forget. We had driven up a seven-thousand-foot mountain not far from Penticton to look for alpine wildflowers. We left the car at the bottom of the last steep slope and went the rest of the way on foot. We skirted bare outcroppings of rock and patches of late snow, and walked through masses of pink heather and short, brilliantly red Indian paintbrush and clumps of vivid blue lupine. As we climbed, the clouds seemed to come down to meet us, and when we reached the top, we were surrounded by swirling white mist. The flowers were gone and there were only bare rocks, clammy with damp and the snow that lay deeply in the hollows.

We heard them before we saw them. A muffled thundering, far off at first, but getting quickly louder and closer. Then through the mist and up over the flank of the mountain, heads held high, with streaming manes and pounding hooves, galloped a herd of wild horses. The leader was a big white horse, and he tossed his head when he saw us but didn't break his pace. As though they were urged on by an invisible charioteer in an invisible chariot, they thundered straight across the rocky slope in front of us and disappeared down the other side. Then the clouds seemed to draw in again and, like spectators leaving after the show is over, we went back down to the car in silence.

3. OUTINGS

CAMPING

Summer, 1947

In 1933, when Dick and I were married, we were oddities among our friends. None of them were getting married; no one had enough money. But we didn't let that deter us. Even then eighty dollars a month wasn't very much to live on, but we managed somehow. When it came to holidays, we went camping. Camping, at least our kind of camping, wasn't popular then. We had the highways and byways pretty much to ourselves. Organized campsites were conspicuous in their absence.

At first we managed to borrow a tent and filch knives and forks, pots and pans from our own kitchen. Then we bought a little equipment trailer. And later we drove to Seattle and bought quantities of war-surplus tents, sleeping bags, camp stoves.

Eventually our camping trips were highly organized, well-supplied affairs. The whole family grew to prefer them to any other holiday. We camped and explored and fished in all sorts of out-of-the-way places in this big province of British Columbia.

GOOD MORNING. YOU KNOW, SOME WEEKS AGO WHEN I WAS TALKING OVER these programs with the people here at CBR, we decided that you might be interested in hearing how one family goes camping, and everybody enjoys it—even Mother! We thought, too, that a subject like that might help to introduce you to the Phillips family, about whom you will be hearing something, at least indirectly, in the next few weeks, because (perhaps because I'm a woman) I find it next to impossible to stay absolutely impersonal when I'm talking about anything. And I share with most other women the habit of relating things to those people and even places that I know best.

Years ago, my husband and I used to discuss which we'd buy first when the far-off day arrived that we could buy either: a car or a boat. It seemed to us, living here on the British Columbia coast, that all adventure lay just around the corner, if we only had a boat. However, as with most of us, when the day came that we were able to afford a car or a boat, practical considerations won the day, and we bought a car. We soon found that even in the Chevy—we'd invested in a slightly dilapidated '29 Chevy coupe—we could still have our adventure, although it didn't consist of exploring out-of-the-way bits of the B.C. coast, and sailing sparkling waters with salt air and sunshine in our faces. But it did consist of exploring the great Interior of our province, fishing in out-of-the-way lakes, and gradually learning to enjoy what we now think is one of the greatest of all sports, fly fishing.'

That first trip "up-country," with a borrowed tent, borrowed fishing rods, and everything packed in and on and around that little car, was the first of many that have been a never-ending source of pleasure to us all (yes, even to Mother). That first trip wasn't without its complications, either. I remember that during the last day or two of our holiday a forest fire crept closer and ever closer to the camp; we couldn't decide whether discretion was the better part of valour, and we should get out of there in a hurry. We were still dithering when the decision was made for us. There was a cloudburst in the night, and since we were sleeping on the ground, and hadn't thought to dig a trench around our tent, many little rivulets started to run through the tent, and we were soon thoroughly and most uncomfortably wet.

I think it was that trip too, that we made our first acquaintance with the slippery qualities of gumbo, and that acquaintance gave us a very healthy respect for the deceptive-looking stuff that is mud with a difference.

Then our family started to arrive—two boys, two years apart—and for a while our interests were very much focused on other things, things like formulas and routine and first teeth. But as soon as they could both walk and talk we started planning for our first holiday with the boys. And it took planning! We decided that for this first venture we probably shouldn't rely on tents for our housing, and after much correspondence we found a cottage on the Interior lake of our choice. That, however, was only the beginning. We also decided that if there was to be any holiday for anyone, we should take someone with us to help with the boys. Finances, never very far from the surface, reared their ugly heads at this point, and positively leered at us. We simply couldn't afford a children's nurse. That problem was finally solved by the simple means of advertising for a girl who would like a holiday in the Interior in return for part-time help. We got so many answers to our ad that we began to think that all of the junior female population of Vancouver wanted to holiday in the Interior. So we were able to make a careful selection, a selection that proved to be a very happy one for all.

Then we had to plan supplies. The place to which we were going was too far from the nearest town to make it practical to go there for food more than once during our two week stay. And then, too, we weren't very sure just how well our cottage was supplied with things like bedding and pots and pans and dishes. We made countless lists; every day or so we seemed to mislay them and start all over. We checked and rechecked and checked again. At last we seemed to be complete. My husband had built a sort of luggage carrier that fitted on top of the car—which, by the way, was no longer Chevy, but a car more suited to the size of our increased numbers—and into that we packed the supplies. What wouldn't go on top we put in the back.

After weeks of preparation, we were ready to start one Friday evening. It was also Friday the thirteenth, but that daunted us not at all. We should have been warned. And to tell you this part of the Phillips saga, I'll have to go back a bit. About a month previously, my husband's attention had been caught by an advertisement in the paper for a Springer spaniel hunting dog for sale at a most extraordinarily reasonable price. Out he went to see it, and about an hour later came back with Peg. She was a lovely dog, affectionate and gentle, and we told each other that after all, females were the best dogs to have. She did seem awfully fat, but we thought we could fix that with proper diet and no tidbits between meals. But Peg went on getting fatter, and at last it dawned on us that she was shortly going to produce a family. This realization hit us about three days before we left for our holidays. And of course we couldn't leave Peg behind. We decided that we'd just have to chance it, and take her along. So we did. Into the back seat went Peg and the two boys. Into the front seat went Margaret (the girl who was going for the trip) and the two of us. The car was pretty well loaded, and the roof every so often gave a sort of ominous creak, and the straps that my husband had devised to hold the luggage carrier on had a tendency to come loose, making it necessary to stop and tighten them up again. We ate a picnic supper beside the tumbling water of Spuzzum Creek, and made up a bed for the boys on the back seat of the car. They were still small enough that they fitted very comfortably end to end. They went off to sleep just as we had hoped they would, and we proceeded on our way. We like driving the canyon at night, particularly on a night such as that one was. It was full moonlight, and far below us the Fraser flowed, a ribbon of gleaming silver. The boys slept peacefully in the back seat, and the three of us talked quietly about many things.

It was just outside Spences Bridge that it happened. There was a little cry from Peg. "Perhaps we'd better stop and let Peg out," I suggested. "We'll stop in Spences Bridge and get some coffee for us and cocoa for the boys. Peg can get out there," answered my husband. We were very nearly there, and there was no further sound from Peg, so we went on.

In the little town of Spences Bridge we stopped in front of the all-night coffee stop. I got out and went round to open the back door of the car. In the glow from the lighted windows of the coffee shop, I sensed rather than saw a small black object rolling towards me down the slope of the car floor. Instinctively I put out my hands to catch it—and it was a tiny pup!

We made Peg as comfortable as we could, and after having our coffee and cocoa we drove on. Every half-hour we stopped, gave Peg a drink of water—iced, because all we had was thermos jug of ice—and every time we stopped there was another small black puppy, until there were five altogether, and even then we could tell that they definitely were not Springers. No wonder Peg was for sale at such an extraordinarily reasonable price.

There's not much more to tell about that first trip with the boys, except that all our other plans worked according to our careful reckoning. The boys had the thrill of catching their first fish, and they splashed happily along the lake's edge attired in the life belts we'd bought for them and insisted on their wearing in the water and in the boat. And we all got very brown and ate mightily. Yes, it was a most successful holiday. As for the pups, they were the admiration of all beholders. Peg throve on the praise and admiration of everyone, and when we finally started on our homeward drive, the puppies provided an endless source of amusement for the boys. It was rather like having a five-ring circus in the back of the car.

That trip was a good many years ago now, and gradually, as the boys have grown older and we have grown wiser in the ways of camping, we have developed a pattern for our camping trips that make them possible even on an ordinary weekend. A small equipment trailer makes it possible to pack everything on Thursday night, and Friday evening we pile the boys and the dog, which is now, I should tell you, a male Labrador of mighty proportions. Then we attach the trailer on behind, fasten our light five-ply boat to rods on top of the car, and take off up the valley for two days of outdoor relaxation. Often we don't even fish. We just sit. And there's always plenty for the boys to do to keep them happy and interested. And when we come home on Sunday evening, we're rested and relaxed and ready to face all over again the serious business of living.

We still plan a camping trip for our two-week holiday, though. And let me tell you, they're planned for the maximum of comfort and the minimum of work. Perhaps you'd like to hear what we think are necessary items for that kind of holiday. Let's see, now. Three tents, complete with pegs and poles, two for sleeping and one for a work tent to be used in wet weather (and it does rain in B.C., even in the summer, and even in the Interior!). Two good-quality camp stoves, because, while it's fun to cook over a camp fire, it does rain some-times. A good assortment of dishes and pots and pans and cutlery—and all those things should be articles that you've bought specially for your trips, not things that you weed out of the kitchen drawer. A good lantern (those gasoline ones are well worth the investment when you wash dishes in the dark, or if you come in late after a specially good day's fishing). Two folding tables and enough folding chairs for everyone. Oh yes, and fairly comfortable camp cots with light mattresses and sleeping bags and pillows (it isn't any holiday if you can't sleep at night because your bed is hard and uncomfortable!). And last, but by no means least, a good supply of water. That means that when you're choosing your campsite, don't forget that the water supply is even more important than your surroundings.

Does all that sound like a pretty tall order, not only in quantity but in financial outlay as well? If you do it gradually, and plan it carefully, you hardly notice the effect on the family budget. And think what it means in saving once you've got it all collected. You're a self-suffi-cient unit, quite independent of resources other than your own. You can go anywhere where there's anything like a good road. And there's nothing like that kind of a holiday if you want to discover the country you live in and to meet the people who have made the same discovery.

And for both you and your children there are all the wonders of nature to discover: the wild laughter of loons, the lonely howling of coyotes over the distant hills at night, a bear scrambling up a tree at your approach, deer coming down to the water's edge in the dusk, a moose swimming in the lake, the sudden flurry of duck getting off the water, a flight of geese high against a sunset, squirrels and chipmunks and toads and even snakes.

I guess, though, you'll have to put your feelings about the little creatures of the lakes and woods into a tight little compartment. If you're scared of toads and mice and things like that, you'll have to make up your mind that they're part of the great outdoors and just ignore them. Perhaps I'm lucky in that those things have never bothered me; they're just all part of the great discovery—British Columbia!

Just before I say goodbye for today, here's a picture of the Phillipses at a campsite. Evening has fallen. Across the lake the sun is going down in a blaze of colour behind the hills. The campfire is sending leaping tongues of flames into the gathering dusk. Dinner is beginning to send up delectable odours. Down at the water's edge, the older boy is intent on making a job of cleaning the day's catch of trout. The younger boy stands outlined against the dying day as he fishes for minnow with all the concentration of a Simple Simon catching whales in his mother's pail. Off in the deeper shadows of the trees, the dog is rustling leaves and branches, on some small business of his own.

And now goodbye, until tomorrow!

Picnics

July, 1949

To picnic or not to picnic. Well, I guess it's a matter of taste. If you like picnics, there's nothing more fun. If you don't, there's nothing more uncomfortable, more trouble, or less fun. The Phillipses like picnics. And since, in this coming two weeks, you're probably going to hear a good deal about the Phillips family in one way or another, perhaps you'd better meet us right away. We are four: Dick, Sallie, and two sons, Tony, age fourteen, and Ted, age twelve. And we have been picnicking since the boys could walk.

I still remember our first picnic with the boys because it involved the necessity of putting them down for their regular afternoon nap, and that involved fitting one into the front seat and the other into the back seat, and somehow creating the illusion of peace and quiet so they'd go to sleep. I won't say it was an unqualified success, but I think they did get a little rest, and in any case, they loved the picnic.

Just recently, though, we reached a new high in picnics. It was on this occasion that Tony, the older boy, said, "Mum, I think you should make a program out of this." So I decided to make a program out of Phillips picnics generally and this all-time high in particular.

But let's go back to the beginning, that very first picnic. We went to pick blackberries. In my colossal ignorance, I had overlooked the fact that blackberries held little, if any, interest for a three- and a five-year-old. But ponds and frogs and mud puddles did. So did the wayside flowers—at least they did for my younger son, who shares with his brother a tendency towards hay fever, and who insisted on seizing every flower he saw and sniffing up its fragrance like Ferdinand. We did pick some blackberries, though, and the boys didn't get too terribly wet and muddy in the various pools and puddles from which we lifted them, more or less patiently.

Then there was the picnic supper we took with us the first time that we ever took the boys on a long fishing trip. That was a picnic par excellence. Mother really went to town on that one! I carefully packed fried chicken in waxed paper. We had potato salad in jars. There was even dessert: strawberries in cream. But nobody enjoyed that supper at all. And the reason? Well, we had our dog Peg along, and it so happened that she was at that time expecting the arrival of a family, and she picked that particular night to have it. At supper time, she was a very restless and unhappy dog and puppies started arriving in the car about ten o'clock that night at Spences Bridge. The family of five was finally on the scene at four the next morning, just before our arrival at our destination. Fortunately, the boys slept soundly on the back seat in their sleeping bags all through it. The boys were very surprised to find five puppies under the kitchen table of our cottage next morning when they woke up.

From the point of view of the orthodox picnicker, I'm afraid the Phillipses would never qualify. Seldom, if ever, do we take large supplies of sandwiches with us. If our meal is to be a simple one, we usually put a couple of loaves of bread, some butter, various fillings (such as cheese and cold meat and jam), cookies, and fruit into a carton with a couple of knives, a quart of milk, and some paper plates, and that's our picnic. On a fishing expedition, we enlarge the commissary with a frying pan and bacon and some extra utensils. No, we aren't formal picnickers.

Last New Year's Day, we had one of our very best picnics. Somewhat exhausted by the previous night's festivities—it was the first time that the boys had really stayed up to see the new year in, and perhaps I should add that Mother and Dad had stayed up considerably later—we decided that there would be nothing more refreshing than a picnic bonfire on the bank of the Fraser, quite close to our house. And we did. A huge fire, and the early dusk closing in with a metallic light on the waters of the river, tugboats passing up and down. It was cold, but not wet, and we ate our hot supper and drank in the freshness of the winter wind and enjoyed every minute of it.

The bank of the Fraser has proved to be a grand place for picnics. Almost any night in the summer, the Phillipses can be seen packing their supper into the car and driving thitherward. It's usually only for an hour or two, but for that short time we have left behind us the four walls of our house and the hustle and bustle of our everyday city life. And somehow, however much we love the four walls of our house, however familiar the hustle and bustle, it is still a very pleasant and restful thing to leave them behind for a little while, to breathe fresh air, to feel the wind on our faces, to smell wood smoke, and yes, even to get sand in our shoes.

No description of our family picnics would be complete without some mention of Point Roberts. Over the years, we have gone down to that queer little section of the U.S.A. set in the middle of Canada a great many times. For many people, the attraction has been something other than a picnic. For us, quite honestly, it has been the point with the lighthouse on it. To us, that treeless, windswept point with the white wooden tower topped by its flashing light has always held a magical fascination. There is something so alone about it—the sunshine seems clearer and hotter; the sea seems more like the real ocean with breakers and an authentic sea-smell of hot sand and seaweed and salt. And the shore is a never-ending source of adventure and delight. Because of its exposed position, the point receives on its shores the flotsam and jetsam of the whole sweep of the gulf. There are great timbers, washed silver-grey by the waves; there are wooden floats from the fishing nets; there are bits of boats—here a hull, there a broken oar. There are bottles that might contain a message from a shipwrecked mariner. There are crab shells and dead dogfish and bits of rope. That shore is a treasure trove; for who knows? At any moment one of us might find real treasure washed up from the sea!

One Sunday, we took a picnic to the point. It was a beautiful day, cloudless and clear. The sea was deep blue, heaving gently towards the shore, where it broke in little creamy waves along the pebbly beach. We set ourselves up as always, building a table from the endless choice pieces of driftwood and a fireplace from the rocks and pebbles that lay for the taking, and then proceeded to bait hand-lines for the boys so that they could throw them into the surf and perhaps catch a flounder or a plump perch. Suddenly, we heard a tremendous splash. We lifted our heads and looked out to sea; there certainly was some sort of commotion out there. In a minute we saw what it was, and couldn't believe our eyes. A tremendous black bulk rose from the sea, literally standing on its tail; and then, with the tremendous splash we had heard before, fell back into the water again! Then another and another. Finally, we realized what it was. There, in front of our eyes, not more than a couple of hundred yards away, a school of killer whales were at play. One by one, the great sea-mammals, weighing at least two or three tons apiece, would rise into the air, stand on their tails, and fall back into the water. Meanwhile, the others were enjoying themselves by blowing great spouts of water into the air. The noise and commotion were quite indescribable. Gradually, they moved away, and after a while the surface of the sea was as peaceful and undisturbed and blue as before. But it was a sight that we will never forget.

Perhaps at this point I should tell you about the picnic that caused my son to suggest that I tell you about our picnics. The occasion was my younger son's birthday. Now we had found that a picnic *à la* Phillips was something definitely new and different for most of the boys in our neighbourhood, so we decided that Ted's birthday party would take the form of a picnic. Where? Yes, to the bank of the Fraser. Our supplies this time were a little different than other times. We took forty-eight wieners and forty-eight buns as a starter. (We had invited twelve young guests.) To that we added a dozen Dixie cups of ice cream, three dozen pop (all the varieties we could remember), three packages of marshmallows, two packages of popping corn, sundry pickles, mustard, and a huge birthday cake, complete with the requisite number of candles—twelve and one to grow on. Believe it or not, no one was sick. A couple of them took time out to rest and recuperate, but there were no real casualties. Which all goes to prove that picnics carry their own special immunity!

Anyway, we attached the trailer—we have a small equipment trailer for carrying tents and so forth—behind the car, and the twelve guests proceeded to draw for the privilege of riding in it. We had decided we could carry five and ourselves in the car and the rest in the trailer. We put mattresses and cushions on the floor of the trailer, although I don't think they would have minded the bare boards. Finally, we started off, and never was there such noisy excitement. Excitement is never exactly quiet, but the excitement of twelve boys between the ages of ten and fourteen is the noisiest thing you ever heard. The noise didn't begin to subside for some two hours, when the third hot dogs were finished.

When Ted had invited his guests, he had issued strict instructions that every boy should wear old clothes, bring a heavy sweater or jacket, and a flashlight. The first two carried the flavour of Mother; she knew what to expect on a picnic. The last was Ted's own idea. It was born of experience. He had found that tugs passing up and down the river in the late twilight responded magnificently to the beam of a flashlight accompanied by loud and prolonged yells; almost invariably they resulted in responsive yells and in the search-light of the tug being flashed on the shore. So each of the twelve that night carried flashlights. After supper, when Dick and I had decided that we could relax for a few minutes from our ceaseless job of counting heads to make sure that no one had fallen into the river or somehow got mislaid, someone suddenly spotted a tug coming up the river. It was nearly dark by this time, and we could see the red and green port and starboard lights of the tug, as well as its masthead lights. In a second, over-full tummies were forgotten, gone was all the pleasant after-supper lethargy; twelve boys sprang into action. Twelve boys lined the river bank. Twelve flashlights shone on the tug. Twelve throats yelled lusty hullos. Suddenly the tug did what was expected of her. Her searchlight came on, swung in a wide circle, and focused on twelve dancing and leaping figures outlined on the bank. Figures appeared on the deck of the tug, and as long as the tug remained in sight, it kept its searchlight trained on the boys, whose excitement had reached fever pitch. Dick and I had also reached fever pitch, tearing up and down, counting noses, cautioning this one to keep away from the edge, that one not to yell so loud and long (we feared for a permanent damage to his vocal cords).

Then we said it was time to go home. And the boys rallied round like young heroes. Each one helped pack something back to the car. One contingent put out the fire—really put out the fire. Others gathered pop bottles. Everybody did something, and all of them wanted to carry back far more than he could possibly manage. Back at the car, there was a momentary argument as to who should ride in the trailer, an argument quickly settled by the simple expedient of saying that those who had come down in the trailer would go home in the car. On the way home, the boys made the welkin ring with the strains of "Pack up Your Troubles," and even "Lavender Blue, Dilly Dilly." We deposited them one by one at their homes, tired and dirty, but happy. It was a good birthday party!

One word, though, should you be thinking of a party like that one: be sure and take along a towel and some soap. Even twelve-year-olds get to a point of dirtiness where they want to wash. Believe it or not, at least ten out of the twelve took advantage of the chance and washed their dirty hands and hot faces. And another tip: don't let the boys—or girls—roast all the wieners. Cutting roasting sticks is a grand thing to keep them busy while you're getting the fire just right and the improvised table of driftwood set; but if you let them roast all the wieners, there will be more lost in the fire than find their way into small tummies. Let each one roast just one, and take along a pot big enough to boil the rest. And still another tip: use paper plates and burn them up in the fire afterwards. A good supply of the cheapest paper napkins also pay dividends; they're useful to wrap around the dogs, and for wiping off greasy hands.

But, believe me, it was a successful birthday party.

FISHING

July 21, 1949

WHEN I STARTED THINKING ABOUT THIS MONTH'S SERIES OF TALKS, I ASKED A good many people, in a hopeful sort of way, "Do you have any ideas about what would make a good program?" Because I very much wanted to make the series an interesting one. Somebody—I've forgotten who—said that it might be interesting to talk about salmon fishing. Well, I thought there had been a good many programs of one kind and another done on salmon fishing. But I bet there hasn't been one done on herring fishing. Or, at least, a part of one.

I remember how astounded Dick and I were the first time we really saw anyone herring fishing. It was a calm, quiet morning. Not a ripple disturbed the surface of the water, such a morning as only happens once in a long while. We saw this man standing up in the bow of his boat with what at that distance looked like nothing more or less than a long stick. With this long stick, he apparently swept the water every now and then, much the way a canoe paddler uses his paddle. When we came closer to him we saw that the long stick had quantities of tiny prongs set into it, like a woman's so-called "rat-tail comb" is set with teeth at one end, with its long handle at the other.

It was with this comb arrangement that the man was sweeping the water. Every so often, the herring would break water, skitter along the surface in a bright, silvery broken splash of brilliance, and disappear. The man in the boat would follow them, stand up in the bow again, and sweep the water with his herring rake. If he was lucky, he would bring the dripping rake from the water with many tiny, wriggling silver bodies impaled on the prongs. Presently, though, the wind came up, and his herring fishing was over for that day.

It was last fall that I first saw commercial fishing for herring. That was a day I'll never forget. I saw herring caught in three-hundred-ton lots—something like forty-two million herring to every three hundred tons. When we approached the fishing ground—they happened to be running in Nanoose Bay—we saw what seemed like thousands of screaming seabirds, wheeling and screaming over a huddle of fish

boats. We learned that the birds were hovering over a set. A set
means that a seiner (a fish boat with a seine-type net) has let out its
net there, and is in the process of bringing in to the surface its
tremendous load—that is, it is tremendous if it's a good set—of wriggling silver herring. The huddle of four or five boats, which at that
distance looked for all the world like four or five old market women
with their heads together for a good gossip, included the boat that
had actually made the set, another boat that was helping this one to
bring up its net (it takes two to do this, one on either side of the net),
and a couple of others who were standing off with ropes attached to
the first two, pulling to keep them on an even keel. Alongside the
boat making the haul was the packer, into which the catch was to be
loaded. We were interested to learn that every man on all those boats
would receive his share of the take, not only the men on the boat
that had made the original set, but all of the men involved. In the
case of a two-hundred-ton set, for instance, each man would receive,
in addition to his regular wages, some twenty dollars as his share. I
guess commercial fishing can be a profitable business!

We were on another packer, and pretty soon it was told on the
intercom radio to go over to a certain seiner and load its catch. As
we came closer, we could see what looked like an enormous pan of
simmering water between the two seine boats drawing in the net.
The pan, of course, was the net, and the simmering water between
was literally boiling with millions of silver fish. And the noise they
made! It was an indescribable sound, something like a magnified
sizzling in a giant frying pan, a sound that never stopped until the
net was empty. The packer drew alongside the seine boat with a
scarcely perceptible bump. The lines were secured, and almost at
once the business of loading was begun. We saw the great brail net
(a purse-shaped affair open at the top and closed at the bottom with
a drawstring) swing out from the seine boat over and into the
seething cauldron of fish, and then sweep, dripping, across the hull
of the seiner, and over into the open hold of the waiting packer.
Once in place, there was a jerk, the drawstring was released, and two
tons of twisting, wriggling herring were plunged into the packer's
hold. And, once again, the noise and movement were almost impossible to describe. The winch creaked and puffed, the boom rattled
and groaned, and the whole seine boat rolled and rattled from side
to side, with all the rigging clashing and clattering. The fish sizzled
in the seine net. The brail net swished through the air. And the fish

fell into the packer's hold and flapped there with a sound rather like all the gutters of your house overflowing in a cloudburst.

Meanwhile, over on the other seine boat, the one that was helping to pull in the net, five or six men in flapping yellow oilskins were slowly and laboriously pulling in the great bulk of the net. And the net, as it was drawn up the side of the boat, glittered and sparkled in the sun like a spangled shawl, with thousands of tiny opalescent herring scales caught in it. Overhead, the white seagulls still wheeled, screaming, dipping, and diving, and sometimes swooping to the water to snatch a wriggling fish in their beak and fly off triumphantly. We saw gulls sitting on the railing of the boats, too full of herring to fly! I even saw one so full that the tail of the last herring was sticking out of his beak. There's a great deal more that I could tell you about that day we spent with the fishing fleet; we finally came home up the Fraser River with a full load at about three o'clock that morning. It was quite an experience! It made our ordinary, more mundane methods seem tame by comparison.

Just the same, there are exciting moments when you catch just one salmon on the end of a light leader and a long rod. There was the day, for instance, that we went out to the Point Grey bell buoy in a small boat in a choppy sea. It was a really choppy sea, too. The boat went up and down like a bobbing cork. If there'd been time to think about it, we could have felt very seasick, but the fish were really running that day, and we were much too busy to stop and think about the way our tummies were feeling.

And there was another morning in Cowichan Bay when I really tied into a big one. That was an unforgettable experience. It was cold and frosty—the time of year was early November—so frosty that there was a coating of white all over the boat when we climbed into her at about six o'clock. We were bundled in heavy clothing, and I was wearing a pair of heavy gloves as well; when that fish struck, I couldn't move fast enough! With my line screaming out from the reel, I mutely held out one hand, and then the other, to have the gloves taken off, and then concentrated on getting that fish in. I thought he'd never stop taking line out. When he did, it was to pull every trick that any fish ever knew. He jumped. He skittered along the top of the water on his tail. He ran back towards me as fast as he had run out. He dived straight down, and stayed there, standing on his head, sulking. When I finally did land him, I felt battered and bruised. But he was a big one: seventeen and a half pounds of fighting coho.

And over there at Cowichan Bay in coho season they give you buttons: a copper one up to twelve pounds; up to fifteen pounds rates a silver one; to eighteen it's a gold one; and eighteen and up it's diamond. I'm still proud of my gold button.

We've all heard fish stories. But how many of you ever heard of catching a fish without hooking him? And I don't mean in a net, either. I mean on the end of a line. But it did happen. And it was quite a sizable salmon, too; about eight pounds, I think. When the fish struck, he wasn't hooked, but by some strange freak of current or twist of the fish's body, the line made a perfect half-hitch around it just behind the main fin. And it just so happened that in fighting it, the fish never got enough slack line to loosen the half-hitch. We netted that salmon without ever hooking it!

Well, I could go on with good fish stories from now until next Christmas. I guess people who fish always can. But, for me anyway, the pleasures in fishing aren't all in catching them. It's a pleasure made up of many things. It's made up of watching the summer morning spread over the water, of watching the mist rise and disappear in the early morning sunlight. Of watching the shore, the trees, the waves washing on the rocks. The good smell of low tide. (All low tides don't smell the way they do in False Creek, you know!) It's a pleasure made up of the smell of fresh fish frying in the open air after a session of before-dawn fishing, and the aroma of coffee boiling when you've landed on a stretch of smooth rock that's warming in the early sun. It is even the rocking of your little boat on a day of grey skies and choppy sea. And it's coming into a warm room in the evening, after a long day of salty fresh air and wind and sunshine.

I know lots of people who find fishing merely boring. "But what do you do all the time when you're not catching fish?," they'll say. Well, you can always think. And it seems to me there's always plenty to think about: ships and shoes and sealing wax, cabbages and kings. And there's always plenty to look at. The shore is always changing, and so are the sea and the sky. No, it doesn't seem to me that there's ever anything boring about fishing.

And in B.C. we're pretty fortunate when it comes to fishing. There are so many kinds of fishing to do. And each of them provides a different way to see and get to know our province. You can fish in the sea, and get to know what the coast looks like. Even if you only jig for flounder in the waters of English Bay, you discover that the city looks quite different seen from a small boat. You can fish in the rivers, and watch how the water rushes past you, walk the banks and see the trees and flowers, and hear how the water sings. You can fish the lakes, and wonder at the way the light is always changing on the water, at the way the wind can run in little riffles across its surface, at the way sudden raindrops make miniature waterspouts and run hissing before the wind. Fishing isn't just catching fish; it's all these other things, too. The fish are really quite incidental!

And now, about tomorrow's program. It's going to be quite a special interview. Last year, Mary Pack came here to tell us about her crusade against arthritis, the great crippler. And this year she is coming back again to tell us that crusades can be successful. She will tell us just what is happening in the fight against arthritis, and particularly what is happening in B.C. I'm sure you'll find her story an interesting one.

And so, until tomorrow. So long!

HIP BOOTS AND LIPSTICK

February 9, 1950

The special talk "Hip Boots and Lipstick" was commissioned by Ross McLean for national broadcast. How disappointed I was when, on the morning of the broadcast, I woke up with what could only have been strep throat. I could hardly speak, and that evening my special broadcast was read by someone else.

PROGRAM: HIP BOOTS AND LIPSTICK
WRITER: Sallie Phillips
READER: Peg Dixon
PRODUCER: Ross McLean
RECORDED: Monday, February 6, 1950
BROADCAST: Thursday, February 9, 1950
TIMES: 7:30–7:45 p.m. E.S.T., 9:15–9:30 p.m. C.S.T., 8:45–9:00 p.m. P.S.T.
NETWORK: Trans Canada
MUSIC: Three O'clock in the Morning: in and under

ANNOUNCER: You might say that SALLIE PHILLIPS'S married life was going to the ducks. No, not the dogs, where married life has also been known to go. To the ducks. Here at CBC Vancouver, we're pasting discarded sheets back onto the calendar to make the scene look like a certain morning in October. Like three o'clock of a certain morning in October, as a matter of fact. And here begins a monologue for radio entitled HIP BOOTS AND LIPSTICK.

MUSIC: *Three O'clock in the Morning: up full briefly: interrupted rudely by sudden peal from a loud-voiced alarm clock.*

SALLIE: Ho-hum! Sometimes I think I'm carrying this business of being the playmate as well as the helpmeet of my husband just a little too far. Three o'clock in the morning; we've danced the whole night through. No, that's wrong! It's three o'clock in the morning, and time to get up. Such a beautiful morning, too—for ducks. The wind is howling and the rain is driving against the windows. You know, it's the most amazing thing. Ordinary mornings I have to take major measures to get that man up, but on duck-shooting mornings he leaps from the bed with all the alacrity of a bird dog confronted with a nice fresh scent of pheasant. Where's my long underwear? Oh, I remember; I left it in the bathroom over the radiator to keep warm. There! If my friends could see me now! Even in mail-order catalogues there's something ludicrous about the female form in long woollen underwear. And heaven knows I don't even have the perfection of the female form in mail-order catalogues! Oh well.

Now that old flannel shirt of Dick's, and my tin pants. Whoever named them tin pants knew what he was saying. Every time I put them on I wonder how I manage to walk at all in them. But they do keep me dry. Now what? Lipstick? Well, yes, I guess that is one concession to my sex that I'll always make. I wouldn't feel dressed without lipstick, even duck-shooting. Now my heavy sweater and my dry-bak coat and my hip boots. I wonder why they don't make hip-boots for women? I suppose because there just aren't enough women crazy enough to go duck-shooting at three o'clock on a wild wet windy morning in the middle of winter to make it worthwhile to manufacture them. I wish they did, though; even with two pairs of socks, the smallest men's size have an alarming tendency to slide off completely when the mud is more than ankle-deep.

And finally, my hat. What a travesty of a hat it is! Maybe it keeps the rain out, but that hat, more than anything else, outrages my sense of the fitness of things.

MUSIC: *A few bars of John Peel or a hunting horn.*

SALLIE: When did all this get started? It all began a number of years ago when Dick, my husband, somewhat belatedly took up shooting. He wasn't then, and isn't now, a good shot. But what he lacks in accuracy, he makes up in enthusiasm. It took me a couple of years to realize that I was fast becoming, maybe had already become, a shooting widow. Every weekend during the shooting season, he arose in the chill hours of very early morning and disappeared until the evening when he returned, usually dirty and wet, sometimes with birds, sometimes without, but always filled with stories of what had happened during the day. Stories of a particularly spectacular retrieve by the dog, or just why he had missed a shot, or of how he had actually had a double on a pair of mallards.

Now, I had always had a theory about wives being actively interested in their husband's activities. At gatherings of the girls, I was wont to hold forth on that being one of the ways to keep a man once you had him. And after it became quite evident that shooting was a definite interest on the part of my husband, and likely to remain so, it also became evident that I would have to put up or shut up. In other words, I'd either have to start showing an active interest in shooting or stop holding forth at those gatherings of the girls.

Actually, I'm not sure that part of it wasn't good healthy feminine curiosity. I wanted to know what it was all about. Anyway, one day—I picked a time when the weather looked reasonably dry—I tentatively suggested that maybe I could go along and watch. Dick, who is perhaps a more than usually co-operative husband, seemed to welcome the idea. I went along. And, believe it or not, I enjoyed it.

I enjoyed watching the dawn break, sometimes over bleak salt marshes with the wind rustling the dry stalks of the reeds and the lonely crying of seabirds, sometimes over mountain peaks at the end of a lake, sometimes over wide clipped stubble fields. I enjoyed watching a flight of ducks pause in the air and circle down to where our decoys floated. I enjoyed the plunging eagerness of the dog as he tore into the water to make a retrieve. I enjoyed the cold winter sunsets and the creaking sound of the ducks' wings as the evening flights came in. I honestly did.

So, of course, the next step was getting me a gun. After much consultation with other members of the shooting fraternity, Dick decided on a lightish twelve-gauge double-barrelled shotgun with an offset stock. And if I secretly hankered for a ladylike sixteen-gauge, I was also rather proud of being the possessor of a masculine twelve.

But I was scared to death of firing it. I remember the first time. Dick and another chap who was with us set up a tin can on a fence post, backed well out of range, and told me to go ahead. Shaking inwardly, I loaded, trying to remember all the things I'd been told to do and not to do. Then, with a complete certainty that the gun would explode in my hands the minute I pulled the trigger, I aimed, closed my eyes tight, and fired. I guess I hadn't remembered enough things. And possibly it was well that the men had moved out of range. I missed the can altogether, and nearly knocked myself over backwards in the bargain. I opened my eyes cautiously, my ears ringing from the noise of the explosion, but otherwise still in one piece. I might say here that not until this year have I completely got over being scared of my beautiful gun, and although when I shoot at a bird, I dutifully lead it or aim over it or under it, according to the direction it is flying, as I have been told to do, it is only this year that I have ceased to close my eyes tightly just before pulling the trigger. So that my recurring surprise at finding myself in one piece after a shot has only been surpassed by my exceeding wonder when I open them to find that I've actually brought down a bird!

My pride at overcoming my fear of the gun is tempered, alas, with the conviction that I'll never, at this late date, be a good shot. I guess I'll remain a sort of walking bird sanctuary with a gun, for the remainder of my shooting days. Perversely, I still enjoy duck-shooting.

SOUND: *Up sound of car. Establish and fade through.*

SALLIE: Ho-hum. The long drive up the valley to Hatzic in the wet dark with the rain slicing across the beam of the headlights and the windshield wiper swishing hypnotically is not the best part of the day. My eyes feel as though they were full of sand. Eyes really can feel like holes burned in a blanket. Four hours sleep isn't enough— at least it isn't enough for me. And neither of us feels much like conversation. If I could only stop yawning. Guess I'd better light us a cigarette. Want a cigarette, dear?

SOUND: *Car engine up and out.*

SALLIE: I suppose that anyone in this part of the world who has ever done any bird shooting cherishes a dream of the day when he—or in this case, she—can count a Canada goose in the day's bag. Once, I almost got a Canada goose. Almost, but not quite. I still blame that idiotic grouse, but actually I know that it was all my own fault.

We had been shooting over potholes in the Copper Creek country back of Savona. Pothole shooting is an exasperating pursuit at the best of times when you can drive your car from one to another. But we didn't have a car. We had driven in to the camp with a group of moose-hunting enthusiasts, lured by the promise of innumerable ducks just sitting and waiting for the Phillipses to arrive. There were not innumerable ducks, and someone in the party had miscalculated the amount of gasoline necessary to take us in to Copper Creek and out again, so if we ever wanted to get out again, we couldn't use the car to drive from pothole to pothole. We walked instead. I've no doubt we spent a very healthy holiday, but at the end I felt as though I never wanted to walk again. In between walking, we crawled. That's because these little potholes dotted around that particular part of the country are fairly open, and our only hope of getting a bird was to sneak unseen to the water's edge and surprise them. Nine times out of ten, they got up just out of range and flew off unconcernedly to another pothole. It wasn't any use waiting for them to come back. With literally hundreds of little lakes to land on, why come back to the one where someone had taken a shot at you? I'm sure that was the ducks' reasoning, and I don't blame them. Then, off we would tramp to the next hole and repeat the process.

One day we had walked further afield than usual and come upon a hitherto unexplored lake set high on a little hill and ringed around with a dense growth of jack pine. We approached it as quietly as we could, and when we came to the edge of the water, we saw that the lake was bigger than we expected, and that away up at the far end there were about twenty-four big ducks floating peacefully on the water. They hadn't seen us, so we retired hurriedly among the trees to lay a plan of action. The plan of action involved a sneak done by me to put the birds up, while Dick hid in a strategic position over which we figured the birds would fly. You see, we had long ago conceded the fact that the odds were heavily against me hitting a bird, but I did possess nuisance value. I would put the birds up for Dick to get a shot. So sneak I did. And what a sneak! The wiliest redskin couldn't have been quieter. It took me an hour of creeping and crawling to reach a point where I could once again see the ducks. I lifted my head cautiously and looked over a log. There they were. Only they weren't ducks. They were Canada geese. And they were about a hundred yards away from me.

My heart began to pound madly with excitement. If I could sneak about another fifty yards distance, just to where I could jump up and run to the water's edge, I'd have trouble missing those drifting battleships of birds! Barely moving now, I inched my way forward. I'd gone about half the distance and still the birds were all unsuspicious. In my path lay a log I would have to cross. I stopped to consider the best way of getting over it. Suddenly, just at eye level as I lay flat on my tummy, a grouse appeared, walking along the fallen trunk of the tree. We saw each other at the same time. The grouse stopped and we eyed each other for a long minute. And the grouse chuckled—I'll swear it chuckled! Just loud enough for the geese to hear. And everything happened at once. Like a flight of Cansos taking off, the geese began to lumber slowly across the water. I stood up, cleared the log with a standing jump that surprised me even then, and dashed to the water's edge. Cocked the gun, brought it to my shoulder, and stood like a frozen image. Yes, just stood there and watched the geese trail across the water and into the air and away across the lake and vanish into the distance, never passing anywhere near the spot where Dick lay hidden. Buck fever? I had goose fever. I couldn't have pulled the trigger if my life depended on it!

SOUND: *Wind up and fade through.*

SALLIE: No, I can hardly blame Dick for doing his own sneaks after that. He's out there now, sneaking up the slough to where a flight of mallards landed in the stubble field. *Br-r-r-r,* I'm cold. And wet. The rain's bad enough without that wind. There's his head now. I can just see it over the top of the bank. He'd better get down. Those birds will see him.

I remember a time, though, when the joke was on him. It was up at Hatzic in the middle of winter, when the lake was very low and mostly mud instead of water. It was very cold, too. We had decided that we would really get out there in the middle of things to that spot all the birds seemed to cross in their flight. We would build a blind of reeds and we'd sit right there in the mud and have, for once, really good shooting.

Building that blind was a real labour of love. We cut the reeds on the shore, piled our arms full of them, and then started out to our selected spot. Hatzic mud possesses most unusual qualities of give and take. First of all, it lets your rubber hip boot sink well into it—about midway up the calf of your leg. Then it does its gluey best to take the boot off as you lift your feet to take a step. Every two or three steps I had to deposit my reeds in the mud, firmly grasp the top of my boot and yank hard. With a reluctant sucking noise, the Hatzic mud would relinquish its prey and, retrieving the reeds, I would stagger on for a few more steps. And repeat. Finally, however, the job was done, the blind erected, and we sat down on a convenient log to wait. I say "convenient" log only because it was the only log lying in that particular area of mud on which we could sit. So we built the blind around it. Unfortunately, it was lying in the wrong direction. We couldn't sit side by side. The only way to sit on it and still to face the direction in which the birds were flying was astride it, one behind the other. Now, I've already mentioned that I don't often hit a bird when I do shoot, and naturally enough, it seems to me, I've become a little hesitant about firing at all when a shot from me might spoil one for my spouse. Well. Things had been pretty quiet, when suddenly a flight of teal materialized out of thin air, flying low and fast. Although I was first on the log, I held my fire, hoping that Dick would get one. I waited for the shot, but behind me there was only silence. Silence, and then a gentle plop! I turned around then to see my husband slowly settling in the mud. He had learned too far backwards aiming at the birds as they flew over! I did try not to laugh.

SOUND: *A distant shot, and another.*

SALLIE: My goodness! Two of them! Next week we eat duck! (CALLING) Nice shooting, dear! Hmm? Oh yes, I still enjoy duck shooting.

ANNOUNCER: Here at CBC Vancouver, ROSS McLEAN has been producing a lighthearted duck-umentary written by SALLIE PHILLIPS and read by PEG DIXON. It was known to us as HIP BOOTS AND LIPSTICK. We recorded it earlier.

GRAND COULEE DAM

August 22, 1950

GOOD MORNING. IT SOMETIMES SEEMS TO ME THAT OUR NEIGHBOURS TO THE SOUTH of us are very prone to lay claim to having the biggest and best of everything and anything. Especially the biggest. And it also seems to me that most of us these days are very apt to judge civilization and progress in terms of size. Every year something bigger and better than the same thing last year is hailed as a step forward in human development. Surely that is not a true evaluation of man's growth? But I suppose it comes as a result of the fact that it's practically impossible to measure man's spiritual and mental growth. It's too intangible, and sometimes, perhaps, a little open to question. But there's no doubt about our material progress, and it can be measured. Mostly by size. This summer, we saw something conceived and built by those same neighbours of ours to the south, which is not only measurable in terms of size, but which is also making a direct contribution to man's well-being, and thus, indirectly, to his mental and spiritual growth. At least, so it seems to me. This something—and believe me, it is something—is Grand Coulee Dam.

For a long time now, my father, in his capacity of civil engineer, has been making detours whenever possible on his trips to see how the construction at Grand Coulee was getting along. Unfortunately, though, none of his engineering curiosity was passed along to his daughter, and I never paid much attention to his descriptions of the things that were happening down there on the Columbia River, one hundred and fifty miles below the American-Canadian border. So I wasn't at all prepared for the amazing structure that we went to see one blistering hot summer day during our holidays. We had been visiting my sister in Penticton, soaking up sunshine and disporting ourselves in the waters of Skaha Lake, when we decided that it was about time we did something with a Purpose—purpose with a capital P, that is—so we settled on a day's trip to Grand Coulee as an interesting and instructive "doing something."

There was another reason, too. Incredible as it may seem, our boys had never been across the border except for our trips to Point Roberts, and they didn't get any feeling of being in a different country. I don't really know just how they expected it to look like a different country. But this time, they eventually found ways in which it did. They found it strange to be somewhere where B.C. licence plates on the cars were few and far between, and they noticed the difference in the ever-present advertisements along the highway. Otherwise, except for the dam itself, I'm afraid the country through which we passed was very much like the country we had left behind at the Canadian border. Not so many years ago, we would, of course, have noticed the difference in the roads. But actually, nothing that we drove over on the other side that day could match the excellence of our own Hope-Princeton Highway and the highways around Penticton. Of course, we did see the Stars and Stripes floating in the sunshine several times, and that, I confess, gave me a bit of a twinge, because for many years I called the Stars and Stripes my flag. And in any case, it is a beautiful flag, don't you think? As a matter of fact, I had the same funny little twinge when I saw the Southern Cross of the Australian flag the day when Prime Minister Menzies of Australia was in town. Because it was once my flag, too.

On our way to Grand Coulee Dam, we passed through many little towns, most of whose names began, surprisingly enough, with the letter *o*: Osoyoos and Oliver and Oroville and Omak. I began to wonder if the old joke they tell about Osoyoos applied to other places, too: it seems that Osoyoos used to be called just Soyoos, but at some undetermined period after it was settled by an Irishman, they added the *o*! We also passed through a small place called Nespelem, and here we saw the annual get-together of all the Indian bands thereabouts. Their big wigwams of canvas, painted with signs and symbols, were set up in a large field. Apparently, they get together in this way every year for ten days of dancing and feasting and talking over the problems of each band.

At last, without any warning at all, we were at the Columbia River. And as we dropped down to the water level, the air, which had been hot and dry, as only the air in the Interior can be, grew noticeably cooler. And then there was the dam.

You know, it's just a little bit difficult to put into words one's impression of something as tremendous as Grand Coulee Dam. Our neighbours to the south call it the greatest man-made structure of all time, and the statistics concerning the amount of concrete it took to build the dam, the amount of electricity generated by it, the huge quantities of water that flow over the top of it, and so on, are simply fantastic.

There are, for instance, ten and one-half million cubic yards of concrete in it; that's enough concrete to make a cement sidewalk twice around the world! It is 4,173 feet long, 500 feet thick at the base, and 550 feet in height. The central spillway is 1,650 feet wide and forms a waterfall more than twice as high as Niagara Falls. Inside this huge structure there are eight and a half miles of galleries for inspection, operation, and maintenance. We went down into some of those galleries to see the enormous turbines, and it's a little like getting into the catacombs in Paris, except that it's brightly lighted, and instead of innumerable bones and skulls, there are innumerable arrays of control panels and strange-looking mechanisms at whose uses I wouldn't even venture a guess. The galleries open into one another in the most confusing way, and if one falls behind the official touring party as we did, people seem to vanish in a matter of minutes, and you are left with the almost panicky sensation that you might wander around those empty, echoing corridors of concrete lined with nameless instruments of electrical power forever.

The power plant at Grand Coulee is still incomplete, but even now it is the mightiest in the world. During the war, although still being constructed, its power production was equal to the labour of one million men working eight hours a day for seventy-eight years. See what I mean when I said that the statistics are fantastic?

When the irrigation system is in operation, water from the dam will serve more than a million acres of land in a two-million-five hundred-thousand-acre expanse, land that will be divided into family-sized units. Buyers will only be permitted to buy one such unit, and landowners will only be allowed to retain one family-sized unit. It's interesting to note that already all the land to be irrigated has been surveyed, examined, classified, and appraised (the appraisal based on dry-land values), and these values are available to prospective settlers, who are warned not to pay more than the dry-land value of any family-sized unit of land. So there won't be any profiteering.

When the Bureau of Reclamation began the tremendous project back in 1933, they were more than a little aided by the Grand Coulee itself. The Grand Coulee is a geological phenomenon. It was cut through a lava plateau by the Columbia River's mighty ice-age ancestor when its channel was blocked by a glacier flowing across it at the same place that the dam now stands. The Grand Coulee is fifty-two miles long, one and a half to five miles wide, and has perpendicular walls rising nearly a thousand feet—what a wonderful natural reservoir! But finding and deciding to utilize Grand Coulee were really only the first tiny beginnings. All over the irrigation and reservoir area, plans had to be made for the readjustment that would come about when the dam was built. Towns had to be moved, bridges built, new highways laid in. One large graveyard had to be moved onto higher ground. Property soon to be flooded had to be bought by the government. Abandoned buildings had to be removed, dismantled, or burned. The small percentage of fish that normally go up the Columbia beyond that point to spawn had to be caught at another dam farther down towards the river mouth and transplanted into tributary streams below the Grand Coulee Dam for spawning. This activity alone extended over eleven years, the time needed to form new spawning habits for the salmon that would normally go higher up the Columbia. And on either side of the river a town site was planned and the houses built for the hundreds of men employed on the construction and maintenance of the dam. The town is already a very pleasant place, cool even in the blazing summer heat, with green lawns and bright flower beds and neat white homes.

You could write a book, and probably someone has, about the actual construction of the dam, and the gargantuan problems that cropped up and had to be dealt with. Things like running into a great bank of plastic clay that kept slipping and finally was held back with an ice dam built of six miles of pipe through which a freezing solution was pumped to harden the slippery mass; and the more than one million cubic yards of faulty and eroded rock that had to be blasted from the perpendicular walls of the canyon. Someone said to me after I mentioned that we had visited Grand Coulee, "But what is there to see? After all, it's just water flowing over a dam." Taking into account, though, all the things that went into making the dam, and the reason for it, and the dam itself, it seemed to us that there was plenty to see. Just watching the water fall over the top into the depths below held us spellbound for a long time. It was almost impossible to grasp the immensity of the water tumbling and churning down into a seething, frothing cauldron that tossed great clouds of silver spray far back upwards towards the heights from which it had just fallen. It was beautiful, and at the same time rather terrible in the feeling that it gave of unleashed power. And when we considered the fact that the water falling over the spillway was as nothing compared to that which poured into the great turbines to create electricity, well, it was almost more than we could grasp.

With the unerring sense of the dramatic that our southern neighbours have, they have made a wonderful vantage point below the top of the dam, overlooking the place into which the water falls. They have built a sort of miniature stadium there, where one can sit and just look. Inside, there is a lecture room where every so often someone gives a lecture to the ever-present crowds of sightseers. With the aid of a wonderful little working model of the dam, the lecturer tells the story of the dam. Then, with the crowd in the properly awestruck state of mind, there is a short tour of the actual dam itself. I believe that at times it is possible to travel through the dam on a little railroad, although the day we were there continuing construction—because there is still a great deal to be done to finish the project—had temporarily suspended these trips. But we did see the huge turbines in the powerhouse and the simply enormous shafts of the generating units.

One of the things that impressed me most was the fact that the floors in this "factory for manufacturing power" were all of beautiful marble squares such as one might see in a very swish office building. And in one place were diagrams, all made from marble inlaid into the floor, explaining the process of turning water into electricity, rather the way we've seen the signs of the zodiac or the points of the compass inlaid in the floor.

Oh yes, we found something to see at Grand Coulee Dam. It was rather a silent family that emerged outside again when the tour was over. We were all busily trying to grasp the bigness of everything we'd seen.

And think what it all means in terms of benefit to people. Water for lands that only need water to grow flourishing crops. Power to operate all the complicated mechanisms that modern man finds necessary in order to live. The ideal behind all that hugeness seemed to me to be quite touchingly and simply expressed in the way in which the opening ceremony was handled. Do you know who was the first person to tap this power, the first person to turn a switch in the house and utilize the electricity? Why, an old Indian woman, a woman whose people had lived in the Grand Coulee for goodness knows how many hundreds of years before the white man came, before electricity was ever dreamed of. And she bought a new washing machine for the occasion, and when she turned that switch, she released the power of Grand Coulee Dam to do her weekly wash!

Until tomorrow then.

OPENING DAY

October 19, 1950

GOOD MORNING. I DO HOPE THAT, WHEN YOU HEARD I WAS GOING TO TALK about a day's shooting, you didn't quickly turn the radio dial, muttering to yourself meanwhile, "What's hunting got to do with 'Morning Visit'?" because, really, opening day was quite a unique day. And, believe it or not, it was a family day.

It happened this way. For some, oh, twelve years now, I've been traipsing the countryside every shooting season. Sure, I carry a gun, but I imagine I could count on the fingers of one hand the number of birds that have fallen to my gun in all that time. I took up shooting because I made up my mind that I was darned if I was going to be a shooting widow. My husband and I have always gone fishing together and when, rather late in life, he took up shooting, I didn't relish the idea one little bit of being left behind on weekends. So I persuaded him to buy me a gun, too, and I guess it doesn't really matter if I close my eyes tight when I squeeze the trigger! As time has gone on, I've grown to love our shooting trips. I love the long tramps after pheasant across the stubble fields. I love watching the sunrise on a frosty morning from behind a screen of bulrushes, and the night flight coming in against the setting sun. I love the autumn colouring on the hillsides in the early part of the season. And is there anything lovelier than those mornings in early winter when every branch and twig and blade of dried grass is rimmed with white frost?

But this year, on opening day, something was added. Tony, our eldest boy, has been waiting impatiently for the last two years until he should be old enough to carry a gun and go out with us. We decided that this year he was old enough—he's fifteen and a responsible youngster. So there was a period when he watched the "For Sale, Miscellaneous" columns in the newspapers every night, and almost every evening when Dick walked in the door from work, he'd say, "Daddy, there's a good one in the paper tonight, a double-barrelled twelve-gauge for only $75." The address would invariably be somewhere the other side of town, but after dinner, out they'd go to inspect the gun. Finally, they found one, a good one, and a great bargain. For the next few days, small processions of Tony's friends passed through the house on a conducted tour to the cupboard where the guns are kept, and I heard him enlarging on the merits of his gun over all other guns. And then it was a week until opening day. He began counting the days, then the hours, and the night before the great day, I strongly suspect that he stayed awake all night counting each minute as it passed on leaden feet.

Now, taking Tony with us posed a bit of a problem. What about our younger son, Ted? We couldn't very well go off and leave him. After all, he'd always been camping and fishing and picnicking with us. So we decided that he could go along, too, and act as a superior sort of bird dog. Not, I must hastily add, that we needed any more dogs. Rocky, our big black Labrador, has been our bird dog for the last six years, and he's wise in the ways of ducks and pheasants. He, of course, would go along. But then there was Tony's own dog, a young cocker. Under Tony's tutelage, Mike has been showing distinct signs of turning into an excellent retriever, too. So Mike must go. And then, what about Ted's dog? Ted recently became the master of a Labrador puppy. Stormy is three months old now, still much too young to be left alone all day. So I suppose that it was inevitable that Stormy would come along. Now do you see why I said opening day, 1950, was for the Phillipses a family day? The only members of the family not present were the parrot, the budgie, and the goldfish.

Now, if your husband is a huntin' man, or if by any chance, you go out, too, you'll know that opening day, in fact, any day's shooting, involves getting up at an ungodly hour in order to reach your chosen shooting grounds by daybreak. We got up at three a.m.! I've never enjoyed getting up at that hour, anyway, but add two eager-beaver children to general dismal greyness, and the outlook is bleak indeed! We got through breakfast somehow, and a weird meal it was. Bacon and eggs may taste good at three in the morning after an evening's dancing, but to get up at that hour and look a fried egg in the face—ugh!

Then we were all in the car—how, I don't quite know, since it involved quite a packing problem: two boys, two adults, and three dogs, not to mention three guns, supplies of ammunition, and very plentiful supplies of food. Having Tony along, whose size-twelve feet are hollow, made the latter a necessary part of the day's equipment. We hadn't been driving long when we ran into fog, not just drifting wisps, but really thick fog, the kind that doesn't respond to head-lights at all. The situation wasn't helped any by the fact that for the first part of our way at least most of the other nineteen thousand and ninety-seven hunters who had taken out licences this year seemed to be going in the same direction. It was rather like trying to drive home from town during the rush hour on a foggy night in November. Even-tually, the crowd thinned out, turning off down side roads to their chosen shooting grounds, and then the fog thinned, too, and finally disappeared. We drove on towards Hatzic Prairie in that pre-dawn greyness that lightens imperceptibly into daylight. By half past five we had arrived at our destination.

The weekend before shooting opened, we had driven up to Hatzic and arranged with a friendly farmer to shoot on his land. I don't know why it didn't occur to us that if he was friendly to us, he probably was equally friendly to other people, but it didn't. And we were surprised, maybe even a little bit aggrieved, to find a goodly number of other cars parked in front of the farmhouse. However, we were there, and it was too late to change our plans and go some-where else, so we started down into the fields, all of us and the three dogs. I still don't know why at some time or other during the day one of our pack of hounds didn't tangle with a dog belonging to another hunter, but by some miracle they didn't. (It may have been because we tried very hard to keep well away from them.)

We managed this business of keeping well away from other people so well at first that we soon found ourselves in deep, tangled bush, where it was actually difficult to know where to put our feet next. We had just about reached an impasse, and were standing around helplessly with brambles twined around our legs and branches poking into our eyes when, with a swish and a clatter, a beautiful cock pheasant rose awkwardly into the air, gained altitude slowly and gracefully soared over our heads into even deeper bush. By the time we recovered our wits and fired, Mr. Pheasant was safely out of range. That was our first shot—a perfect one, and a perfect miss. Disgusted, we waded out of the bush, leaped a couple of ditches, and emerged into an open field. However, it soon appeared that at least four other groups of hunters liked the same field. They seemed to be all around us. And I began to feel nervous. Some years ago, when we found ourselves in a crowded field, I got in the way of some shotgun pellets that lodged in my face, and ever since, I've been—understandably, so it seems to me—distinctly nervous about crowded fields. Just then, a solitary duck flew overhead, very high, but since ducks seemed to be very few and far between that morning, everybody fired at it anyhow. It seemed to me to be a veritable barrage. My nervousness increased. And then it happened. Suddenly, just over to our right, a regular flock of pheasants, there must have been at least seven of them, and four of them cocks, blew out of the grass and flew in every which direction. "Get down!" I yelled to the boys, and, obedient to Mother's command, they both dropped flat on their faces. I looked up from my crouching position to see a cock flying directly over my head. Shot number two and another miss. That one, though, I didn't mind. Tony said afterward that he was sure some shot whistled past his head, and I wouldn't be a bit surprised, because somehow or other we seemed to be the focal point of that second and much too personal barrage.

We left that field in a hurry. In fact, it wasn't long before we went back to the car, determined to try to find a less populated spot. A family council settled on Matsqui as our next port of call. On the drive over a new difficulty developed. It's fortunate that after bringing up two children and numerous puppies, I'm no longer squeamish about such things. We merely stopped the car and cleaned it out. And Mike, the cocker, was having his troubles, too. His long fine hair had come into close and intimate contact with a numerous variety of burrs, and, poor little dog, he didn't enjoy having them removed. So we went our way to the accompaniment of yelps of woe.

It was in the neighbourhood of Matsqui that we got our first pheasant. Later still, we spotted some mallards dropping into a slough. Dick and Tony did a sneak to the stop of the dyke, and Dick dropped a beautiful green-head. Tony, I should mention, was manfully potting away at everything, but without visible result. I guess it'll be a while before he really catches on. Of course, if he takes after his mother, he probably never will catch on; however, I hope that, in this respect at least, he doesn't resemble Mama. Ted, meanwhile, was sticking pretty close to me, from time to time uttering wistful little remarks to the effect that he just couldn't wait till he was old enough. Something tells me that by the time he is old enough to shoot, too, I'll gladly relinquish my gun to him. I just don't think I could stand the strain!

Along about this time, the pangs of hunger overcame the family. Actually, I don't know why they hadn't overtaken Tony long before. I guess excitement must be a meal in itself. But now it was definitely lunchtime. Optimistically counting on the weather, we'd packed the makings of a leisurely lunch that involved lighting the camp stove and heating soup and making tea. But the weather didn't co-operate. At that time, there was a fine Scotch mist blurring the windshield of the car, and there was a cold, damp wind blowing. So, uncomfortably sitting in the car, I attempted to fill the aching void in my menfolk with sandwiches made on a small plate held on my lap. I seemed to be making sandwiches for an eternity. At last, they were satisfied, and the dogs were fed, too. I forgot to mention earlier that we had brought along each dog's individual dish and a plentiful supply of dog food; they don't ordinarily get fed in the middle of the day, but this day they deserved a treat. They'd all behaved wonderfully well. Rocky worked the fields as he always does; Mike worked, too—I don't think he was quite sure what he was looking for, but he was certainly looking—and little Stormy kept right along with us, mostly minding his own business, and keeping pretty much to heel.

Eventually, we repacked ourselves and started off again to find yet another likely field. During the afternoon, Dick brought down another pheasant amid great excitement. Each bird, of course, created a commotion among all concerned that quite defies description. Later in the afternoon, too, the sky cleared, and the last part of the day was lovely, the hillsides ablaze with colour and the distant mountaintops standing clear and snow-covered against the sky. Then the light began to fade as we tramped one last field, and before we knew it, darkness was falling and opening day was over. That is, the shooting was over. We still had the long drive home. But it was a happy drive. The excitement of the day still lingered, and Tony had a final crowning moment of pride when we were stopped by the RCMP at a roadblock at the Pitt River Bridge, and he was asked to show the officer his shooting licence. He withdrew it from his wallet and flourished it grandly. In that moment he felt every inch a man.

And so ended the Phillipses' first opening day *en famille*. I don't mind stating that I was tired, more from playing the role of mother as well as hunter than from any other reason. Perhaps next time we go out, I'll be able to relax a little. I guess some family adjustments take a little time!

I'll be back again soon. Goodbye for now!

OGLING THE ANGLER

July 25, 1951

OGLING THE ANGLER PRESENTS A VERY INTERESTING SUBJECT FOR CONSIDERATION. I suppose that anglers have been ogled, in one way or another, since time immemorial. Only I never happened to think of it just that way. And, of course, this province of British Columbia offers unlimited opportunities for ogling as well as for angling, for I don't suppose that anywhere else in all Canada are practised so many forms of the angler's art. But before we consider the various forms of angling there are to be ogled, let's think, first of all, about the different kinds of ogling the angler undergoes.

First, every angler has experienced the ogling of his friends—and at such a time he has many friends—when he returns from a fishing trip well supplied with gleaming trout. Upon which ones will he bestow his favour? Who will be given some of the treasure trove later to provide a meal of succulent fish, crisp and sizzling from the pan? However, if you're like most anglers, such ogling doesn't often come your way, mostly because such angling doesn't often come your way, at least within reasonable distance for successful transportation. Many an angler has packed his catch and happily imagined the longing glances of his friends, only to find that the long, hot drive back to the coast has made his haul fit only for fertilizer for the garden. I remember one year, though, when the salmon run was unusually good right close to home, just off Spanish Banks, as a matter of fact. That year it finally got so that you couldn't give salmon away. Everyone, even your enemies, were sated with salmon.

Then there's the ogling the would-be angler in pursuit of his art gets from the non-angler. Unless you're an angler yourself, nothing in the world—not even golf—looks so purposeless to the onlooker. At least in golf there's a ball to hit from one place to another. But it's seldom indeed that the watcher sees an angler catch a fish; all he sees is an apparently normal fellow human being solemnly and patiently throwing a line into the water. Not only that, but he knows that the fisherman has spent untold sums on his equipment, and spent long hours perfecting his technique—and all, apparently, in order to watch his line go out a certain distance, and land on the water in a certain way. And even if the angler does hook a fish, what is the fascination about hauling it in, cracking it on the head, and tucking it into his creel? (And then, for goodness' sakes, repeating the whole process.) What's more, if the ogler's patience were as enduring as the angler's, he would see the process go on until time or tide put an end to it. Oglers, however, at least in my experience, don't have that kind of patience. And if the ogler only knew! If he only knew the kind of pleasure a well-placed cast gives any angler. It is not important if a fish doesn't rise to it; the cast is a satisfaction in itself. Should a fish rise to his fly, should its nose break the water and its body turn over with a sudden gleam of scales in the sun, and should the reel begin an angry scream in a rising crescendo until at the end of the line the fish suddenly leaves the water in a desperate leap for freedom, then the angler's joy is complete. He feels the power in his straining, curving rod. He senses the smoothness of his reel as he alternately reels in line when the tension eases for an instant, or lets it run free as the fish takes another run with another shining leap at the end of it. He has confidence in his gossamer line and leader and in his own knowledge of just how much stress to place upon it. It is for this that he has invested those untold sums in his equipment. It is for this that he has spent those long, patient hours perfecting his technique. I'm sorry for the non-angling ogler who knows nothing of this!

Then there are the oglers who are themselves anglers. One fly fisherman eyes another and snorts, "What does he think he's doing, lashing the water into foam?" Or a grudging, "Not bad—for a woman!" And sometimes, the completely unenvious admiration of a perfect cast perfectly executed.

Occasionally, one kind of an angler ogles another kind of an angler. The fly fisherman watches the troller boating his fish in a tangle of spoons and wonders what pleasure there is in such unsporting methods. Or vice versa, when the troller watches the fly fisherman and wonders why he goes to all that bother when it's so much less trouble and you catch so many more fish with a string of spoons. Being a fly fisherman myself, I must confess to belonging to the type of ogler who wonders what the troller sees in hauling them in wholesale. Mind you, there was a day when I trolled, too, but that was before I discovered the incomparable thrill of fly fishing, when it's your skill against that of the fish and the odds are pretty even as to which will win. And I wouldn't exchange accepting the challenge of wind and water; the never-ending interest of trying out a new fly; the tremendous controlled excitement that seizes you when you see a trout, far down in the clear water, change course and swim up to snatch the little contraption of feathers and thread on the end of your line. No, I wouldn't exchange all that for just rowing up and down, up and down, trailing behind you deep under the surface a string of heavy spoons and a worm on a hook.

Let me hasten to add, however, that all this refers to lake fishing. I'm certainly not above trolling all the accepted hardware when it comes to sea fishing—even to unsavory strips of herring bait and as many ounces of lead weight as the experts consider necessary. But, even then, tucked away in a corner of my mind is the thought that it's all pretty hard on the fish. Especially when, as sometimes happens, you catch a small grilse and don't even know you've got him on, and when you finally bring your line in because you're not catching anything, there is the poor little creature, drowned. Just the same, if I had plenty of money and plenty of time, I'd always do my sea fishing at Cowichan Bay when the coho are running. It's the closest approximation to fly fishing in the ocean, in my experience; a lightish rod, sixty feet of cuttyhunk line, a bucktail fly, and no weight at all. Along with that lightish rod, though, you need a reel that'll hold a lot of line. When a prime fourteen-pound coho hits that bucktail fly, you need plenty.

One kind of fishing that holds a certain strange fascination for ogler and angler alike is jigging. The fascination is due to the fact that you never know what you're going to catch. Undersea denizens such as cod and flounders and bullheads and dogfish and catfish, and even, yes, ratfish! Jigging requires a minimum of equipment and effort, and is conducive to meditation. All you do is anchor your boat over a likely piece of sandy bottom, bait two hooks with almost anything, let your line down until it touches bottom, and then just sit there, gently jigging the line up and down. Even a purist sometimes enjoys jigging.

As a matter of fact, there's always the element of the unexpected when you fish in the sea. A few weeks ago, some friends of ours got the surprise of their lives when they caught an eight-foot basking shark. And once my husband brought in his line to find a half-drowned hell diver. It's not unusual either to hook a small fish, generally a cod, and have another, larger cod gobble it greedily, so that the angler finds himself in a sort of marine version of Red Riding Hood—you remember how the woodcutter chopped open the wolf to find Grandma inside! A classic story my husband tells is of fly casting late one evening on Buttle Lake. It was nearly dark, too dark, really, to be fishing at all, because he couldn't even see where his fly was landing. That's why just at first he didn't realize that something was wrong: where was his line? Apparently it wasn't behind him. Certainly it hadn't landed in the water in front of him. He finally realized that it was going straight up in the air. Since he did not number the Indian roper trick among his accomplishments, he was, to say the least, a bit bewildered. He reeled in this elusive line far enough to perceive that he had caught a bat! Dick's antics as he tried to land the bat would have been an ogle-worthy sight for anyone.

Having been an angler for many years myself, I've ogled many another angler in pursuit of his art. I remember one misty summer dawn when the tyee, the great king salmon, were running in Comox Bay. Catching one of these monsters required just the right combination of time and tide, and this particular morning conditions were ideal: low tide slack just at dawn. In order to be on the spot at the magic minute, all the fishermen rose while it was still dark, and began rowing up and down in the black darkness. The good fishing ground was fairly small in area, so even in the dark the boats fell into a sort of rude procession, up the length, a wide semicircle, and down the course again. As the daylight came, gradually the procession of boats became visible and they were a ludicrous sight. All sorts and types of craft, solemnly playing follow-the-leader up and down an apparently unremarkable stretch of the sea. One small boat that looked rather like a kayak with the bow and stern cut off was propelled by a serious gentleman in a derby hat. Maybe it was because of the hat, I don't know, but he caught the biggest fish taken that morning, a forty-five pounder. That was the morning that I lost the biggest fish I've ever hooked. I suspect that the passing of time has increased its size. But I'm willing to bet that fish would have weighed in at forty pounds. He came in to the boat on his first run, right up to the side, gave me one startled look—maybe I should say one startled ogle—and departed, taking most of my tackle with him. I guess I should have been wearing a derby hat.

And I remember one cold and stormy twenty-fourth of May up at Lac Le Jeune. Once again, the best fishing centred in one spot, just off the place where the waters of a wide shallow bay fell off steeply into fathomless—literally—depths. The water was very choppy in a strong cold wind, and the rowboats bobbed and manoeuvred clumsily while the fishermen tried to get into a position where they could cast downwind. All except one boat. This one was expertly managed by an elderly gentleman who, during all the hours we fished there, was never heard to utter a word. With his passenger it was a different matter. In an extremely cultivated English voice, she carried on a more than slightly profane conversation with her silent spouse, all the while casting the most amazingly long line into the teeth of the wind from a semi-reclining position in the stern, holding the rod in one hand, and in the other, a large umbrella well positioned over her head. We were catching a lot of fish that day, and suddenly we were favoured by a stentorian blast. "I say, what fly are you using? I've been using a New Zealand green sedge, and I'm blanked if I've caught a blank thing in the last half hour!" That was one angler who was well ogled, I'll bet, whatever part of the world she happened to be fishing. And, of course, it never would occur to her that she was in the least unusual.

Then there was the young couple who camped near us up at Big Bar Lake. They carried with them all the necessary equipment for tying their own flies, and he spent the evenings painstakingly putting together little scraps of feather and tinsel and thread, and all day long fishing with a long string of spoons and a worm. And that's not a fish story, either; that's just exactly what they did. You can imagine our state of wonderment, especially as they were an extremely pleasant and normal young couple in every other respect.

As you can see, ogling the angler, especially if you're another angler and can appreciate the peculiarities of the species, can be a most rewarding occupation. Should you want to do a little ogling on your own account, and if you live within reachable distance of Stanley Park, betake yourself to the southern end of Lost Lagoon any Thursday evening between half past six and dark, and there you can see upwards of seventy-five would-be anglers earnestly learning to angle. They stand in two rows, back to back, on a float, and throw lines into the water according to their several styles and abilities. In case you should think them quite mad, the occasion is the free fly-casting instruction classes sponsored by the Vancouver Angling and Game Association, and these classes not only provide a wonderful opportunity for the layman to ogle the angler, but open the way for the specialized ogling of one angler by another. Try it sometime!

4. HERE AND THERE

ENGLISH FOR NEW CANADIANS

July 7, 1949

THE OTHER DAY I MET AND HAD A GOOD LONG TALK WITH A MOST INTERESTING person who is doing a most interesting and worthwhile job. She is Dr. Edith Lucas, and her official title is Director of High School Correspondence Courses, Department of Education. The specific job I found so interesting, though, is quite out of the usual run of correspondence courses. Dr. Lucas has developed—as a matter of fact, is still developing—a course in English for New Canadians.

When Dr. Lucas was asked to work out some means by which these New Canadians, most of whom are Displaced Persons who have come to B.C. to live, could learn to speak English quickly, she hadn't the faintest idea how she would do it. Her own wide experience in languages came to her aid (she had won university honours in Latin and French and was awarded the Nicol scholarship for post-graduate study in France) and soon she had devised a course that is producing the most astonishing results.

First, she hunted through existing courses to find something suitable, but soon came to the conclusion that only a course specially prepared for the purpose would be any good at all. There are several reasons for this. In the first place, most of the people who are helping the New Canadians with their instruction are not professional teachers; they are farmers or farmers' wives, or quite ordinary citizens without formal teaching experience. The course had to be easy to teach, as well as easy to learn. And then, too, existing courses that might have been used were too juvenile in content, and were intended to cover a much longer time period than was desirable. You can see that the time element is very important; these people who have come to live in our country want to learn English quickly. The barrier of language can make living a very difficult business. Too often we become impatient with trying to understand, and exclude from our activities those whose language we don't understand. For the foreign-born person in our midst, it's practically impossible to adjust to our way of life without a knowledge of English. So Dr. Lucas made her course functional, rather than basic. Her method concentrates on familiarizing students as quickly as possible with the sentence patterns of everyday speech—not academic English, but English as she is spoke.

And Dr. Lucas is succeeding. The response to her first papers was immediate and enthusiastic. Amateur teachers found her manual of instruction easy to follow and apply. And the students began to learn English, the kind of English that would help them to become real New Canadians—quickly!

I think perhaps you might like to hear just a little of what the course is about. In order to fit the new words into sentence patterns and situations that best show how they should be used, Dr. Lucas invented two or three families, the members of which are put into everyday situations in a simple story. For instance, in one story, the mother goes shopping. In another, the daughter decorates her room. The way to open a bank account is told in another, and in still another, insurance is discussed. As well as the story, each paper—I believe that in all, ten papers have been completed, and that ten more are planned—contains a dialogue, a simple and realistic conversation that explains or supplements the story. And, of course, there are many pages on word pronunciation and meanings, and on simple, everyday sentence construction and grammar.

One of the reasons that I thought you might be interested in hearing about Dr. Lucas's course for New Canadians is that I don't think it's as widely known as it should be. The other day, I heard about someone working in an out-of-the-way place who had become so concerned about the need for an English teacher for a group of Displaced Persons that he was seriously considering trying to make a course of his own. Well, he knows about Dr. Lucas's course now, and soon another group of New Canadians will be learning English the easy way. Perhaps some of you know of such groups, and could help them in their wish to become good citizens of their new country. Canada needs her new citizens and she needs good citizens; if we shut them out of our lives and activities because they can't speak English, we force them to stay together in tight little language groups, and how can they ever become good Canadian citizens that way?

Did you know that from June 1947 to June 1948, some 25,244 Displaced Persons came to Canada? I don't know how many settled in B.C., but I do know that over one thousand New Canadians are studying Dr. Lucas's course at the present time. And I feel sure that there will be many more as the course becomes more widely known.

When Dr. Lucas was asked to prepare the course, it was intended for use mainly in rural areas, because it was felt that night schools in the larger centres would look after the Displaced Persons there. But when Mr. Graham Bruce, Director of Vancouver Night Schools, heard about the course and saw the material, he asked for it for his classes. And it wasn't long before more than two hundred copies of each paper were going out to Vancouver, and the teachers here were following, step by step, the instructions outlined by Dr. Lucas. And that was just the beginning. Now the High School Correspondence Branch is supplying copies of the course to night schools in Chilliwack and Vernon, and school boards in smaller centres, such as Prince George and Prince Rupert, started courses when they heard that instructional material had been prepared for teachers and students alike.

There are two English courses for our new citizens. The first is for beginners, those who came to our country with no English at all. The second one is more advanced; it is intended for those new immigrants who had studied English as a foreign language in the high schools of their native land. This second course is the one with which I'm most familiar, because I'm helping with the very interesting job of preparing some of the stories and dialogues. It is this second and more advanced course that is meant to prepare our New Canadians in B.C. for citizenship in the fullest sense of the word. Dr. Lucas, realizing this, knew she must include information about all aspects of Canadian life. I understand that the dialogues are great favourites; the students just love taking the different parts. Some of the papers yet to be completed will contain information about our social services, our history, and our municipal, provincial, and federal government systems. In other words, English II is a course in Canadianization, and all done in the most interesting and informal way possible. I wonder if you learned Canadian history the way I did? In my far-off school days, it was the most boring subject! And, of course, it needn't be; it shouldn't be. And it's good to know that our New Canadians are going to learn it the really interesting way.

The course tries in every way possible to encourage the foreign-born student to go on and explore the language of the country of his adoption. No longer will we have citizens who have lived in Canada for years and years, and who still cannot speak more than a few words of English. And as their interest in the language grows, so will their interest in becoming Canadians in every sense of the word. The course also helps the student to express his thoughts in English. We have, among our immigrants, many cultured people with a wide range of thinking, and the English II course will do a tremendous amount to remove that sense of isolation and inferiority that I mentioned before that exists where there is the barrier of language. The New Canadians will be able to take their places beside the people of their own degree of culture in Canada.

English II is being used in night schools, but it has been compiled in such a way that students in isolated districts may send in their papers for correction to the High School Correspondence Department. Dr. Lucas told me that almost every day the department gets appreciative and enthusiastic letters. The Superintending Principal of the Prince George High School wrote, "Progress has been amazing. One group of elderly people from Greece is already becoming fluent. Two and a half months ago, they could not speak one word of English." Another teacher bemoaned the fact that nothing similar has yet been written for the teaching of French in our schools. He may get his wish. Who knows?

Meanwhile, a thousand of B.C.'s New Canadians are learning to speak English. I can just picture it, can't you? In classrooms, some of them. Others gathered around the table in a farmhouse kitchen by the light of an oil lamp. Or maybe in the lounge of a YWCA. Wherever there are New Canadians, you will find groups of them learning our strange and difficult tongue, learning about Canada, learning to be Canadians.

You know, it must be a pretty painful business, transplanting oneself from one country to another. But Canada must seem a far cry from places of horror like Buchenwald and Dachau. And it must be very pleasant looking over the rolling hills of our B.C. Interior, or up at the tree-covered sides of the Coast Mountains, or the lush green fields of the Fraser Valley, or the rolling swells of the Pacific Ocean washing on the long beaches. It's easy to understand that these New Canadians want to become part of our land and to learn our way of life. To Dr. Edith Lucas goes a great deal of the credit for helping them achieve their wish. She is doing a job, which, to me anyway, rates her as one of our really outstanding citizens.

And now, just a word about tomorrow's program. This morning, I'm going out to the university, where the summer sessions have begun. These special classes always have a great fascination for me; they seem to teach all the really interesting subjects there are to learn, things like drama and short-story writing and handicrafts. I'm going to see some of these classes in action, and tomorrow I'm going to tell you all about what I've seen.

Till tomorrow, then. So long!

JUNIOR FOREST WARDENS

July 13, 1949

SOME TIME AGO, I TOLD YOU ABOUT A VISIT I PAID TO THE JUNIOR FOREST Warden Camp out at Point Atkinson. Perhaps you'll remember how impressed I was by the feeling of being miles from anywhere the very minute we turned off the highway into the beautiful stretch of eighty acres of parkland that has been loaned (more or less loaned, that is; I believe there's a nominal rental of a dollar or so a year) by the City of West Vancouver. They are eighty acres of virgin forest, with towering evergreens, and at their base the lovely-smelling soft brown mould that is the result of hundreds of years of falling leaves, and growing in the springy carpet, the delicate green of fern fronds. Great moss-covered tree trunks lay where they fell, goodness knows how many years ago.

The road winds up hill and down dale until it reaches Point Atkinson, that rocky promontory topped by the white lighthouse and flashing light that marks the entrance to Vancouver Harbour. Tucked away in the rocky crevices are a number of buildings that at one time housed a naval unit set there to guard the entrance. Now these buildings are used to house the boys of the Junior Forest Wardens, that offshoot of the Canadian Forestry Association that is doing so much to make our young people aware of the value of our forests, so much to educate them in methods of conservation and preservation, of what is, after all, just about the greatest heritage of British Columbians.

The Junior Forest Wardens of the Canadian Forestry Association were first organized in 1930. Membership was determined on the basis of the recommendation of schoolteachers. About one in every hundred students was chosen. That, as a matter of fact, is how my son, Tony, came to be a Junior Forest Warden. Once we understood what it was all about, you can imagine how proud we were! At first, though, when he came home one day and told us that he had been chosen to join the ranks, we were quite bewildered. In those days, we didn't know such an organization even existed. Today, though—

and at the risk of putting the tail end of my story first—I should tell
you just how glad we are that it does exist. Because of Junior Forest
Wardens, Tony has decided at fourteen what he wants to do when
he grows up. He wants to go into forestry, and is planning his
courses in junior high towards the requirements for that particular
training. These chosen students were between the ages of ten and
sixteen. Since 1930, when the organization was begun, twenty-five
thousand young British Columbians have entered the ranks, and of
these about nineteen thousand five hundred have had their training
and joined the honorary ranks of the organization, all of them
pledged to carry the message of conservation and preservation for
the rest of their lives. It's a pretty fine thing to know that we have
such a wonderful backlog of citizens educated in how to maintain
that precious heritage that I mentioned a few minutes ago, our
forests.

Right now, today, there are about fifty-five hundred youngsters
involved, boys and girls—yes, girls, because Junior Forest Wardens
may be girls as well as boys. No longer is this a purely masculine
world! There are fifty-five hundred boys and girls being trained in
forestry, woods travel, first aid, signalling, swimming, and lifesaving.
There are, throughout B.C., one hundred fifty-two Junior Forest
Warden clubs with a membership of nearly thirty-five hundred.
These clubs meet once a week all during the fall and winter months
for study and to take part in hikes, field trips, and other outdoor
activities.

At this point, you're probably wondering what happened to the
other two thousand or so. And I think this is a very interesting point.
Just because a boy or girl lives too far away, in one of our more
isolated communities, doesn't mean that he or she is barred from
Junior Forest Wardens, no indeed. These youngsters get their instruction by correspondence, through pamphlets, and through the official
publication *Outdoor Boy*. By the way, it just occurred to me to
wonder why the magazine is called *Outdoor Boy?* Especially since we
just finished saying that it's no longer a purely masculine world, at
least among the Junior Forest Wardens. Perhaps we should set our
brains to work, and devise a title that would be a bit more representative, such as, well, *Our Outdoors* or *Your Forests*. Anyway, it's a
very good little magazine.

During the hot, dry summer months, the young wardens in our
province are always on the lookout for that great destroyer of our

forests, fire. So firmly is this responsibility ingrained in them that, one night driving down the Fraser Canyon, we had to forcibly restrain our young son from leaping from the car to report a grass fire at the edge of the road. He was only finally persuaded by the fact that there did seem to be a number of people already on the job. And one really important thing we've noticed since Tony has been training is his sense of responsibility about campfires. We have been very impressed with the way he examines the proposed site of a camp-fire, looking overhead for hanging branches, scouring the site for encroaching underbrush, actually taking the precaution of making a cleared space around the fireplace so that the flames can't run along dry grass or twigs. And then, when the time comes to put out the fire, it gets really put out. Well scattered and doused with water, till there isn't even a wisp of smoke, and the stones have stopped sizzling when the water is poured over them. Reporting fires is one of the very real contributions the junior forest wardens living in isolated commu-nities can and do make towards preservation and conservation.

Another summertime activity of the Junior Forest Wardens is assisting the Canadian Forestry Association by taking part in commu-nity parades. And very smart they look, too, in their fire-red shirts with the green junior warden insignia, their forest-green caps and ties and their khaki trousers. They also help in distributing posters and poster stamps; they even give talks to their schoolmates and warn travellers about the dangers of fire. One of their most recent projects is a very interesting one: woodlots. Woodlots are usually a commu-nity project. A lot is donated to them by the city or municipality, and the young wardens advise about the best way of cutting and marketing the timber on it. They will also, I understand, do the cutting, too, as they arrive at that stage in their training. Then they replant the lot with replacement trees as the others are logged off. And all this, you can see, not only gives the young warden a prac-tical application of the knowledge he has gained over his course of instruction, but also spreads the good word about the very best way to obtain the highest yield financially from our forests, while at the same time preparing for the future, so that we won't suddenly find ourselves minus our greatest resource. Right now, the Junior Forest Wardens have six such community woodlots in the province, and it seems to me that that is a project that should keep right on growing.

This year, there was another camp for young wardens held at Kimberley. I think it is hoped that more and more centres will operate camps that are distinct from the one at Point Atkinson. At present, though, aside from the one in the Kootenays, Point Atkinson remains the main training centre. All summer the camps go on. They last for an eight-day period each, and at the end of that time, the young wardens who have attended return to their districts all over the province as leaders in conservation work. In August there is a camp for girls. During the Christmas and Easter holidays there are camps, too. The training the young wardens receive acts as a finishing school for leaders.

Here are some of the courses of instruction held at camp. Advanced forestry includes timber cruising, tree falling, elementary surveying, and vocations. In elementary forestry, the young wardens are told all about the functions of a tree, how to identify the different variety of trees, and the value of forests. The course in woods travel and camp lore teaches them how to travel and live in the woods; they learn camp-cooking; how to make camp, keep it, and break it; and the principles of rifle safety. The first aid course is the St. John Ambulance course for a certificate. The course in fire prevention teaches not only prevention but the use of fire-fighting equipment and how to fight fires. Swimming and lifesaving are studied under YMCA instructors and under the association's own Red Cross–trained instructors. Tests are held by Red Cross examiners. Then, of course, there's signalling. I must admit to having been greatly mystified the first time I came upon Tony waving his arms around in a little-frequented corner of the house. I found that he was only practising semaphore, and that I didn't need to be worried about his sanity! In signalling, they learn Morse code, too, and for days, strange tappings echoed through the house—all, I'm sure, highly intelligible to the initiated. Finally, under the heading of recreation, we find swimming, games, sports, boxing, special games that make use of woods-travel knowledge, and, of course, hobbies.

There's another interesting way in which a general knowledge of forestry is being spread through the province, and that is through the Junior Forest Wardens' course in forestry, as it is outlined in their text-book *Forest and Woods-Travel*, which is being sent out to more than two hundred school forestry information clubs. These groups also receive monthly bulletins, the magazine *Outdoor Boy*, and films from the Canadian Forestry Association's own film library.

I suppose that ten boys doesn't seem a very impressive total out of all those who have been Junior Forest Wardens in the last nineteen years, but here are the facts about those ten: of ten boys who completed not only their high school course, but also the junior forest warden three-year leadership course of instruction, nine have entered into forestry. Five of these are attending the UBC forestry course, one is a plywood technician, and two are employed with the B.C. Forest Service. Among the things to remember when you think that ten out of all those boys is not very many boys, is that it is only comparatively recently that there was a forestry course open to our boys at UBC. And add to that the fact that it is only recently that any branch of forestry as a profession has become a matter of serious consideration by mothers and dads. And, after all, it's the mothers and dads who have the largest, and perhaps the final say, in what their sons will choose as a life work.

But the Canadian Forestry Association itself will be the first to tell you that, important as it is that boys take up forestry as a vocation, probably the most important work of the young wardens still lies in the field of education. Not only that they themselves know about forest preservation and conservation, but what they can do to bring their knowledge to a tremendous section of B.C.'s population that otherwise would never know anything about the importance of a knowledge of forestry, what it can mean to them in terms of actual financial security and profit. Our forests are the backbone of our province's economy, and the intelligent use of them is the basis for not only our own prosperity, but that of the generations yet to come.

Junior Forest Wardens are doing a real job in our province, and if you have a son or a daughter—don't forget the daughter!—who might make a Junior Forest Warden, get in touch with the Canadian Forestry Association, 509 Burrard Street, and find out all about it for yourself.

And now, until tomorrow. So long!

CHILDREN'S DAY AT THE ROYAL VANCOUVER YACHT CLUB

July 28, 1949

A LONG TIME AGO, WHEN I WAS FIRST MARRIED, MY HUSBAND AND I HELD long discussions about which we'd buy first—when we could afford either—a boat or a car. We had both done quite a lot of sailing, and it somehow seemed that, with all the Pacific Ocean at our door, and the wonderful coast of British Columbia waiting to be explored, it was all wrong not to have a boat of our own. Of course, in the long run, when the time came, we bought a car. It was the lesser of two luxuries. But even now, we often have wistful thoughts about that boat we never bought. Saturday afternoons are such times. Especially if there's a bright sun and a brisk breeze, and all the sailboats are bowing and curtseying over waves just tipped with white out there in English Bay.

Yesterday I went on a most memorable sail. In fact, the whole experience was unforgettable. Because yesterday was the third annual Children's Day at the Royal Vancouver Yacht Club. It was the day when sailboats and power cruisers of all shapes and sizes take children from six welfare organizations on a cruise around the bay.

This year, there were nearly three hundred of these children. They came from the Vancouver Preventorium, that Red Feather Service that does so much to remove the dread shadow of tuberculosis from the lives of children. They came from Alexandra and Gordon Neighbourhood House, and from the Vancouver Children's Aid Society, all organizations whose work is to make, in their several ways, the lives of boys and girls richer and fuller and happier. They came, too, from the Loyal Protestant Home, and from the Children's Hospital. They came on crutches, they were carried, they limped, or danced happily along. Three hundred of them.

As I stood on the dock watching them stream down to the boats, I thought of the Pied Piper of Hamelin, and the children who followed so gaily where he piped. These boys and girls wore paper hats with flowing coloured streamers, and they waved the brave red, white, and blue of the Union Jack. Quickly and efficiently they were assigned to their boats, and soon the railings of cruisers and the decks of sailboats were alive with excited children.

Here and there, though, was a little group washed in some way from the main stream, waiting, more or less patiently, for someone to notice them and tell them where to go. One of these little groups consisted of four small boys who were holding out for a sailboat. They stood off to one side and announced plaintively at intervals that "We want to go on a sailboat. We don't want to go on a motor boat." And every so often the smallest of the four, a small, dark, plump little boy, would begin to jump up and down with irrepressible glee, and say, "Which sailboat d'you think we'll be on? Which sailboat d'you think we'll be on, huh?" The flowing streamers on his paper hat danced up and down with him, and his flag waved wildly.

I turned to look up the dock at a little spastic girl who had been sitting patiently in a chair, to see her picked by a stalwart club member and carried down the ramp, and when I turned back, the little group of sail-minded boys had gone. I saw them again later. They were on a sailboat. All four of them. The biggest was leaning nonchalantly against one of the mainmast stays with his hands in his pockets, every line of body saying, "See? No hands!" The fact that he was in imminent danger of falling overboard didn't seem to bother him at all, although it did the skipper of the boat. I saw him remonstrate with the boy, and persuade him that there's nothing unmanly about using your hands to hold on with when you're in a sailboat. The small, dark dumpling of a boy was gleefully trailing his flag in the water, and the other two were scrambling about like agitated monkeys.

Meanwhile, I was sailing, too, on a sailboat. And we had four boys on board. They were from the Children's Hospital, and their names were Bert, Doug, Don, and Ron. Bert was a quiet boy. He hardly said a word, but his eyes took in everything. He saw the great span of the Lion's Gate Bridge pass high over our heads. He saw the tugs towing barges with railroad freight cars from the Island to the mainland. He saw the great, towering freighter pass by us, sending out a running wake of waves that set us rocking. He saw the clouds break and the sun come through and light up the water and the mountains. He looked up and saw the great white spread of the sail as it billowed out, filled with the wind. And he felt the sun and wind on his face.

Don was a tow-headed youngster with an eager, pointed face. At first, he was very quiet, too. Filled with speechless wonder at every-thing. But soon he began some quiet activities of his own. He leaned over the side and trailed his flag in the water. He wordlessly made a tour of inspection below. He drank Coke and ate chocolate bars with great, if silent, appreciation.

Ron was more vocal and also more venturesome. He wanted to steer, please. He was cold, and could he go down to get warm? He thought he was going to be seasick (he wasn't). Could he go up front? Finally, he settled down to an occupation that held his interest for the duration of the cruise. He lay flat on the stern and grasped the rope that towed the dinghy and pulled it towards him until it almost touched our boat, then let it go again. Endlessly. He was playing speedboat. Later, when skipper, crew, and I came to go ashore, the seats of the dinghy were too wet to sit on.

Doug was the littlest boy. He was also the life of the party. There was nothing quiet or the least bit awed about Doug. He wanted to know about everything. He wanted to get into everything. We answered all the questions we could. Such as, "How deep is the water here?" "How long is a fathom?" "Is this a lake we're on?" "Have you got a deck of cards?" "Can we play poker?" "Can I steer?" "Is there a bathroom on this boat?" "Can I have another Coke?" And at regular intervals from the time we were out of the inner harbour and into the bay, "How soon do we get hot dogs?" And he certainly got into everything. One minute he would be sitting beside you asking another question and we were answering it, or trying to, and the next instant, he would disappear and for a frantic moment we would think he'd surely fallen overboard; then up would pop his head through the forward hatch like a jack-in-the-box! We were breathless trying to keep track of Doug. But we couldn't get annoyed with him. There was something about the impish smile and long-lashed, guileless eyes that prevented us from getting annoyed with him, even if we'd wanted to. Which we didn't. He was having the time of his life.

Sometime during the afternoon, when I was savouring the sunshine and the wonderful sailing breeze, I made the remark that it would be wonderful if we could keep right on sailing across the Pacific Ocean. Later Doug remarked, "I like sailing on the Pacific. It's nice. You know, I wouldn't have know this was the Pacific if she hadn't said so!"

All the boys were interested when the skipper wrapped a heavy jacket around Ron and told them its history. That jacket had been present at a good many of the most exciting naval events of the war, including the landing in Normandy. Later, I saw Doug unobtrusively slip it on, too, so he could say he'd worn the historic garment. And they were all very impressed by the array of silver trophy cups down in the cabin: "Gee, did you win all those?"

Then we came into the yacht club anchorage, picked up our mooring, and sent our young passengers ashore in the club tender with those hot dogs in sight at last.

Anchored close by was the great cruiser belonging to the club commodore. On board was the whole contingent from the Preventorium. These TB-threatened boys and girls couldn't mix with the others, and so they had their own band on board, their own private party, complete with all the good things to eat and the balloons and the fun that the others on shore were having.

All around us, children were being landed on the yacht club dock. Up the ramp they streamed, this time following an invisible Pied Piper who piped of hot dogs and ice cream. On the lawn of the club, long tables were set up, each marked with the name of the organization, and loaded down with hot dogs, ice cream bars, chocolate milk, Coke, candies.

At the top of the ramp, balloons and favours were dispensed, and pretty soon loud pops were heard from here and there. And soon after that, a trickle of boys and girls began to return: "My balloon bust, kin I have another?" And then there began another question, a question born of the knowledge that there wasn't much chance of getting those balloons home whole unless the air was let out of them. It was: "Will you untie my balloon, please, I wanta let the air out so's it won't bust." The women who had spent hours blowing them up and tying them all were, well, a little taken aback, but this was the children's day, and they struggled to undo what had been so carefully and painstakingly done. And there's nothing harder to undo than a really tightly tied balloon!

Of course, there was no way to keep track of how many balloons each child got, so no one was really surprised when someone pointed out a solemn boy sitting on the bumper of a parked Ford, methodically cutting the string off balloon after balloon and stuffing the deflated ones in his pockets. When someone else suggested to him when he came back for yet another one that the scissors he had somewhere acquired would be very useful to her, he replied airily, "Oh, if anyone wants to let the air out, just send 'em over to me. I'm working over there on that old Ford."

There is a very small cannon on the lawn in front of the yacht club, its muzzle pointing out to sea. Around it there was gathered a gun crew of three small boys. With balloons as ammunition supplied by one member of the crew, placed on the cannon by a second, and whammed with a stick by the third, the resulting POP gave a most satisfactory likeness of firing the cannon. It was lucky that there were plenty of balloons!

But even balloons lost their fascination when the entertainment began. There were cowboys who sang and strummed guitars, there was a wonderful magician, there were acts by the young guests themselves. Boys and girls of all sizes and colouring, pretty and plain, straight-limbed and crippled, stood and sat and leaned. And watched and laughed and clapped. Most of them had started the afternoon looking reasonably neat and tidy, but now they showed signs of wear. One little girl, whose hair had been done in careful ringlets, was wearing her paper hat atop a stringy mop from which the salt air and the wind had removed all trace of curl. Her face was besmeared with ice cream, and she clutched a balloon under each arm, two bags of candy dangled from her wrist, and her flag, also somewhat bedraggled, stuck out from the load at a rakish angle. Maybe they didn't all look like that little girl, but they all felt like her. Tired and dirty and bedraggled and—happy.

And that was the third annual Children's Day of the Royal Vancouver Yacht Club. Can you think of a better way to give three hundred children a good time? I can't.

CANADIAN MUSIC SYMPOSIUM

March 7, 1950

GOOD MORNING. IS IT TOO EARLY IN THE MORNING TO ASK YOU A QUESTION? Well, I'm going to ask it anyway. How many of you really know what the word symposium means? SYMPOSIUM? You don't know? Neither did I. I had a sort of vague idea that it had to do with a discussion, but it was a very vague idea. So when one day, some months ago, I heard about the forthcoming joint project of the Community Arts Council and the Vancouver Symphony Society, a project called the First Symposium of Canadian Contemporary Music, I decided that I'd better find out exactly what a symposium was.

Now it so happens that our Oxford dictionary is a good, convenient volume for taking to school, and spends most of its time in our older son's desk in those halls of learning. The only other dictionary that we own is a tremendous tome, full of the most amazing information, and weighing about twenty-five pounds, very useful for pressing wild-flowers, and, occasionally, for finding the meanings of unusual words. Scattering long-forgotten four-leaf clovers as I went and the remains of a gardenia and a rose or two, I leafed through this book and finally came upon "symposium" and here's what I read: "1. A drinking together, a compotation; a merry feast; a convivial meeting." This, to say the least, was a little surprising, partly because it wasn't anything like my preconceived idea of the meaning of the word, but more particularly because it didn't sound in the least like a Community Arts Council and Vancouver Symphony Society project. Then I read on. "2. Hence, in a loose way, any collection of opinions, as of commentators on a disputed passage; in a recent use, a collection of short articles, as in a magazine, by several writers, on various aspects of a given topic; as, a symposium on the Indian question." Well, that was more like it. By substituting a collection of musical compositions by different composers for the short articles by various writers, we had, broadly speaking, the First Symposium of Canadian Contemporary Music.

Feeling that there was a definite need for a serious look at Canadian music in all its aspects, the Vancouver Arts Council and the

Symphony decided to sponsor this four-day symposium. It was to consist of four concerts, and the programs were to include only works by contemporary Canadian composers. Then, at the end of these concerts, there would be a panel discussion by musical experts—the symposium proper—and it would be a critique of the aims and trends of Canadian music as they had been exemplified by the four concert programs. And so it was arranged. A general invitation was issued to all Canadian composers wherever they might be living to submit manuscripts for consideration by the symposium committee under Jacques Singer. Mr. Singer is, as you know, the permanent conductor of the Vancouver Symphony Orchestra. In all, there were about one hundred and fifty manuscripts sent in, and from these, the committee selected the best and most widely representative program possible, bearing in mind orchestra facilities, difficulties in orchestration, and all the thousand and one considerations that govern the selection of any program. The final programs include the works of thirty-four Canadian composers. Of these works, some have already been accorded worldwide acclaim, and some are receiving their first performance.

Each of the four programs contains groupings of different kinds of music. The first, which will be held next Sunday afternoon, will be played by a string orchestra with woodwinds. The second, on Monday afternoon, will be chamber music. The third, Monday evening, will be choral. And the fourth, symphony. This last will be on Tuesday evening in the Denman Auditorium, and for that one, the entire program of the regular Pops will be devoted to Canadian music. That night, our western music lovers will be able to hear, for the first time, some of the works that have made Canadian composers world famous. They will hear, for instance, John Weinzweig's "Red Ear of Corn," conducted by the composer himself. They will hear Paul de Marky's "Concerto in B Major," with the composer at the piano. They will hear Alexander Brott's "From Sea to Sea," and others. There will be four guest conductors that night, as well as Paul de Marky as guest artist. I wish there were time to tell you all the items on all the programs, but, of course, that's quite impossible; all I can possibly do this morning is tell you about some of the compositions and their composers that I think all of us out here in B.C. will find most interesting.

Most of us will probably be interested to hear that there are compositions by a number of westerners on the symposium programs. Jean Coulthard, as we all know, was born and brought up and married in Vancouver, and has already brought musical recognition our way with a number of her compositions. The most recent was just a little while ago, when she won an award in the CBC International Service Song competition. She is represented on the program by one of her piano sonatas. At the piano will be Frances Marr, the talented pianist, who, with her violinist husband, Harry Adaskin, has enjoyed such success in New York during the past two years.

Another Vancouverite on the program is Burton Kurth, whose song, "The Christmas Lullaby," will be sung by the Robson Choral Group at the choral concert next Monday night. Other westerners are Charles Palmer, of Victoria, with three songs on the same program; John Beckwith, also of Victoria, whose "Music for Dancing" will be played on the Tuesday night Pops program; and Barbara Pentland, who hails from Winnipeg, but who is at present attached to the Music Department at UBC. Barbara Pentland will have two works on two different programs, "Quartet for Strings" on the Monday afternoon chamber music concert, and "Sonata for Violincello and Piano." She will play the piano part of the sonata herself, with Barton Frank as cellist. You'll be interested to hear that there are four women altogether whose compositions appear on the symposium programs—interesting because, for some reason or other, down through the years there have been very few really outstanding composers who were women. Who knows? Perhaps one of these four Canadian women will one day rank among the great composers of the world's music.

I said before that I could go on indefinitely with details about the symposium, but I must leave something for you to find out for yourselves, either over the air or at the concerts themselves. I hope that just as many people as possible will attend at least one concert. Remember that you'll not only find out for yourself just what Canada is doing in the field of music, but you'll be helping to do your part towards encouraging the development of a truly Canadian music. And in so doing, you'll help to make the thorny path of the musical composer just a little easier to travel, by helping them to gain recognition while they're still alive and can enjoy it! In the past, far too many of our great musicians starved in garrets. That mustn't happen today.

Oh, and one other thing. Those of you who are interested in the opinions of musical experts will thoroughly enjoy the final panel discussion. You will hear Jacques Singer, Harry Adaskin, Barbara Pentland, and John Weinzweig in a critical appraisal of the symposium programs that should provoke much interesting discussion and food for thought for all of us for a long time to come. Proof positive to my mind of the worthwhileness of the First Symposium of Canadian Contemporary Music is the fact that the CBC is carrying parts of three of the programs over its networks, so listen on the air if you can't be present in person. And for those of you who can be present in person, tickets are on sale now at Kelly's, 698 Seymour Street.

So much for the symposium. Now I want to talk about another interesting event, this time in the drama field. During the past thirty-four years, we've come to look forward to the University Player's Club spring production. To us here in Vancouver, it has been a dramatic must on our calendars, and when the club goes on tour after varsity closes for the summer, many of us throughout the province have looked forward to the annual visit of this dramatic group, the oldest club on the university campus. This year marks a sort of milestone for the Player's Club. The spring production will be the thirty-fifth annual play to be staged, first of all here in Vancouver, and later taken on tour throughout the province. And this year's play is called *An Inspector Calls*. It is by J. B. Priestley, and is a story of mystery and intrigue set in the England of thirty-five years ago. I don't know whether the choice of play was governed in the slightest by the fact that the period makes it the same as that in which the Player's Club originated, but it seems like a good idea anyway. *An Inspector Calls* will be seen in the University Auditorium March 14, 17, and 18, and, of course, later in the season, on tour. Tickets for the Vancouver performances are on sale now at Modern Music Ltd., 536 Seymour Street. That's all about the Player's Club for today.

In the few minutes we have left, I'd like to tell you about an interesting experiment that a group of Vancouverites are trying. The group calls itself the Palette and Loom Cooperative Society. They have opened their doors one day a month at 1642 West Broadway, and they are featuring a picture rental service. Yes, a picture rental service. It works like this. Suppose you have a blank space on the wall of the room you are redecorating this year. You know you want a picture for that space, but you aren't quite sure just what kind of a picture. Well, you go to the Palette and Loom, and look at the pictures on their walls. They are all originals, mostly flower pictures and landscapes, and they're not expensive. You choose the one you think would best suit that blank space, and rent—rent, not buy—the picture for a very small sum a month. If, at the end of that time, you decide you don't want the picture, you simply return it. If you do like it, and think you want to own it, you buy it. That way, you're sure of not making a mistake, and that seems to me to be a very good idea when you're buying such an important and permanent thing as a picture. If, of course, you are the sort of person who likes variety in your surroundings, you can have a different picture each month, ad infinitum.

To mention the schools again, almost all schoolchildren hear some classical music and learn to understand it just a little (some of them understand it a lot!). In Vancouver, schoolchildren have a wonderful opportunity, once a month, to actually go to the symphony. On the last Tuesday afternoon of every month, they may go down to the Denman Auditorium to hear the Vancouver Symphony Orchestra play an hour-long, specially arranged program of familiar classics for the price of four ice cream cones. That's only one of the things the Symphony Society does. In the three years that Vancouver has had a symphony orchestra on a full-time basis—and there are only two such orchestras in Canada, the other one being in Toronto—it has brought the people of Vancouver the Pops concert (a weekly program of the lighter classics), as well as the regular Sunday Symphony concert every two weeks. And there's more to the story than that. Every Tuesday night, the CBC broadcasts an hour of the Pops concert for everyone in the province to hear and enjoy. Every Sunday afternoon concert is also broadcast over the CBC for a full hour.

If you enjoy symphony music, you know what a pleasure this has been to you. But, like everything else, it costs money to maintain a symphony orchestra full-time scale. So every year we have Symphony Week to remind us that our Symphony Society needs the support of everyone who is interested in music. Good, strong support, too! This year, someone came up with what sounds like a pretty sound idea to me. Since everyone in the province is able to enjoy the music of the symphony through the radio broadcasts, why not build up a radio membership group of listeners throughout the province, exactly the way the New York Philharmonic Orchestra has its radio membership. For the membership fee of, oh, let's say two dollars, the member would receive advance programs, complete with program notes about the works to be played, something about the guest artists, and so on. Well, why not? It sounds, as I said, like a pretty good idea to me. If you are interested, you could write the Symphony Society at 630 Seymour Street, Vancouver. If there are enough of you, something like that might be begun, and you'd have the satisfaction of knowing that you were doing your part to maintain the work of the Symphony Society, work that so many of you enjoy when the music comes over the air into your homes every Tuesday evening and every other Sunday afternoon.

And that about clears up the agenda for today. One of these mornings I'll be back again with more items of interest about the local scene. Till then, goodbye.

LIFE BEGINS AT FORTY

August 16, 1950

GOOD MORNING. AND IT IS A GOOD MORNING, AFTER ALL! I MUST CONFESS THAT I opened my eyes this morning and looked at the world with a feeling of some trepidation. Would it look a little more tired and dingy, a little more worn around the edges than usual? Or would it, on the other hand, have become rejuvenated overnight and look bustling and fresh and bursting with purpose and energy? I wondered, because one hears such conflicting stories about one's fortieth birthday. Some people who should certainly know say that life is practically over at forty and that one might just as well settle down on the shelf and let the dust collect gently on one for the remaining days of one's life. Other wiseacres insist vehemently that life begins at forty, and with a vigour that I'm sure they never possessed at twenty, set out to prove it.

However, to these now forty-year-old eyes, things generally look pretty much the same this morning. And I'm relieved. I should hate to have to let the dust collect on me while I occupied an inactive corner of a shelf. But, on the other hand, I should equally hate to find myself suddenly filled with that boundless and undirected energy that filled my life at twenty.

I think I'm going to like being forty. Looking back over other birthdays that remain vivid in my memory, they all seem by comparison to have been most uncomfortable.

The first of these occasions that seemed to me to be in any way remarkable was my twelfth birthday. At that time, I was suddenly and frighteningly aware that I was growing up. And I didn't want to. I wished violently that it were possible to remain twelve forever. I remember that my younger sister at eight wished that she could grow up so that she could wear earrings and drink coffee, but at twelve neither of these dazzling possibilities held any charm for me. Perhaps it was because I was fortunate in having eight idyllic childhood years living near the seashore in Melbourne, Australia. Looking back, those years still seem to me to have been composed of warmth and sunshine and golden sand and blue sea. I remember the wonderful wind-twisted grey trunks of the ti-tree along the beaches. The flashing brilliance of a flight of parakeets landing in a cloud of colour in the eucalyptus tree in our backyard. The incredible beauty of the bush land, with gullies filled with giant tree-ferns, with mimosa dropping its golden balls of blossom into the clear brown water of a creek. The smell of billy tea made over a fire of eucalyptus branches on a picnic in the mountains. Oh, I could go on and on spinning word pictures about those years. Maybe it isn't any wonder that I didn't want to grow any older!

And then I was twenty-one and insufferably pleased with my own sophistication, university just behind me, and romance and marriage the most exciting possibilities in the world. That was an uncomfortable birthday, too, with everything quiveringly just about to happen. Whatever anyone says, anticipation is uncomfortable.

Was your thirtieth birthday horrid? Mine was. I felt really old and finished at thirty. That day the world did look worn and dingy, and I resented it very much. I wonder why we cling so hard to the idea of youth? Of course, it's wonderful to retain one's freshness of outlook and a reasonable amount of energy and enthusiasm. But youth? To be young? I don't think it's so wonderful. And that's not just whistling in the dark. Today, on my fortieth birthday, I honestly would rather be forty. I wonder why. Well, at forty, we are mature enough to apply the sum total of our experience to our living. At forty, most of us have had experiences that were unpleasant, done things that we wish we hadn't done; but out of all those things, it is possible to achieve a certain serenity, a peace of mind that I wouldn't exchange to be twenty again for all the tea in China. Most of us have learned patience. At least, a certain measure of it. And if we haven't, we haven't had any happy birthdays, and there's not much point in wishing us many happy returns. Another quality that most of us have acquired is tolerance, tolerance for the other fellow's point of view, for his way of life, for his peculiarities, and even for his faults. Tolerance, of course, is built on understanding, and when we've really learned to try to understand other people, we can find something to like in almost everybody. I've heard people say that they quite enjoy their pet dislikes, and I guess we'd be just too Pollyanna-ish if we didn't have some; but really, it's a lot more pleasant and far more comfortable to like people and things.

Another thing we've learned by the time we're forty, if we're lucky, is how to take it. Small irritations and upsetting incidents don't have the same power to throw us that they once had. And maybe, just maybe, we've learned to take personal criticism. I don't mean the kind that is meant to hurt, but the good constructive kind that is given to us by someone who cares about us.

Perhaps the most important thing of all that we've gained by the time we're forty is a good, solid, workable philosophy for living. I wonder if most forty-year-olds, like myself, have finally discovered that a dependable philosophy for living is to be found in the worn old adages whose meaning is apt to have been a little blurred by time and usage. Sayings like "Do unto your neighbour," and "To thine own self be true." A good many of us have done a lot of pooh-poohing of sentiments like those, myself among the rest. But at forty, I'm not ashamed to admit I was wrong and the sayings right.

And our children. If you other forty-year-olds have been as fortunate as I in having your children while you were young, you, like me, are just beginning to discover what a pleasure your children can be. There's an awful lot of sentimental reminiscing about Johnny and Mary's baby days, and of course they were a very pleasant time. But do you remember six o'clock feedings, and formulas, and daily washings? Do you remember our struggles as we tried to cope wisely and well with behaviour problems, and the terrible time we had getting babysitters for those rare, special occasions when we went out? Would you honestly exchange those days for the teenagers in your home today who help, even if a bit unwillingly, with the dishes; who can scrounge a meal for themselves now and then; who don't mind if you sometimes sleep in on a weekend; who can run errands and carry bundles and make their own way to the dentist? I wouldn't. You know, I've been almost dreading this supposedly difficult period of adolescence with my boys, but I can honestly say that this summer is the first time that I've thoroughly enjoyed my children. They're real companions now. They carry on interesting conversations. Their sense of humour is growing up and we can enjoy family jokes that seem to us excruciatingly funny. And we like to do the same things together, fishing and picnics and camping and going to the theatre and even small doses of listening to music. We can iron out difficulties with discussion, instead of punishment. No, quite definitely, I wouldn't change the status quo. Don't, I hasten to add, run away with the idea that all is peaches and cream in our family. We have our moments. And they're humdingers. But even our moments are on a different level somehow these days, and they're not nearly so upsetting or so long-lasting.

Of course, being forty does have drawbacks. Such as the necessity for acting one's age. One is expected to have a certain dignity, a certain *savoir faire*. That's hardest of all for me. It seems so silly, somehow, that when I have an irrepressible desire to hippity-hop along the street, I must quickly curb the urge and proceed at a matronly walk. And if I feel skittish, I want to act skittish. Well, I've been hearing for some time now that skittishness does not become one of my years, so I guess that now I've finally reached forty, I'll have to become settled and staid.

And another thing is that it is no longer the thing to do to indulge my occasional desire for a ruffle or two on a very full skirt or an off-the-shoulder blouse because, "They are charming on young people, my dear, but you're really not the type, are you?" And then there is the painful necessity of paying more than cursory attention to my face. Once upon a time, a good soap-and-water wash did the trick, but nowadays I feel in duty-bound to my sex to employ all the correct creams and lotions. The same thing applies to the hair. Of recent years it has become more and more necessary to have frequent hairdos for that well-groomed look. Actually though, I've watched the gradual invasion of gray hairs with considerable interest. It would be fun to have what novelists call "a wing of snow-white hair." However, I'm afraid that mine is just going to be plain everyday pepper and salt, or worse, that it will turn that ugly colour so aptly and horribly termed "iron gray." One thing, though: I'm among the fortunate few who don't have to worry about extra pounds. It must be dreadful to have to carry on an eternal battle of the bulge.

And now, looking forward. Well, I figure that there's life in the old dame yet. A good many years of active and enjoyable living. Years for fishing and camping and cooking and canning. Years for reading and writing and going to plays and listening to music and all the other things that make life pleasant. Maybe not in such large mouthfuls, but surely after forty we've learned not to be greedy. And if the pace is a little slower as time goes on, there will be more leisure time for thinking, for putting into practice that hard-earned philosophy of ours.

Last night, just for fun, I looked up forties in my *Bartlett's Quotations*, and rather to my surprise I found something. It was this stark and somewhat cryptic statement from a poem by a man called

Howard Mumford Jones: "They say the forties are the dangerous ages." Well, perhaps so. We shall see! Having found that one, I looked up some more. Bartlett always affects me like that anyway; I never can stop once I start. This time I looked up age. As you can imagine, I found plenty there. Here are a couple of them. "Count your garden by the flowers, Never by the leaves that fall; Count your days by the golden hours, Don't remember clouds at all; Count your age by friends, not years." That one, too, is open to a bit of speculation, it seems to me. Think it over: "Count your age by friends, not years." Hmm. The last one is from John Webster: "Is not old wine wholesomest, old pippins toothsomest, old wood burns brightest, old linen wash whitest? Old soldiers, sweetheart, are surest, and old lovers are soundest." How about it, those of us who are forty and facing the future?

And now, just a word about tomorrow's program. As some of us are already aware, New Westminster is about to launch a symphony orchestra. That this is a major undertaking, we in Vancouver, who have weathered the buffetings of many storms in the effort to keep our symphony, well know. The story of how the Royal City came to want a symphony of its own, of the trials and tribulations of those who have been working towards the accomplishment of their objective, will be the subject of my guest tomorrow, Mrs. W. A. Thompson. Herself a musician, and I believe a member of the orchestra, Mrs. Thompson will, I am sure, be able to tell us a very interesting story.

Until tomorrow then.

Postman, Pound Man

July 17, 1952

GOOD MORNING. THIS IS SALLIE PHILLIPS. WELL, THIS MORNING I WANT TO TALK about two members of the community whose job is community service. The job of one of them is taken so much for granted that he's an almost unnoticed figure as he trudges on his rounds day after day, bringing us our mail. Yes, I'm talking about the postman. Of course, I realize that in the country you have either rural mail delivery—and well I remember what a thrill it is to walk out to the big metal mailbox when the flag is up—or else you make a daily expedition to the post office and pick up your mail from your own glass-fronted box in among rows of other boxes. In the country, as I remember it, the arrival of mail is an event not to be lightly taken. Here in the city, though, I think we're more inclined to take our daily mail delivery just as casually as we accept our milk delivery. The only thing to upset us would be if something happened to disrupt this service that we accept so unthinkingly. And most of us never stop to consider what it means to be a postman. If we think about it at all, we say airily, "What a healthy occupation—out all day in the fresh air!" And sometimes in winter we clear the front steps of freshly fallen snow, "So the postman won't slip." And there our interest ceases. Because, like everything else in life that doesn't affect us personally, we don't use our imaginations. I never would have given the life of the postman a second thought either, if I hadn't been brought face to face with its somewhat grim reality.

It happened this way. Early in the new year I took a new kind of job, for me anyway. It involved house-to-house selling, and this in turn involved a sort of groundbreaking process, delivering letters to the houses we were to call on before we, so to speak, arrived on the doorstep with the goods we were to sell. These introductory letters were a bit of an experiment on the part of the firm for which I was working, so they didn't want to invest a great deal of money in the experiment. The firm saved money by having us deliver the letters ourselves, thus cutting out postage. Well, after my experience, I have no kick whatever against three-cent postage! I allotted myself a certain number of blocks for the first morning, and set forth, firmly clutching the necessary number of letters in one hand, and in the other, my purse and my umbrella, for the weather looked uncertain. At this point, I'm sure you're saying to yourself, "The postman doesn't carry an umbrella and a purse." Of course he doesn't. And I soon discovered why.

The first house was plain sailing. A neat concrete path led up to a front door in which was set a letter slot at a normal height and that operated in a normal way. I managed to slip the letter through it by only shifting the handful of letters into my left hand—already, you'll remember, somewhat encumbered with the purse and the umbrella—and poking it through. The next house, though, was a bit tougher. The letter slot was placed about six inches from the ground and had an abnormally stiff spring on the flap. The letter wouldn't poke. The only way to do it was to set everything down on the doormat and use both hands, one hand to open the slot, and the other to drop the letter through it. By the time I had gathered all my belongings together again, I had begun to have more respect for the postman. The next house along the row was surrounded by a neat picket fence with a small, securely fastened gate. The fastening was one of those hook and eye arrangements, and since either the gate or the fence had sagged a little, it took a little heft of the gate—this way—at the same time as undoing the hook. In view of what I was already carrying in both hands, it took a bit of figuring out. Maybe you can put everything down on a doormat, but you just don't lay your belongings down on the sidewalk while you wrestle with a gate. I began to wonder what I'd do if there were many gates like that. After all, this was only the third house. In addition, having been thoroughly impressed in my youth with the importance of always closing the gate behind one, I was faced with the necessity of repeating the whole performance on the other side, not to mention a complete repeat performance after I had delivered the letter! Because sometimes there are young children who are kept in the garden by that gate. Not to mention dogs. Well, I did it . . . once. After that, I'm afraid I forgot my upbringing, and left the gate open while I delivered the letter, and only closed it on my way out again. I always did, though, remember to close it as I left . . . almost always. Once, however, as I proceeded on my way, I thought that I had deftly closed the gate behind me with a muscular flick of the wrist, to find that either I wasn't as deft as I thought I was, or my wrist wasn't as muscular. I was walking away when I heard an irate female voice shriek, "Don't you know enough to close the gate?" Scarlet to the ears I slunk back and carefully reclosed the gate.

A minute ago, I mentioned that fences and gates are often intended to enclose dogs. It is with much feeling that I add, "With reason!" You can be halfway up the front steps when Fido 'round the back becomes aware of an alien presence and advances growling to the attack. There's something most terrifyingly ferocious about a strange dog who makes menacing dives at your ankles. It isn't even particularly reassuring when his mistress, her head done up in pin curls, pokes her head through the door and says soothingly, "Don't mind Fido, he wouldn't bite anyone. It's just that we like to have a watch dog 'round the place." Ordinarily I'd agree with her. I have dogs myself. But while I was doing that job, I was in imminent danger of becoming a dog hater instead of a confirmed dog lover, which I'd always, until then, considered myself. Here and there on my route I'd encounter a sign, "Beware of the Dog!" I'd beware all right. That gate remained unopened, and the inhabitants of that household remained unenlightened as to the wonderful opportunity they were missing in not having the chance to buy the product I was selling. Another sign I met along the way was the terse, "No Agents or Peddlers." Upon self-examination, I decided that in my present capacity I was both agent and peddler, and, especially if the steps were long and steep, I'd pass that one by, too.

And speaking of steps, if you are familiar with Vancouver you've undoubtedly noticed how many of the older houses have steep flights of steps, particularly houses built on hillsides to encompass one of the many wonderful scenic views we have here, of mountains or water or both. And along my route there was one long block of these houses, with not one but two flights of steps, a garden one and a house one. The first two I laboured all the way up and all the way down, once again because I was brought up to believe it was bad manners to cut across people's gardens. And once again my upbringing went by the board, and I grew very adept at jumping flower beds and even low hedges and in following a faint but well-defined path already worn there by the paper boy and possibly by the postman.

Which brings me back to the postman. Pity the poor postman! Consider what obstacles he faces as he starts out each day on his

rounds. An infinite variety of gates and fastenings, since man's ingenuity seems to enjoy devising new and unusual gadgets of this kind,
from loops of bent wire to spring catches of fiendish complexity. And
inside the gates, dogs. Dogs of all shapes and sizes and dispositions.
And steps. And doors. And in the doors, letter slots that are set in at
every conceivable height from ground level up, and with flaps that
slide, stick, or spring, and, oh so few that open with a finger pres-
sure to let the letter slip through easily! Sometimes I think that there's
a good deal to be said for standardization, for eliminating the right of
individual determination, especially for gates, dogs, and letter boxes.
Most particularly if you're a postman!

Well, so much for my personal acquaintance with that community
service. The other one that I mentioned at the beginning carries with
it even less thanks and, in addition, a lot of unpopularity, too. I'm
referring to the pound man, the officer of the town government who
enforces the laws concerning dogs. It was not an altogether happy
accident that caused me to come to understand the point of view of
the pound man. As some of you already know, we have dogs. And
since we do not have a fence all the way around our property with
a well-fastened gate at the entrance, our dogs do at times leave our
garden and roam at will through the neighbourhood. And not everybody appreciates having somebody else's dog wandering through
their garden, burying bones and scratching up grass as dogs will do.
You can't blame them. If we didn't have dogs I probably would
object, too. As it is, I long ago resigned myself to simply hoping that
the seedlings will grow up, and being quite blind to the divots the
dogs dig in the lawn. So, things being as they are, it was inevitable
that I should meet the pound man.

One afternoon, the doorbell rang and I went to the door. A man
stood there in an olive drab uniform, his cap pushed back on his
head, and the cold light of battle in his eye. "Madam," he said coldly,
"your dogs are a nuisance in this neighbourhood. Something will
have to be done about them."

Now, ordinarily I'm a pretty polite person. But something in the
suppressed belligerence of his voice made me suddenly furiously
angry. "Excuse me," I said, "but I think I'd better go into the other
room for a minute and find my temper. I'm in danger of losing it."
And I left him standing on the doorstep while I did go into the other
room and try to calm down.

In a minute I came back. "Okay," I said, "Won't you come in and we'll talk about this." He did come in. And we did talk it over. For nearly an hour. By the time he left, a couple of cups of coffee and several cigarettes later, the pound man and I thoroughly understood each other. It took a while, though. First of all I asked him how he knew the dogs in question were our dogs. He told me that everybody said they were, and anyway they were two big black Labradors. I pointed out that in this neighbourhood there are a lot of black Labs, and just the fact that they were seen together didn't mean that they were our two. As it turned out later, one of them was ours, and the other was a friend of his, and not a Phillips at all. Anyway, I insisted that he couldn't prove anything on this basis. Then I asked him why he had to be so belligerent about the whole thing, and explained that it only made me feel belligerent, too.

"Lady," he said, "somebody phones in and complains that a dog is tearing up their garden, and I drive right out there, by which time the dogs have disappeared, and I can't do anything anyhow. But I'm greeted at the door by the person who put in the complaint as though I was the owner of the dogs. She scolds me and takes out on me her disapproval of all dogs and of these dogs in particular. By the time she's finished with me I'm hunting around for someone to take out my irritation on—"

"And today it's me," I continued. "You'd get much further and have everything much more pleasant, if you didn't. Take me, for instance. I'm really quite a reasonable soul—"

"Most of 'em ain't, lady, most of 'em of get nasty right away, so I might just as well start off that way." Once again I saw his point, even if I didn't quite agree with him.

So we chatted about dogs and their habits and people's reactions to them, and he ended up by telling me a very funny story. A call came in to the pound office one day to come immediately to a certain address, where a lot of dogs were ruining a newly seeded lawn. The pound man climbed into his truck, and as he was driving down the street on which the man lived he saw a black spaniel walking sedately down the sidewalk. Since the new law prohibiting dogs from being off their own property without their owner was in effect, he stopped the truck and wheedled the dog into the back. He might as well show some results. When he arrived at the address in question there were no dogs anywhere in sight, and the owner of the lawn, which did show signs of a rampage, was furious. He told the pound man in no uncertain terms what he thought of dog owners who didn't keep their dogs on their own property. "Why," he bellowed, "my dog stays right in our back yard where he belongs!" The pound man finally got away, drove back to the pound, booked his lone catch, and took his place at the desk. In a few minutes a car that he recognized as having been parked in front of the complaining gentleman's house drove up, and the erstwhile irate one entered the office sheepishly. He stammered a little, "When you were over our way, you didn't happen to pick up a black cocker did you?"

"Why, yes," said the pound man, "I did."

"I was afraid of that," said the irate one. "My wife was sure of it. You see, it's our dog!"

And now you know how I found out first-hand about the troubles of the postman and that the pound man is a very human person. And, oh yes, our dogs did not go to the pound—not then!

This is Sallie Phillips, saying goodbye until tomorrow.

5. HISTORIES

THE LEGEND OF THE THUNDERBIRD

September 30, 1946

The B.C. School Broadcast script I've chosen to include here is one of many that I did over the years. This one is called "The Legend of the Thunderbird." It was the first in a series, and to get the material for it I went down to the office of the Native Brotherhood on Hastings Street, near the intersection of Hastings and Main. Back then, as even today, to visit that neighbourhood was considered quite venturesome. I climbed the dark stairs to the Brotherhood's office. There I was fortunate enough to find, and to interest in my project, the one man with the inherited right to tell the story of the Thunderbird. He spoke so slowly and in such a carefully measured way that I was able to write down what he said word for word. Which is why, in dramatizing the story, I have so often used Dan Cranmer's own words.

CBR
Dress Rehearsal: 12:30 p.m.
On the Air: 2:00–2:30 p.m.

CAST:
Frankie (Girl)
Thunderbird
Don
Dan Cranmer
Uncle
Great Spirit
Aunt
Gwanalis

BIZ: *Music up.*

ANNOUNCER: Thunderbird Tale! Don and his sister Frances—or Frankie as she was called—still remember that holiday they took this summer up the coast. It all began one evening when they and their uncle were on the deck of his fishing boat, (FADING) looking at the stars.

BIZ: *Up sound of fishboat chugging, hold through.*

UNCLE: Nice night, kids.

FRANKIE: Oh, Uncle, it's grand. And pretty soon there'll be a moon, too, won't there?

DON: Will we be at Alert Bay in the morning, Uncle?

UNCLE: Yes, Don. Getting bored with the trip?

DON: Well, I'll be glad to get there.

UNCLE: Kids these days don't take time out to enjoy what they're doing. Always wanting to be at the next thing.

FRANKIE: How d'you mean, Uncle?

UNCLE: Take me, for instance. Ever since I made enough money to buy this boat, I've fished up and down this coast, and I never get tired of it. The sea looks different every day. So does the sky.

FRANKIE: Like stormy in winter and quiet in the summer?

UNCLE: And bright and glittery in the sun, and all colours in the evening and shadowy and mysterious in the moonlight. Why, on a night like this, I can imagine all sorts of things.

FRANKIE: What sort of things, Uncle?

UNCLE: See that deep shadow over there? Near that little island? I can just imagine that a great war canoe filled with Indians is about to come shooting out of the shadows in pursuit of us.

DON: Indians! Indians are old stuff! Who cares about those old times!

UNCLE: That's what I meant when I said that you modern kids don't take time to enjoy things. After all, the Indians are part of this country we live in. Their history is part of ours. We should take an interest in them, in their way of living, their legends, their skills.

DON: But Uncle, kids can't be bothered with all that old stuff.

FRANKIE: I think it's interesting. Will we see many Indians at Alert Bay?

UNCLE: Uh huh. And see a lot of their totem poles, too.

DON: What's so int'resting about an old totem pole?

UNCLE: For one thing, Don, they tell the story of the Indians. And for another, the carving of totem poles is a dying art. There aren't many Indians left who can really carve a totem. There are a good many who make imitations of the real thing to sell to tourists, but precious few who really know what they're doing.

FRANKIE: And there are a lot of the real ones at Alert Bay, Uncle?

UNCLE: There's an old Indian cemetery up there where there are some of the best left in the country.

FRANKIE: And they all tell a story?

UNCLE: Each one tells the story of a family or of a tribe. Each one of the strange birds and animals and figures has a meaning.

FRANKIE: Why didn't the Indians write their stories, Uncle?

UNCLE: Because before the white men came, the Indians had no written language. Matter of fact, there's an old legend about that.

FRANKIE: Do you know it? Will you tell it to us?

DON: Pooh! Fairy tales and stuff.

UNCLE (CHUCKLES): Why not hold your pooh-poohing till you know a little more about it, young man! Yes, I know the story, but up at Alert Bay there is someone who can do a much better job of storytelling than I.

FRANKIE: Who is he?

UNCLE: An old Indian who is practically the only one left alive now who can tell the true story of the Thunderbird.

FRANKIE: The Thunderbird! I've heard about the Thunderbird! That's the big bird on top of the totems, isn't it?

UNCLE: That's right. A lot of Indians use the Thunderbird symbol, but actually only one tribe has the right to use it. And this old Indian I was telling you about is one of the few of the tribe left alive.

FRANKIE: Would he tell us the story, d'you think, Uncle? Would he?

UNCLE: I think he would. That is, if Don didn't keep saying "Pooh!" every two minutes!

FRANKIE: Oh, you wouldn't, would you, Don?

DON: Aw, I dunno. Might be all right, I s'pose.

FRANKIE: Oh, but it is exciting, Don. Promise you won't be rude to him?

DON: Well . . .

UNCLE: Rude or not—and if you want to hear the story, you'd better not be rude—you kids'd better trot off to bed now. We'll be anchoring at Alert Bay early in the morning, and you'll want to be ready to go ashore and see your Aunt, (X) and she'll be wanting to see you!

BIZ: *Start fading on (X) into sound of wind.*
HOLD B.G. [background] *thru and children talking.*

FRANKIE: Golly, Don! I just couldn't wait to walk over here and see the old cemetery! Oh look! There are the totems, just as Uncle said.

DON: They're awfully ugly looking!

FRANKIE: I don't think so. They look kind of nice, leaning at all those funny angles, and the colours all soft from being out in the rain so many years, and the carving on them. Specially when you think of all the things they mean—you know, like Uncle said.

DON: Give me a real streamlined airplane any day.

BIZ: *There is a slight pause.*

THUNDERBIRD: Why?

DON: Aw, I dunno. Say! Where'd you come from?

FRANKIE: Yes, where did you come from? I didn't hear you coming.

THUNDERBIRD: Oh, I just came. This place is especially interesting to me, so I'm around here quite often. Tell me, Don, why would you rather have an airplane than a totem pole?

DON: Aw, totems are old stuff. And besides, what good's a totem?

FRANKIE: Say, how did you know my brother's name? And how did you get here without us hearing you? Who are you, anyway?

THUNDERBIRD: I'm the Thunderbird, Frankie.

FRANKIE: How do you—the Thunderbird! But . . .

DON: Pooh! I don't believe it! The Thunderbird is only a stuffy old bird in an Indian fairy tale.

FRANKIE: Don! Don't be so rude. Tell me, are you really the Thunderbird, like that big bird up there on top of that totem pole?

THUNDERBIRD: Yes, you might say I am that bird up there! But I was a man, too, you know.

FRANKIE: Why did you come to talk to us?

THUNDERBIRD: Because I was interested in why Don would rather have an airplane than a totem. It seems to me that they both have their uses.

DON: But an airplane . . .

THUNDERBIRD: Just a minute. Look, Don. Your airplane can carry you over the country. But can it tell you the story of that country?

DON: Nooo . . .

THUNDERBIRD: A totem can.

DON: Who wants to know the story of the country anyway?

THUNDERBIRD: Don't you want to know how things came to be the way they are in British Columbia? Aren't you interested in how B.C. grew and why?

DON: We-ell . . . I don't like history much, if that's what you mean.

FRANKIE: I am, Mister Thunderbird. I'd like to know all the things that have happened to make things the way they are today.

THUNDERBIRD: See that building over there? Come with me and we'll go over and see it.

DON: But I didn't see that building there a minute ago!

FRANKIE (WHISPERING): Don't you see, Don? That proves he's the Thunderbird! He can probably do all sorts of things.

THUNDERBIRD (OFF MIKE): Come on. Hurry up!

FRANKIE: Come on, Don. Hurry! I want to see what's in that funny-looking place.

DON: Okay. Okay. I'm coming.

BIZ: *Up gradually sound of drums (as in disc) thru.*

THUNDERBIRD: This is a community house. In the old days it was the meeting place of my people. In it took place all the ceremonies and celebrations of the tribe. Around the great bonfires that blazed beneath its high roof, the sacred dances of my people took place. Look! I will show you.

BIZ: *Drums beat for an instant, then fade and hold B.G.*

THUNDERBIRD: Come on, we'll go into the Community House. It's smoky, isn't it? But look over there, directly below the ridge-timber high overhead, you can see two great bonfires blazing, spitting red-hot cinders onto the hard-packed dirt floor. And there, at a safe distance from the fires, see that low wooden railing, completely encircling the fires? Those people standing around the railing are the Indian spectators, watching the dance that is taking place within the circle.

DON (WHISPERING): Say! Look at the feathers and things they're all wearing!

FRANKIE: Ssh! We'd better be quiet.

THUNDERBIRD: That tall man wearing the white moccasins and the brown trousers, and the shiny jet-black tunic of bearskin is a young brave. See how the black fur sets off the rows upon rows of snow-white beavers' teeth that are sewn on his back and breast.

The dancer who is performing now is dressed like a rooster. See! His entire costume is of white feathers with great tufts of them on his head and around his ankles. You can't see any of the man himself, can you? Not even his face. Look how he's clutching that long wooden spear, also decorated with feathers.

FRANKIE (WHISPERING): Look, Don! All the dancers have their faces streaked with black and yellow and red paint!

DON (ALSO WHISPERING): Just look at that guy over there!

THUNDERBIRD: That guy over there is one of the Indians who is waiting his turn to dance. Do you notice the colours—the bright green blanket about his body, the brown fur headgear, and the many chains of scarlet beads around his neck? And everybody here seems to be under the strange spell of the drums. See, even barefooted children, scarcely old enough to walk, are weaving back and forth in time to the rhythm. And there are the old women with papooses slung over their backs, waving their hands and nodding their heads.

BIZ: *Drums up full, then face under and out.*

DON: Whew! Boy! That was super!

THUNDERBIRD: You found it interesting after all?

FRANKIE: Oh yes, Thunderbird! It was wonderful! To think that all really happened!

THUNDERBIRD: Yes, it still does happen sometimes when my people, what are left of them, get together for a great celebration.

FRANKIE: And we never heard about it?

THUNDERBIRD: And you never heard about it. It seems to me that you and Don would do well to learn a little more about this wonderful province you live in.

DON: But how? How are we to learn the really int'resting things?

THUNDERBIRD: Some you can learn by asking questions, and some you will learn by keeping your eyes open and seeing them. And if you want to find out about something very badly, just ask the Thunderbird! (PAUSE)

DON: Hey, Frankie! He's gone!

FRANKIE: So he has. Wasn't he a nice person?

DON: Yeah. I liked him. I wonder if he meant what he said about telling us more?

FRANKIE: Yes, I think he did. But I think he meant us to find out things ourselves in those other ways he mentioned, too.

DON: Maybe there's more in this than I thought.

FRANKIE: Let's see if we can't learn more about the Indians, Don.

Let's ask Uncle. And maybe we could look up that old Indian he talked about.

DON: And get him to tell us about the Thunderbird!

FRANKIE: (X) Oh Don, this should be fun!

BIZ: *Start fading on (X). Fade in children talking to Dan Cranmer.*

FRANKIE: We've come to ask you if you will tell us the story of the Thunderbird, Mr. Cranmer. You are Dan Cranmer, aren't you?

DAN: The story of the Thunderbird? Well now, and who told you I could tell you that?

FRANKIE: Our uncle said you knew the story better than anyone else. Won't you please tell it to us?

DON: Yes. Please tell us the story, Mr. Cranmer!

DAN: Your uncle was right. I am the only man now alive who can tell the story of the Thunderbird. The young men no longer care about the story of their people. Only I of the tribe know. Perhaps I will tell you, and you will remember, and tell other white children, and then the true story will not fade forever from the memories of men.

DON: We will! We promise we'll remember every word just as you tell us!

FRANKIE: And when we go home after the holidays we'll tell all our friends.

DAN: Well. Then I will tell you. Many, many years ago, before the deluge, there lived a man by the name of Gwanalis (GWAH-NAH-LIS). At that time, the Great Spirit was fixing everything where it should be. One day, the Great Spirit came to Gwanalis and asked him.

GREAT SPIRIT (ON ECHO MIKE): What would you rather be, Gwanalis? A big mountain?

GWANALIS: No. I do not wish to be a big mountain. Maybe before the end of this world I might break into pieces.

GREAT SPIRIT: Would you rather be a great big solid rock? Then you'd live forever.

GWANALIS: No, I do not wish to be a rock. Maybe one of these days I would break in two.

GREAT SPIRIT: Would you like to be a river? Then you'd flow forever and ever. There would be no end to you then.

GWANALIS: Yes, I'd rather be a river. Every variety of fish would swim up me, and all the men who came after me would feed on them.

GREAT SPIRIT: All right, then. You will be a river, and you will flow forever. There'll be no end to you. And different kinds of fish will be coming up you.

DAN: Then Gwanalis became a river, and the river is called Gwani (Gwah-nee) to this day. Then the first salmon went up the river. Then this salmon got ashore up the river in one of the places that he liked the best. Then he became a human being. He was just looking around for a place to build a house when the floods came.

BIZ: *Up sound of river. Increase to roar. Establish and fade to B.G.*

DAN: So he entered the river again and became a fish, as he was in the first place. He went up the river and went behind a mountain to get out of the strong current that was flowing. He waited round behind the mountain until the waters went down. When the flood was down he came down the river again to the same place he had got ashore the first time.

BIZ: *River out.*

DAN: There he became a human being again. He was looking around on the banks to find some rocks to make tools with, to make an adze. Then he went to work hewing some timbers to build a house with. . . .

BIZ: *Sound of hewing and physical exertion.*

DAN: He has already put up the posts on which he will lay a big timber when he hears a noise.

BIZ: *Sound of someone clearing his throat loudly.*

DAN: He looked around and saw a big bird sitting on a big rock just a little below where he was working. So he said to the bird:

SALMON: Oh, Master, I wish you were a man to help me with my work.

THUNDERBIRD: I am a man. I shall help you.

DAN: The big bird pushed up his big beak, and showed his human face. Then he pulled his beak down again over his face. He flew up and put his big talons on the beam that Hwahwasa (for such was the name of the salmon when he became man) had hewn, and flew up with it and put it on top of the posts that were already standing there. Then he flew over and alighted again on the big rock, which is called today Quanwaas. (FIRST A FLAT) Then he came out of his feathers and spoke to them, ordering them thus:

THUNDERBIRD: Fly into the skies again, oh my feathers. When you are back in the skies again, do not thunder except when some of my descendents die!

DAN: Then the Thunderbird turned to Hwahwasa and said:

THUNDERBIRD: I will be your younger brother because I became human after you. I will build my house beside your house on the lower side of the river bank.

DAN: And so they became brothers, and the name of the brethren to this day is Gigilkum, which means First Ones. And that, white children, is the story of the Thunderbird.

BIZ: *Music up and fade. (Something narrative yet wild, perhaps "Die Walkure.") Fade into:*

DON: Golly! All that really happened to the man we saw in the Indian cemetery!

FRANKIE: Isn't it exciting, Don?

UNCLE: So you've changed your mind, eh, Donnie boy? Decided you do want to hear more about the Indians?

FRANKIE: Oh, Uncle, he couldn't help wanting to hear more after seeing the community house and hearing the real story of the Thunderbird!

DON: I want to hear more about all sorts of things that've happened in British Columbia, too, not just the Indians.

UNCLE: One thing at a time, my boy, one thing at a time! With a good healthy curiosity like that, you'll learn all you want to, in time!

AUNT (COMING ON MIKE): Did I hear someone talking about learning?

FRANKIE: Oh Auntie, yes! Don and I want to learn all there is to know about the Indians in B.C.! And about a whole lot of other things, too.

AUNT: Well, your uncle's a good one to tell you about our Indians. He's been interested in them for years.

DON: Tell us, Uncle! Tell us, won't you, huh?

FRANKIE: Oh yes! Tell us, Uncle.

UNCLE: Well now, I thought that perhaps we could talk about the Indians of today.

AUNT: You'll have to do it right here in the kitchen then, because someone's going to help me dry the dishes.

UNCLE: We'll all help. Then we can all talk. How's that? Come on, kids, get busy!

BIZ: *Intermittent clatter of dishes. Continue thru.*

UNCLE: Now! How much do you know about Indian children your own age?

FRANKIE: Golly, Uncle, not very much, I guess.

UNCLE: Did you know, for instance, that the boys and girls at the Indian School in Mission scooped all the prizes in the Pro-Rec competitions there?

DON: Golly! They must be pretty super athletes!

UNCLE: They are, if we just give them a chance to show what they can do. And then there are the boys and girls in the school at Bella Bella, who showed they are pretty good in a different way.

FRANKIE: How, Uncle?

UNCLE: Ever hear of the Latham Foundation?

FRANKIE: I know! Our teacher told us! That's the society in the States that's something like our SPCA, isn't it?

UNCLE: That's right, Frankie, the Latham Foundation tries to prevent cruelty to animals, and one of the ways is an international poster competition they hold every year. Well, the children of the Bella Bella School heard about this competition, and entered some posters.

DON: And won a prize?

UNCLE: And won several prizes. Pretty good, wouldn't you say?

AUNT: There, that's all the dishes done. Let's sit round the table and talk. Wait, I'll light the lamp. (PAUSE) There. You know, children, I've always thought that the reason behind those Indian youngsters and their posters was one of the nicest stories your uncle tells.

FRANKIE: Tell us the story, please, Uncle.

UNCLE: It's sort of a nice story at that. Okay, here it is. Many of the tribes of B.C. Indians have a strong tradition that kindness to animals is one of the important rules of everyday living, and they have stories to prove it, too. The Indians around Bella Bella belong to one of these tribes, and it is because of this very strong belief that the Indian children of Bella Bella were interested in entering the competition.

AUNT: Just goes to prove, I always say, that if you believe in something hard enough, you can always do it well!

UNCLE: And then, of course, there are all the Indian schools that have branches of the Junior Red Cross. Why, I heard that there are more than twenty-five active groups, all working to help other less fortunate children than themselves, both in B.C. and in Europe.

FRANKIE: Did they raise money themselves, Uncle?

UNCLE: They certainly did. Yep, kids, the Indian children are pretty fine Canadians, if you ask me! So are the grown-ups, for that matter. The Indians who fought overseas in the army and airforce made a very good showing!

DON: You mean they were brave fighters?

UNCLE: That's just what I do mean, Don.

DON: Tell us more, Uncle.

UNCLE: No, Don, that's enough for tonight. It's off to bed now, for me at any rate. I have to be away off up the coast at dawn.

DON: Fishing?

UNCLE: Yes, Don, fishing. But there's no room for kids this trip.

DON: Oh well, I guess we might as well go to bed, too. Come on, Frankie, let's go up.

FRANKIE: Okay. 'Night Auntie. 'Night Uncle.

BIZ: *General chorus of goodnight. Door opens and closes. Sound of children's footsteps going upstairs.*

FRANKIE: Oh Don, look out the window! Isn't it beautiful?

DON: And doesn't that island look spooky? I wonder if there are any old totem poles or anything over there?

THUNDERBIRD: That's Haddington Island, Don.

FRANKIE: Goodness! You scared me, Thunderbird!

DON: You sure do arrive unexpectedly don't you?

THUNDERBIRD: That's one of the nice things about being the Thunderbird!

FRANKIE: Did you say that island is Haddington Island?

THUNDERBIRD: Yes. And there is something interesting about it.

DON: There is? What?

THUNDERBIRD: Haddington Island has played a very important part in the history of British Columbia.

FRANKIE: Has it? I never heard of it before.

DON: Tell us about it, Thunderbird.

THUNDERBIRD: I'll tell you next week, Don, because you've ASKED THE THUNDERBIRD!

ANNOUNCER: Next week, Frankie and Don will learn about Haddington Island and its place in B.C. history, because they remembered to ASK THE THUNDERBIRD. This has been the first in a series of programs about British Columbia, presented to schools by the British Columbia Department of Education in cooperation with the CBC. May we remind listeners once more that if they have not yet received a copy of the Teachers' Bulletin, they may secure one by writing to the Director of School Broadcasts, c/o CBR, Vancouver, B.C.

BIZ: *Theme up.*

ANNOUNCER: This program was from Vancouver. This is the Canadian Broadcasting Corporation.

INTERVIEW WITH BEA WOOD, PLAYER'S CLUB ALUMNA

March 14, 1950

During my years in radio, I did many interviews with all sorts of people, from artist Toni Onley to actors and actresses in the plays and musicals of the time, like Jean Stapleton, who was appearing in Harvey. All of the interviews—with the exception of this one, with Bea Wood—were done with prepared questions from me and ad-lib responses and conversation. I don't remember why I wrote this one out in full, preparing not only my questions but also her responses. What I do remember is that the process of her reading my prepared responses set us off into the most undignified fits of giggles, which were so uncontrollable that I suspect the engineer took us off the air momentarily—we almost had to go off the air permanently.

SAL: GOOD MORNING. THIS MORNING WE HAVE A VISITOR IN THE STUDIO. WE are going to talk about the Player's Club, and especially about Player's Club tours. Perhaps some of you may have heard me mention one day last week that this year marks the thirty-fifth anniversary of the founding of the University Player's Club, and that this week in Vancouver will see the thirty-fifth anniversary production of this, the oldest club on the university campus. That's why I thought it would be interesting to ask one of the early members to come here and talk about the plays of other years and about some of the amusing incidents that happened on tour. I was fortunate indeed to be able to persuade Bea Wood to draw on her recollections, because Bea has acted, toured, chaperoned, and directed the Player's Club. I can't help but feel that unless we had her husband, Professor Wood, on the program, it would be impossible to have anyone who knows more about all phases of the Player's Club's activities. Perhaps, Bea, you'll start off by telling us when you first became a member.

BEA: That was in 1919, Sallie, just three years after the club began. It was organized, you know, in the fall of 1915 and presented its first spring play in 1916.

SAL: In 1919? That makes you practically a charter member, doesn't it? Tell me, did you make it first try? I remember that I tried out for two years running before I finally made the grade.

BEA: No, I didn't make it on the first try. In those days, tryouts were very slapdash affairs, not a bit like the carefully prepared occasions that they are today. Four of us were handed a Shakespeare play, and told to read the parts on page so-and-so. I think I found myself declaiming the part of Richard III.

SAL: Without any preparation?

BEA: Without any preparation! And I have no doubt that I did it very badly. Anyway, I didn't get in. The following year, though, I tried out again, and this time I was successful.

SAL: And from that day, you've been active in Player's Club doings?

BEA: Well, not so much after 1931. But up until then, yes, I was pretty active.

SAL: First of all as an actress.

BEA: Yes, and then I was chaperone and mistress of makeup for two or three tours.

SAL: And you did some directing, too, didn't you?

BEA: MENTION NUMBER OF PLAYS DIRECTED. NAME THEM.

SAL: And, of course, you've appeared in Player's Club Alumni productions, right up to this year, when you had a part in *The Winslow Boy*, the Club's Dominion Drama Festival entry. So if anybody knows the Player's Club, you do, Bea. Did they have tours when you first joined the club?

BEA: As a matter of fact, Sallie, the way those Player's Club tours of the province began is quite interesting. My husband and I were talking about that last evening.

SAL: Then do tell us about that. But, first of all, I think we should explain that your husband, Professor Wood, was not only the originator of the club, but also its guiding spirit for, what—fifteen years?

BEA: No, seventeen.

SAL: And wasn't yours and Mr. Woods' romance one of the famous Player's Club tour romances?

BEA: Yes, it was. It budded on my first tour, and blossomed forth in an engagement announcement two years later.

SAL: And thereby, I bet, hangs a tale!

BEA: But not for publication?

SAL: No, Bea, we'll respect the sanctity of your romance, even though we'd like to hear about it! Well, though, to get back to the way tours began.

BEA: After the presentation of the first play, the president of the university—it was President Wesbrook then—asked us to put it on in New Westminster and Victoria. And so the annual tour was born in that small way the very first year.

SAL: When was the biggest tour?

BEA: In 1931, I think, when the spring play was presented twenty-five times throughout the province.

SAL: 1931? Why, I did the costumes for that year. The play was *The Young Idea*. I had no idea that any sort of a record was established that year.

BEA: Well, one was. And at different times the spring play has been staged in at least thirty-one communities in B.C. on various tours.

SAL: It was felt, wasn't it, that tours served a very real purpose?

BEA: That's true. In the earlier days, there was a widespread feeling throughout the province that only Vancouver benefited from the existence of a provincial university. These annual visits by the Player's Club did much to bring at least one student activity to the attention of the smaller cities and towns, and the tours did a lot to correct wrong impressions about the limited enrolment of the fast-growing university.

SAL: In other words, the tours did a sort of travelling public relations job for the university?

BEA: That's right. And, of course, the student players had a wonderful time doing it!

SAL: I know. I've always regretted that my dramatic ability didn't amount to enough to get me a part in a spring play so that I could go on tour. I've heard more stories about the things that happened during those scrambled weeks. . . .

BEA: Scrambled is right. One-night stands in strange halls and theatres, hopping on and off trains, lugging our own bags. I remember one tour when we actually made up for the evening performance on a tossing sea when the boat was really going wop with a wiggle between. I was doing the makeup that year, too.

SAL: That must have been an uncomfortable experience.

BEA: It was. In more ways than one.

SAL: Tell us about it!

BEA: Well, that was the year the club put on *Friend Hannah*, and I was chaperone, and also the putter-on of makeup. We had played the night before in Comox, and were due to appear that evening in Powell River. And there was a storm. A really bad one. So bad that the boat was late in starting, and then we had to take the outside passage. It wasn't long before we realized that we weren't going to arrive in Powell River until after the curtain was supposed to rise. So we decided that the least we could do was get everybody made up before we docked. We could save that much precious time. And make up we did, with everything sliding back and forth, and our tummies heaving up and down.

SAL: Oh dear, what a business! Were any of you actually seasick?

BEA: We most certainly were!

SAL: All of you? Even you?

BEA: Not quite all of us. Two of the cast remained disgustingly robust through it all, and they kept poking their heads in at the door and laughing at the rest of us as I desperately applied grease paint to pea-green faces. And, yes, after a while it was too much for me, too, and I was seasick.

SAL: I can just imagine you all. Bright grease paint over pale faces and, every so often, someone making a dash for the rail.

BEA: It was rather grim.

SAL: I should think that was a triumph of understatement. What finally happened?

BEA: We docked eventually at a quarter to nine, and, believe it or not, the curtain went up at a quarter past!

SAL: On, of course, the principle that the show must go on. But how did you ever get the scenery up?

BEA: Oh, we didn't. We used curtains and things. The audience didn't seem to mind. After all, they had been sitting waiting for us to arrive for one solid hour.

SAL: You must have all been feeling pretty wobbly, too.

BEA: As a matter of fact, after the awful effects of the seasickness wore off, we were all starving. Fortunately, however, the good citizens of Powell River had prepared an after-the-theatre supper for us, and it was a real spread. We did full justice to it!

SAL: I can imagine.

BEA: And then there was the time in an Okanagan town when we were presenting a long four-act play by Bernard Shaw, called *You Never Can Tell*. The theatre was the local movie house, and, since that was the day of the silent films, music was supplied by the regular three-piece orchestra. It so happened that the third act curtain of that particular play found the two young principals in a clinch. The orchestra, accustomed to movie endings, struck up "God Save the King," whereupon the audience rose with one accord and began to stream from the theatre. As far as they were concerned, the play was over!

SAL: How very disconcerting! Whatever did you do?

BEA: Freddie rushed out in front of the curtain and finally managed to persuade them to return to their seats for the last act.

SAL: That's one instance of anything happening. Were there more?

BEA: Yes. That was the year, in still another Okanagan town, that the lighting failed.

SAL: You mean all the lights went out?

BEA: All of them!

SAL: I don't see how you could get around that one. How did you? Get oil lamps?

BEA: No. It was more ingenious than that. All the cars parked outside the hall were turned facing towards the building, and we finished the play by headlight.

SAL: You turned on the headlights and played by the light they gave through the windows?

BEA: Yes.

SAL: Well. That was ingenious! Tell me, Bea, what has become of these intrepid young actors? Did that rigorous training lead to many professional acting careers?

BEA: Quite a few. Several are well known to radio audiences, through CBC drama programs.

SAL: I can think of some. Lister Sinclair and Dorothy Fowler.

BEA: And Marjory Ellis and Bill Buckingham and Eileen Seaton.

SAL: How about legitimate stage?

BEA: Our very first leading lady, Jessie Todhunter, whose husband, John Taintor Foote, died a short while ago in Hollywood, played with the Henry Miller Co. in California, and later on the New York stage. And then there are Dorothy Adams, Mary McLeod, Beth Gillanders, John Glen, and Art Hill.

SAL: So the rugged training did pay off sometimes. As a matter of fact, Bea, there are a good many old Player's Club members whose names we hear these days in connection with drama in one form or another. Sidney Risk, for instance. He's directing this year's spring play, *An Inspector Calls*. Sidney and I were the same vintage—1931.

BEA: That was the year that three student plays shared the Christmas plays program.

SAL: In some ways, it seems a very long time ago, and in some ways, it seems like yesterday! Sidney has stayed faithfully with the theatre, hasn't he?

BEA: He has. And finally had the reward of seeing his Dominion Drama Festival entry win the regional award.

SAL: Yes, *Noah*. I wish I'd seen it. It certainly was a much-discussed production. Well, the Player's Club couldn't have made a better choice of director for their thirty-fifth anniversary production. I do hope *An Inspector Calls* will be a great success.

BEA: It's a good play by a good author.

SAL: J. B. Priestley.

BEA: And I understand the cast is excellent. Tonight's the first public performance, isn't it?

SAL: Yes, and it will be played for the general public again on Friday and Saturday evenings in the University Auditorium. And I'm told that tickets are on sale now at Modern Music Ltd., 536 Seymour Street. You know, Bea, I envy the cast of that play.

BEA: Yes, I think I do, too. Even with all the hard work that putting on a play involves, the fun and experience outweigh it.

SAL: And they have the tour to look forward to. It won't be long until the hurdle of the spring exams is crossed, and then they'll be packing scenery and costumes and travelling around B.C. in the very loveliest time of year. No wonder romances blossom on Player's Club tours! Think of all the places they'll see and the people they'll meet.

BEA: Very friendly people, too. And very kindly audiences. Well, I wish them luck.

SAL: So do I. All the luck in the world to the Player's Club thirty-fifth annual spring production, *An Inspector Calls* by J. B. Priestley. Thank you ever so much, Bea, for coming here today and reminiscing about some of the things that have happened during those thirty-five years. Let's heave a sigh and say goodbye, feeling just a *leetle* nostalgic and sentimental.

Goodbye, and I'll be back again soon with more items of interest about people and happenings right here in B.C.

So Many Children

February 22, 1951

Annual general meetings were usually pretty dry and boring affairs, so in 1951, when I was honorary secretary of the Board of Directors of the Children's Aid Society of Vancouver, I suggested doing something very different for the occasion of the fiftieth anniversary meeting. "So Many Children" was the result. In addition to being broadcast, a recording of the program was played at the meeting. Production of the program required the co-operation of all sorts of willing volunteers: professional actors and actresses, board members past and present, boys and girls from the B.C. School Broadcasts, and technicians from CBR and CKMO, as well as the use of their station facilities. The program was a success, and fifty years later, I am saying again, thank you to each and every one of you.

NARRATOR: There was an old woman who lived in a shoe; she had so many children, she didn't know what to do; so she gave them broth without any bread; and she whipped them all soundly and put them to bed!

MUSIC: *Short and introductory.*

ANNOUNCER: SO MANY CHILDREN. The story of the first fifty years of the CHILDREN'S AID SOCIETY of Vancouver, by Sallie Phillips.

MUSIC: *Short bridge to:*

MAN: Hmm.

WOMAN: What is it, dear? Something interesting in the paper?

MAN: Uh-huh. I see here where it says that the Children's Aid is having its fiftieth anniversary next week.

WOMAN (THOUGHTFULLY): Its fiftieth anniversary? Why yes, I guess it soon will be fifty years.

MAN: Make you feel a bit ancient?

WOMAN: Yes, it does. Fifty years! I've always sort of felt that the Children's Aid and I grew up together. Fifty years, and in some ways it only seems like yesterday. (PAUSE, THEN LAUGHING A LITTLE) It brings back memories.

MAN: Was it very bad?

WOMAN: Being in the Home, you mean? I guess I thought so then. But no, it wasn't so bad. Not nearly so bad as before I was in the Home.

MAN: You know, in all the years we've been married, you've never talked about that time.

WOMAN: I guess I didn't want to remember. I don't know why not, because every time I read or hear about the Children's Aid, I do remember. Every time I read or hear of some new development in child welfare, I remember. And my heart lifts to know that the world still cares about lost and lonely children.

MUSIC: *Gradually up to high and fade through:*

NARRATOR: Throughout the length and breadth of Canada there are men and women to whom the fiftieth anniversary of the Children's Aid Society brings back memories.

1st WOMAN: I remember the smell of dirty rags I tried to wrap around me to keep me warm.

1st MAN: I remember how my body ached from being beaten.

2nd WOMAN: I was hungry. Do you know what it means to be hungry?

2nd MAN: I was hungry, too. I stole.

1st WOMAN: But the Home was clean and warm.

1st MAN: I worked in the Home, goodness knows, but I was only punished when I was bad.

2nd WOMAN: And in the Home we ate three times a day.

2nd MAN: In the Home I did not need to steal.

NARRATOR: Like most organizations of the day, the Children's Aid had a motto. It was: "We Protect the Little Ones." And we read in the first annual report of the Society that its founders asked government:

VOICE: To so frame the laws that the children of drunken, dissolute, and immoral parents should, by the protection and aid of the law, have such help and assistance as would enable them to grow up to a good and useful life, and not by the force of their surroundings become untruthful, unclean and immoral, thereby adding to the pauper and criminal classes of the community.

NARRATOR: All stories must have a beginning, and the story of the Children's Aid begins in 1901 when the Children's Protection Act, petitioned by the Local Council of Women, was rushed through the provincial legislature and the Children's Aid Society incorporated to give citizens of goodwill the right . . .

VOICE: To protect a young girl from the horrible cruelty practised by her mother when mad with drink.

NARRATOR: The beginning of the story of the Children's Aid coincides very nearly with the beginning of the story of the raw young city of Vancouver, and of a Canada just on the threshold of nationhood. All three of them have grown up together in a world of bewildering changes. A tough time to grow up in, the first half of the twentieth century! Everything grew and increased and multiplied with terrifying rapidity. Things like knowledge and inventions and people. Especially people! And with the people, problems.

VOICE: There was an old woman who lived in a shoe; she had so many children, she didn't know what to do!

NARRATOR: The founders of the Children's Aid must have felt like that old woman. The first annual report, presented on November 25, 1902 stated:

VOICE: Your directors at the time of the incorporation of the Society expected to be called upon to deal with some two or three cases during the year, but they regret to say that their work has by force of the evil conditions existing in the City, been more extensive than could be imagined by any person or persons, twenty-nine children having been made over by law to their care, control, and protection.

NARRATOR: You see? They thought the first home was crowded with seventeen, but before they knew it there were thirty-five children in it. By the end of the year, there were forty-four, with a waiting list of twenty-nine. They moved to a larger·Home, and almost immediately it also was too small for the number of children to come in. Nor were any of these early Homes equipped for the purpose for which they were used and they were always dangerously overcrowded.

SOUND: *Roll of thunder, growing louder.*

JANE: Ooooh, I'm frightened. I don't like thunder. (SCREAMING) Mummie, Mummie, the lightning's coming right in here. Oh, don't let it, Mummie! Don't let it!

MARGIE: It's only a thunderstorm. Stop yelling for your Mummie, Jane. You know perfectly well your mother isn't here!

JANE: C-c-c-can I come into your bed then, Margie? You're so big and brave.

MARGIE: Come on, then. My goodness, you are a crybaby.

SOUND: *Loud thunder.*

MARGIE: Oooh! That one was close!

JANE (SCREAMING AGAIN): Oh save me, save me, Margie, the lightning's going to burn us up.

MARGIE (CROONING): Hush Jane, hush. Margie will look after you.

SOUND: *Up gradually the sound of flames, up through:*

JANE: Margie! What's that, Margie?

MARGIE (UNCERTAINLY): I . . . don't know. It . . . sounds like a fire crackling.

VOICES (SHOUTING OFF AND COMING ON): FIRE! FIRE! FIRE!

SOUND: *Flames up and out.*

NARRATOR: Yes, in that house, overcrowded with children, fire did break out. Mercifully, the flames were confined to the roof, and the children were quickly rushed to safety. None was hurt. The old record reads like this:

VOICE: On March 11, 1906, during a heavy storm, the roof of the Davie Street Home caught fire. It was wonderful the way people came forward to help. The Old Hospital was vacant, and through the efforts of Sir Charles and Lady Tupper and Mrs. Atkins, we obtained the use of that building, and that night the children were sleeping in their new temporary Home.

NARRATOR: But even when, through the efforts of Mrs. Atkins, property was bought on Wall Street, and a planned Home built, it, too, proved inadequate after just six months. The need grew faster than the means to fill the need. The Children's Aid had so many children, it didn't know what to do. Sometimes, though, the directors had very definite ideas about what they ought to do—or not to do. In the annual report for 1910, we find:

VOICE: Your committee has dealt this year with some questions of no ordinary importance, one of which is the numerous applications made to receive the offspring of misguided and unfortunate girls. Several girls have come to the city from various parts of Canada and some from the Old Land with a view to hide their shame, and have made application, sometimes even before the child is born, to have the little one committed to the Society immediately after birth. Your committee is of the opinion that the Society was not established for the purpose referred to.

NARRATOR: That, apparently, was one responsibility the board quite obviously did not intend to accept! But then in 1913, read:

VOICE: Your directors deplore exceedingly that so many young babies have been deserted during the year, which has made it necessary to provide a special ward for them, which of course adds very materially to the cost of maintenance.

NARRATOR: Strange, wasn't it, that those worthy men and women never seemed to connect the Society's refusal to accept illegitimate children and the tragic plight of a number of deserted babies whom circumstances later forced them to take in?

VOICE: There was an old woman who lived in a shoe; she had so many children, she didn't know what to do; so she gave them broth without any bread . . .

SMALL CHILD (READING): Dear Daddy South: I'm sorry you thought I was bad last night. I didn't say there was worms in the porridge, I said there was worms in the carrots, and there was! Your little girl, Linda.

NARRATOR: But perhaps the little girl that was Linda grew into the woman whose earliest memories are of being hungry. Better worms in the carrots than no carrots at all? Anyway, I've found the odd worm in homegrown carrots, haven't you? And remember that all the vegetables, eggs, poultry, and some of the fruit eaten in the Wall Street Home was grown on the five-acre lot the Home stood on. In 1913, the Rev. Mr. Unsworth said:

VOICE: Another attractive thing I like about the report, if you will permit me to say so, is the smell of the barnyard. I can hear the crowing of cocks, the cackle of hens, the mooing of cows. It makes one feel that some boys would rather wish their father would be a defective father and disgrace himself so they can be adopted into this farm.

NARRATOR: I wonder if the boys in the Home would have agreed with the Rev. Mr. Unsworth? The main thing, though, is that in spite of the occasional worm in the occasional carrot, there was both broth and bread in the Wall Street Home. Not fancy fare, you understand, but good—and enough!

VOICE: There was an old woman who lived in a shoe; she had so many children, she didn't know what to do; so she gave them broth without any bread; and she whipped them all soundly and put them to bed . . .

NARRATOR: By and large in those early years of the Children's Aid Society, the children were happy and well cared for. But sometimes things did happen.

MOTHER (AGITATED): Operator, will you give me A1426. Yes, please. (PAUSE) Hello? I want to speak to Mr. South. (PAUSE) Hello, Mr. South? This is Mrs. Wood speaking. Mrs. Wood, yes. You boarded my two sons John and George while my husband and I were out of town. My mother died, Mr. South, and we went up-country to attend the funeral. What? Yes, John and George Wood. We left them with the Children's Aid and paid for their keep because we were assured that they would be well looked after in the Home. Were they? Indeed they were not. I've just found a great bruise on little John, which both boys tell me he got from a beating. Yes, that's what I said, a beating! (ALMOST HYSTERICAL) Can you tell me, Mr. South, by what right your matron beat my three-year-old son? What's that? Really, Mr. South, you don't beat a three-year-old boy just because he wets his bed! Mr. Wood and I are going to prosecute the Children's Aid. I am not being hasty. If things like that are going on in the Home, Mr. Wood and I intend that the public shall know about it! Let the directors investigate first? Why should we? I think it's something everybody should—what? My children do *not* exaggerate. Well, yes, maybe they have sometimes, but I don't think . . . The good name of the Children's Aid? Well, of course, if I hadn't thought the Children's Aid had a good name, I wouldn't have sent the boys there when Mother died and we had to. Give the Children's Aid a chance? Why? Well, yes, I see what you mean. Maybe you're right, Mr. South. I see. You say you'll have the whole thing properly investigated by the board of directors? Well, I know you have very fine people on your board. Can I depend on that? I'll hear from you tomorrow? I'd better hear, Mr. South. If I don't, Mr. Wood and I will proceed with our action. Very well, then, I'll hear from you tomorrow. Yes, thank you. Goodbye, Mr. South.

NARRATOR: The investigation was begun, the matron admitted the spanking, and Sir Charles Tupper, Chairman of the Board, wrote to the matron:

VOICE: Meanwhile you admit you spanked this child of three, though you say you did it in a very mild way. I deem it my duty to suspend you as matron, pending the investigation, for whether you caused the wound to the child or not, no matron should spank a child of such tender age.

NARRATOR: And at the investigation itself, we find Mr. Wade in the chair:

MR. WADE: This spanking has been admitted by the matron. The board would now like to hear if this sort of thing has occurred before.

FIRST BOY: I am eight. I have been here with every matron. We are well treated at the Home. This matron whips about the same as the others.

SECOND BOY: I am ten years old. I have been in the Home a long time. I saw John Wood spanked. She used a hair brush. She didn't hit him very often or very hard. He didn't cry much. He cried just a little while. He stopped before I went to sleep. I've often been whipped. There used to be more whippings then than there are now. They are not as hard now as they were before; we are not as bad now as we were before.

NARRATOR (RUEFULLY): I guess she did whip them all soundly and put them to bed, all right. The committee, though, after seeking several medical opinions, and after closely questioning the matron, withdrew the charge of cruelty because it could not be proved that the bruise was caused by the hair brush, and not by a fall.

INDIGNANT WOMAN: Such goings-on!

NARRATOR: Didn't you ever spank your children, madam? And in those days, spanking was the approved means of discipline. And anyway, who was to judge standards of competence and training for the institutional staff of those early days? There weren't any professional social workers, you know. And you must admit the members of the board did their level best to be fair to everyone concerned, and that they certainly felt a great sense of personal responsibility towards the children in their care.

INDIGNANT WOMAN: Just the same . . .

NARRATOR: Just the same. Fires in overcrowded buildings, worms in the carrots if not in the porridge, whippings without a justifiable reason. It doesn't sound good, does it? Somehow, though, I think maybe it was all part of the difficult business of growing up, and that for each of those incidents, and probably other incidents, unrecorded ones, there were reasons why they happened. You see, the important thing is not that these incidents happened.

INDIGNANT WOMAN: You don't think it's important that these things happened to helpless children? Shame on you!

NARRATOR: You misunderstand me, madam. Certainly no one wants to see children mistreated. But no disease, you know, was cured until someone got sick. There was a reason why these things happened. There had to be. After all, the founders of the Children's Aid and its board members through the years were men and women of goodwill. They saw a need and tried to fill it. They gave a great deal of time and thought and energy to try to help children to be happy, not to make them unhappier. There was, for instance, Mrs. T. E. Atkins, a woman whose name appears and reappears in the early records, a woman whose concept of the Mission of the Society was ahead of the years during which she worked, but who worked, nevertheless, without thought of self for the realization of her ideal. Away back in 1902, she said:

VOICE: To rescue homeless, abused, and neglected children in the earliest age of their misfortune, finding homes for them in well-approved families, to continue a watchful care over them . . .

NARRATOR: Could it be helped that there were more homeless, abused, and neglected children than there were homes for them to live in? Even today, foster homes are often scarce and hard to find, but her ideal is becoming a reality.

VOICE: To give assurance to the poor and needy that their children, if left destitute, shall be watched over with tender care . . .

NARRATOR: Those were not the words of people who would permit the maltreatment of the children they sought to protect.

VOICE: To protect society against its greatest foes, ignorance and vice, by securing proper home training and education for destitute little ones that otherwise might fall under the most evil influences . . .

NARRATOR: And this we know they tried to do. Does a worm in a carrot outweigh the training and education they tried to give the children?

VOICE: To urge upon parents their supreme responsibility for the proper care and training of children so that they may grow up into good citizens and be a credit and honour to the State . . .

NARRATOR: Today these ideals are being realized. Today it is the joint responsibility of government and individual citizens to see that the children of our civilization receive the care and protection Mrs. Atkins wished for them fifty years ago.

INDIGNANT WOMAN: That's all very well for the members of the board. Maybe they were doing their best. But how about the staff? I bet they didn't do more than they were paid to do!

NARRATOR: How wrong you are, madam. J. P. South, founder and secretary of the Society for many years, the Daddy South of Linda's letter, worked virtually for nothing. For, to be exact, the princely sum of one hundred dollars a month, forty of which he paid to his stenographer. And in 1914 we find the staff of the Home, overworked and harassed, cheerfully offering to take a twenty per cent cut in pay when the directors diffidently approached them to accept a cut of ten per cent. And in 1915, a year that was described as one of unprecedented anxiety and unforeseen difficulties, we find that one of these unforeseen difficulties was that seventy-one children went down with measles in a period of five weeks and the matron, Mrs. Lockhart, did all the nursing, whereby, according to the record, the Society was saved the large sum which would have been paid if a nurse had been employed! There was more than love of money motivating the men and women who ran the Children's Aid!

INDIGNANT WOMAN (SLIGHTLY MOLLIFIED): Well then, what was the matter? Why did these things happen?

NARRATOR (CLEARING THROAT): Will you pardon me if I proceed in verse?

INDIGNANT WOMAN (SURPRISED): Why, yes indeed!

NARRATOR:
 Those men and women of early days
 Toiled tirelessly a trail to blaze.
 A way out of the tangled wood
 Where lost-lorn children hopeless stood.
 Some tools they had, a very few,
 The will to help, the urge to do,
 But skills they lacked, they needed gold,
 A dreary story often told.
 The money was the first to come,
 At first a minus minimum
 From government molasses-slow
 In moving on from status quo.
 Yes, government began to take
 A share of future worlds at stake.
 A country's children after all
 Will write its story, rise or fall.
 And now at last our men of State,
 Grown wise, and so, compassionate,
 Give freely of their golden hoard
 For foster children's room and board.

INDIGNANT WOMAN:
 You interest me I must confess.

Go on, I'm all attentiveness.

NARRATOR:

    With pleasure, ma'am. We said before
    Our men and women lacked the lore
    For clearing trails for childish feet,
    To make a wide and sunny street.
    Of working standards there were none,
    To indicate: This should be done,
    This do not do, This person hire,
    This one is not what you require.
    And then on the horizon broke
    The first of a new kind of folk.
    They called them social workers, and
    Skillfully they took command.
    Now out of darkness, doubt, and fears
    That followed them down through the years,
    The people who so long had fought
    For rights of children, dearly bought,
    Began to see their dreams come true.
    Not all, not nearly all, but you
    Don't hope to reach in fifty years
    Perfection, if you're pioneers!

NARRATOR (CONTINUES NOW IN PROSE): Do you understand a little better now, madam? Are you a little less irate?

INDIGNANT WOMAN (NOT INDIGNANTLY NOW, QUESTIONINGLY): But these things still happen. Why, just the other day there were headlines in the papers.

NARRATOR:

    Isn't it most always true,
    A paradox we all should rue,
    That scandal's always headline stuff,
    Good news is seldom good enough?
And after all, the story of the Children's Aid Society, like the story of all things that make progress as men progress, is one of:

MUSIC: *A short sharp punctuation after each word:*

NARRATOR: Castigations . . . investigations . . . recommendations . . .

frustrations . . . reorganizations . . . approximations—in short, growth!

MUSIC: *A rolling crescendo to an abrupt stop.*

VOICE: There was an old woman who lived in a shoe; she had so many children, she found out what to do; so she gave them love along with bread, gave not a whipping but care instead . . .

NARRATOR: Hmm. Mother Goose, modern version. Not bad either, not bad at all! And do you know, in the story of the first fifty years of the Children's Aid you can practically put your finger on the point in time when the new version began to be the true version? It's a point just midway into those fifty years, and it came as a result of two of those paradoxes we all should rue, two headline scandals closely concerning the operation and administration of the Society. The frankness and thoroughness of the delegation of board members who were then called to appear before the Public Accounts Committee brought excellent results. Mr. Ian Mackenzie reported the findings of the committee to the Legislative Assembly:

VOICE: Upon examination, irregularities of a somewhat serious character were found to exist. Your committee finds that these irregularities were largely attributable to a lack of business training on the part of the Secretary. Your committee recommends that steps be taken to ensure that, if necessary, proper assistance be provided in the Home to supervise reports, committals, and correspondence. Your committee points out that although only regularly committed children are provided for by statute, yet a very large proportion of the expenditure is incurred on behalf of non-committed children cared for by the institution, and that the care of these children is a moral, if not a statutory, obligation. Your committee finds that there has been a very unfortunate lack of co-operation between the Secretary of the Children's Home in Vancouver and the Provincial Superintendent of Neglected Children, and respectfully points out that the cause of the children is of much more importance to this Province than the personal career or personal feelings of either of these two gentlemen, and recommends that more co-operation be manifested in the future. Your committee were greatly impressed with these representations (by members of the board of the Children's Aid), especially in view of the fact that these directors have been at great personal sacrifice of time, money, and energy, rendering consistent and devoted service to the cause of the orphans and neglected children requiring assistance, and your committee consider it a duty as a matter of public record to express their appreciation of the services rendered by these public-spirited citizens. The committee also recommends that the present government grant of three dollars a week for each child in the Home be increased to four in view of the fact that the Home does commendable work in receiving and caring for orphan and neglected children from all portions of the mainland, and to assist the cases not regularly committed, and to enable donations to be used for other necessary purposes in the Home . . .

NARRATOR: Along with castigation and frustration and all the "-ations" we spoke about, sometimes comes vindication. This report by the Public Accounts Committee to the legislature was vindication indeed, not only verbal, but financial as well.

VOICE: There was an old woman who lived in a shoe; she had so many children she found out what to do . . .

NARRATOR: The finding-out came with the results of the 1926–27 Child Welfare Survey conducted under the leadership of Miss Charlotte Whitton. The survey report recommended first:

VOICE: The appointment of a thoroughly capable administrative officer.

NARRATOR: Found in the person of Miss Laura Holland, a woman whose ability to inspire others to work for the cause of all is a continuing story today in 1951.

VOICE: Re-housing the children in the old Home on Wall Street, repeatedly condemned . . .

NARRATOR: In 1928, the old Home was demolished. Some of the children were placed in a safer building on the Wall Street property, and many in carefully selected private homes, boarding homes, institutions, and in free foster homes under supervision. And then in 1930 the new building at 1675 West 10th was formally opened. But there still remained the establishment of four new services, one of which would be considered sufficient to justify a separate organization.

VOICE: The creation of a child protection field service, the organization of social investigation and supervision in connection with free home placement, the establishment of a boarding home system, and the development of baby care.

NARRATOR: Miss Holland, with four assistants and in four years, fulfilled all this. An heroic accomplishment by an heroic woman. And in addition to all this she won acceptance for what seemed to many to be untried and dangerous policies. Professional social workers came under this heading, and so did foster homes. But even that wasn't all. Miss Whitton's report had also stated:

VOICE: The administration officer must also plan for the installation of a case-record system, for the introduction of adequate medical and psychiatric services and night supervision . . .

NARRATOR: All this Miss Holland and her four assistants accomplished. But there is still more. The report survey went on:

VOICE: The Society is in a key position to lead in the building up of local standards of child care and the protection of the child born out of wedlock . . .

NARRATOR: The Children's Aid had always led the way in the building up of standards of child care. After all, before the Society existed there was no child welfare program of any sort; its story is the story of child welfare in British Columbia. And as far as the protection of the child born out of wedlock, well, the responsibility refused so long ago by the early directors now became part of the Society's program, and today forms a large part of its work.

VOICE: There was an old woman who lived in a shoe; she had so many children, she found out what to do; so she gave them love along with bread; gave not a whipping but care instead . . .

NARRATOR: So from that time on our Mother Goose rhyme, modern version, is not fiction, but a fact. In the years that followed, the program begun by Laura Holland has developed new strengths, new depth and breadth and meaning.

WOMAN: My family and I have found happiness again because the Children's Aid showed me where I was wrong. . . .

NARRATOR: That's known in the social work profession as preventive case work.

YOUNG WOMAN: I came to the Children's Aid before my baby was born. I knew they'd give me the help and understanding I needed so badly. You see, my baby had no father.

NARRATOR: Good service to the unmarried mother is the best community insurance against haphazard placement of babies. And children born out of wedlock need protection.

LITTLE BOY: How do you know that lady wants children? Do you just knock on the door and ask her?

NARRATOR: Children's Aid Society caseworkers search for, select, and supervise foster homes for the care of children who cannot or should not stay with their own families.

WOMAN: I can't have children of my own, and my husband and I do so want a baby. . . .

NARRATOR: The sooner children deprived permanently of the care and interest of their own parents have the chance to form permanent ties with other parents, the better. By "other parents" is meant, if possible, adopting parents.

LITTLE BOY: I hate you! I hate everybody! Go away or I'll kick you!

NARRATOR: Poor kid! He's been badly damaged already by life. Before he'll be able to form new family ties, he needs the kindly, impersonal, understanding atmosphere of a small institution. Sometimes, too, adolescent boys and girls need the specialized flexible services available only in a small institution.

IRATE WOMAN (NO LONGER IRATE): You know, I was pretty mad at you back there, but now it all begins to make sense!

NARRATOR: We lay no claim to perfection, madam. We only hope for progress. We try to keep the services of the Children's Aid flexible enough to meet the needs of each individual child, and we try to look forward enough so that as our knowledge of the emotional needs of children grows, our program may grow also.

MUSIC: *Sneak in under and hold through*:

And so, today, the Children's Aid Society of Vancouver looks back over fifty years of growth. The path it's followed, by and large, has not been so very different from the one laid down for it so long ago by Mrs. Atkins. Sometimes the going has been rough, but always wandering feet have found the way again. And now ahead of it there stretches an untravelled road. We set our feet on the road and turn our faces to the future.

MUSIC: *Out.*

NARRATOR: And because there are still, and there will always be, SO MANY CHILDREN, we say this pledge, made to children everywhere by the members of the Mid-century White House Conference on Children and Youth:

CHORUS: To you our children, who hold within you our most cherished hopes, we make this pledge:

WOMAN'S VOICE: From your earliest infancy we give you our love, so that you may grow with trust in yourself and in others . . .

MAN'S VOICE: We will recognize your worth as a person and we will help you to strengthen your sense of belonging . . .

MAN'S VOICE: We will respect your right to be yourself and at the same time help you to understand the rights of others, so that you may experience co-operative living . . .

WOMAN: We will work to conserve and improve family life, and, as needed, to provide foster care according to your inherent rights . . .

MAN: We will intensify our search for new knowledge in order to guide you more effectively as you develop your potentialities . . .

WOMAN: As you grow from child to youth to adult, establishing a family life of your own and accepting larger social responsibilities, we will work with you to improve conditions for all children and all youth . . .

MUSIC: *Sneak in under and bring up through:*

CHORUS: So may you grow in joy, in faith in God and man, and in those qualities of vision and of the spirit that will sustain us all and give us new hope for the future.

NARRATOR:
    Using the tools of a united community,
    Working as one for the blessing of all,

Each service together in harmonious unity,
Forward we answer the trumpet call.

MUSIC: *Up to triumphant high and out:*

MR. LORD: The fiftieth anniversary meeting of the Children's Aid Society stands adjourned.

About the Author

Sallie Phillips was born in Midland, Ontario, in 1910. Her father was a civil engineer, and because of his work, the family moved to Melbourne, Australia, in 1915. Eight years later, they settled in Vancouver. Sallie studied at the University of British Columbia and in Paris, then married and had two sons. In the early 1940s, volunteer work in her neighbourhood, the Dunbar suburb of Vancouver, led her into simultaneous careers in freelance radio broadcasting and the emerging field of public relations.

From about 1946 to the mid-1950s Sallie broadcast programs over most of Vancouver's radio stations, but most of her work was for the CBC, which broadcast her programs locally, nationally, and internationally. These were the days before tape-recording came into general use, when it was the spoken word, read from a script—as opposed to tape recordings linked by commentary—that described people, places, and events. With a smooth and expressive voice that "could really take it off the paper," and infinite curiosity, Sallie was a natural for radio. But she was also a natural for public relations, and her highly successful career in that field eventually overtook her work as a freelance broadcaster.

After retiring in the late 1960s, Sallie and her husband Dick travelled extensively in B.C., the rest of North America, and Europe, in pursuit of wildflowers, fly fishing, and other pleasures. They moved to Vancouver Island in 1972, and have lived quietly in Victoria since 1986. Sallie and Dick have six grandchildren and seven great-grandchildren.

Other Titles Available from Sono Nis Press

By Snowshoe, Buckboard & Steamer
Women of the Frontier
by Kathryn Bridge

Florence Agassiz, Eleanor Fellows, Violet Sillitoe, and Helen Kate Woods lived and travelled throughout British Columbia in the nineteenth century. All four women left detailed accounts of their lives and adventures in journals, letters, and sketches, which Kathryn Bridge has incorporated into her perceptive analysis. The rich historical narratives in *By Snowshoe, Buckboard & Steamer* reveal the enormous courage, determination, and compassion of these pioneering women.
Winner of the 1998 Lieutenant-Governor's Medal for Historical Writing!
ISBN 1-55039-086-4 • 231 pp • 6 x 9 • $19.95

Henry & Self
The Private Life of Sarah Crease 1826–1922
by Kathryn Bridge

Sarah Crease was an extraordinary Englishwoman whose long life and marriage encompassed both privilege and hardship, scandal and accolade, in the old world and the new colony of British Columbia. Kathryn Bridge's thoroughly researched biography includes extracts from Crease's letters and diaries, and an annotated edition of Crease's 1880 journal that records her travels with her husband.
ISBN 1-55039-071-6 • 216 pp • 6 x 9 • $21.95

Rattenbury
by Terry Reksten

Francis Mawson Rattenbury was only 25 years old when he was commissioned to design the new Parliament Buildings for British Columbia. The flamboyant "Ratz" soon became the most sought-after architect in the province. He designed almost every important building of his time in BC.

The sensational story of BC's most important architect, his triumphs, his battles, his scandalous life and grisly murder by his wife's lover and the subsequent trial are all carefully documented in this award-winning biography.
ISBN 1-55039-090-2 • 204 pp • 6 x 9 • $18.95

Gilean Douglas
Writing Nature, Finding Home
by Andrea Lebowitz & Gillian Milton

Gilean Douglas is a Canadian cultural icon: nature writer, journalist, farmer, feminist, politician, adventurer, and poet. Born in 1900 into a wealthy family and orphaned at 16, she rejected the expectations of the class and society into which she was born and made her own way in the world as an independent woman.

Douglas's writings span more than 80 years, from her childhood in the early 1900s through four marriages, 10 years alone in the wilds of the Cascade Mountains, and 40 years on Cortes Island, BC, where she died in 1993.

Both a collection of some of the best writings of Gilean Douglas and a fascinating biography, the book includes texts never before published, along with some of the best writing from each phase of her career as poet, nature writer, and journalist. Abundantly illustrated with Douglas's own photographs.
ISBN 1-55039-096-1 • 227 pp • 6 x 9 • $21.95

A Woman of Influence
Evlyn Fenwick Farris
by Sylvie McClean

A must-read for anyone interested in women's history! Evlyn Fenwick Farris (1878–1971), founder of the University Women's Club of Vancouver, was a major force in the establishment and development of UBC, and a key player in the election of the first Liberal government of British Columbia. She was a woman of indomitable spirit and extraordinary political skill, but her Baptist upbringing led her to see women as helpmates of men, not "feminists" working against them. This is a biography of a fascinating, contradictory woman, who both fostered and was caught by change.
ISBN 1-55039-074-0 • 270 pp • 6 x 9 • $22.95